First in the South

FIRST IN THE SOUTH
WHY SOUTH CAROLINA'S PRESIDENTIAL PRIMARY MATTERS

H. Gibbs Knotts &
Jordan M. Ragusa

THE UNIVERSITY OF
SOUTH CAROLINA PRESS

© 2020 University of South Carolina

Published by the University of South Carolina Press
Columbia, South Carolina 29208

www.sc.edu/uscpress

Manufactured in the United States of America

29 28 27 26 25 24 23 22 21 20
10 9 8 7 6 5 4 3 2 1

Library of Congress Cataloging-in-Publication Data
can be found at http://catalog.loc.gov/.

ISBN: 978-1-64336-051-5 (hardback)
ISBN: 978-1-64336-052-2 (paperback)
ISBN: 978-1-64336-053-9 (ebook)

CONTENTS

ILLUSTRATIONS

Tables

Figures

PREFACE

South Carolina plays a pivotal role when it comes to selecting presidents. For both parties, the state's primary is the first contest in the South, strategically scheduled to take place shortly after the Iowa caucuses and the New Hampshire primary. Given that Iowa and New Hampshire almost always select different candidates, South Carolina often plays a decisive tie-breaking role. Further, South Carolina has special significance to each party. For Republicans, the outcome in South Carolina nearly always reflects voter sentiment in other southern states, and the winner of the South Carolina primary has gone on to secure the GOP nomination in all but one contest since 1980. For Democrats, the state is a consistent barometer of other southern contents, demonstrates the importance of black voters, and adds much needed diversity to the early state calendar.

For these reasons, candidates visit South Carolina years before the primary to test their message, interact with voters, and secure key endorsements. After all, a good showing in South Carolina can help candidates demonstrate their viability and build momentum for the primaries and caucuses that follow in close succession. Conversely, candidates who perform poorly in South Carolina often drop out of the race. In simple terms, presidential aspirants know that the road to the White House passes through the Palmetto State.

Despite the importance of the South Carolina primary, academics have written very little on the topic. There is a vast literature on presidential nominations writ large, and excellent books on the Iowa caucuses and New Hampshire primary, but there is no book-length study of the South Carolina primary. We believe this is an unfortunate omission given South Carolina's vital role in the presidential nomination process.

As political science professors in South Carolina, we have seen firsthand the power of the South Carolina primary. At the College of Charleston, we have worked with colleagues to host dozens of South Carolina primary events, many of which provided opportunities for students to meet and interact with Republican and Democratic presidential candidates. As students of politics, we have also been besieged by state, national, and international media outlets with questions about the South Carolina primary. Part of our motivation for writing this book is to respond to these inquiries.

Our book focuses on four key questions about the South Carolina primary:

- How did South Carolina become first in the South?
- Does the state have an uncommon ability to predict each party's eventual winner?
- Is South Carolina representative of each party's national electorate?
- What does it take to win in South Carolina?

To address these questions, we draw on both qualitative and quantitative evidence. We utilize press reports, primary sources, archival documents, and oral histories to better understand the South Carolina primary. We also analyze election results, U.S. census data, and exit polls. While the arguments in the book are evidence-based, relying on statistical techniques where appropriate, the book is written with the general reader in mind. We describe the statistical models and methodology we use in appendix B.

There are two core arguments that run throughout this book: first, South Carolina plays a critically important yet often underappreciated role in the race to secure a party's nomination, and, second, South Carolina's status as the first contest in the South has many positive qualities in the current system.

ACKNOWLEDGMENTS

As with any book project, there are a number of people we would like to thank for their support and encouragement. We benefited from the many resources at the College of Charleston. Gibbs Knotts was granted sabbatical leave to work on this manuscript and is particularly indebted to Claire Curtis for supporting the project and taking on interim department chair duties. Jordan Ragusa has received generous support from the College of Charleston Center for Public Choice and Market Process and would like to thank the center's director, Peter Calcagno. We also appreciate the support from our former dean, Jerry Hale, and the members of his team in the School of Humanities and Social Sciences. Several librarians at Addlestone Library helped us along the way, including Evan Berry, Liza Gadsden, Debbie Larsen, Jared Seay, and John White.

Other library resources in South Carolina aided in the completion of this manuscript as well. We would like to thank Virginia Pierce, a public services librarian at the South Carolina State Library, who helped us access the historical articles from NewsBank. We also benefited from the resources of the University Libraries South Carolina Political Collections at the University of South Carolina. Kate Moore, a reference archivist at South Carolina Political Collections, was particularly helpful providing access to the Republican Party of South Carolina Papers and the Democratic Party of South Carolina Records.

Two early projects fueled our interest in writing this book. Gibbs Knotts collaborated with Winthrop University's Scott Huffmon and Texas Tech University's Seth McKee to write "First in the South: The Importance of South Carolina in Presidential Politics." This paper was presented at the State Politics and Policy Conference in May 2016 and was published in the *Journal of Political Science* in 2017. We cite a number of findings from this article throughout our manuscript. Jordan Ragusa worked with two College of Charleston undergraduates, James Craven and John-Anthony Thevos on an article titled "Palmetto State Primaries: An Examination of South Carolina's Nomination Contests," published in the *Journal of Political Science* in 2017. In chapter 4 of this book, we expand on the analysis first presented in this article. We are indebted to our excellent coauthors on these two projects, and we would also like to thank the editor of the *Journal of Political Science,* Adam Chamberlain, for his interest in our work. We would also like to thank John Holder for his feedback at the 2016 meeting of the South Carolina Political Science Association.

We also received outstanding research assistance from College of Charleston students. In particular, we greatly appreciate the help from members of the Department of Political Science's American Politics Research Team including Nick Catherall, James Craven, Katie Hill, Olivia Rothstein, and John-Anthony Thevos. Catherall provided particularly invaluable research assistance with various aspects of chapter 3. Hill provided excellent index assistance as well.

We also appreciate the support of our colleagues in the Department of Political Science at the College of Charleston. We are especially grateful for the guidance and support from our departmental research collaborators, Karyn Amira, LaTasha Chaffin, and Claire Wofford. In addition, Western Carolina University's Chris Cooper has encouraged this project from the very beginning, and we appreciate the time he has spent reading chapters and providing constructive feedback. Stacy Knotts has also read the entire manuscript and provided valuable assistance.

We received very helpful feedback during a panel at the 2019 meeting of the South Carolina Political Science Association at Furman University. Furman's Danielle Vinson provided particularly constructive feedback, serving as our discussant.

We would also like to thank the College of Charleston's Bully Pulpit Series for hosting candidate forums, debates, and other South Carolina primary events. The Bully Pulpit series is a collaboration between the Department of Communication and the Department of Political Science and has been under the outstanding leadership of Amanda Ruth-McSwain in the Department of Communication. Casandra Foster has also provided superb administrative and event planning support and the Bully Pulpit series has received the backing of College of Charleston senior leadership.

We also benefited from the many conversations we've had with South Carolina journalists and political reporters, including Tessa Spencer Adams, Tom Barton, Robert Behre, Charles Bierbauer, Ashely Blackstone, Andy Brack, Bill Burr, Jon Bruce, Caitlin Byrd, Abigail Darlington, Bill Davis, Emma Dumain, Alan Greenblatt, Leyla Gulen, Victoria Hansen, Brian Hicks, Gavin Jackson, Charlie James, Meg Kinnard, Schuyler Kropf, Jamie Lovegrove, Bristow Marchant, Christina Myers, Cynthia Roldan, Maayan Schechter, Cindi Ross Scoppe, Jamie Self, Andy Shain, David Slade, Glenn Smith, Sam Spence, Dean Stephens, Quintin Washington, and Avery Wilks. We would like to give a special thanks to the late Lee Bandy. Known as the dean of South Carolina political reporters, his four decades of thoughtful reporting on South Carolina politics in the *State* played a crucial role in helping us tell the story of the South Carolina's first-in-the-South primary.

We would also like to thank South Carolina's Republican and Democratic state parties. We are particularly thankful to South Carolina GOP Executive Director Hope Walker and South Carolina Democratic Party Chair Trav Robertson.

In addition, we greatly appreciate the support and encouragement from the University of South Carolina Press. Richard Brown, the director of the press, has been especially supportive of our project, and we appreciate his leadership. In addition, we would like to thank Bill Adams, the managing editor, for his assistance. We also received extremely helpful feedback from three anonymous readers who pushed us to make a number of valuable revisions.

Finally, we would like to thank our families: Stacy, Whitney, Christine, and native South Carolinians, June and Myles. Your support is unconditional, unwavering, and greatly appreciated.

★ 1 ★
WHY SOUTH CAROLINA?

South Carolina's inaugural presidential primary was launched by the GOP in 1980. It was a bold endeavor for a minority party—a plan hatched by entrepreneurial Republicans to exert greater influence over national politics and build support for their party in the state. Democrats had enjoyed near universal control of South Carolina politics since the Civil War, and in 1980 five of the state's eight members of Congress were Democrats, as was the governor, Dick Riley, and Democrats held large majorities in both chambers of the state legislature. From the beginning, GOP leaders branded the primary as "first in the South," working tirelessly to hold this strategically important position on the election calendar.

Holding the first presidential primary in the American South was not something South Carolina Democrats were interested in, at least not initially. Leaders of the state's majority party debated a primary as far back as the 1960s, with those in favor arguing that it would democratize the state's political process. Yet unlike Republicans, Democrats opted for the status quo, holding caucuses through 1988 in an effort to maintain greater control over the party's nominee and out of concerns about the legality of a primary. Facing dwindling electoral support, in part a result of the state's successful Republican primary, the South Carolina Democratic Party eventually held their first presidential primary in 1992, and since 2004, it has maintained the coveted first-in-the-South distinction. Like their Republican counterparts, South Carolina Democrats battled the national party, other states, and sometimes each other to remain the region's first contest.

A Primer on Primaries

Presidential primaries and caucuses are fairly new in American politics, both in South Carolina and across the nation, and there is nothing in the U.S. Constitution that outlines procedures for selecting presidential nominees. During the early years of the republic, nominees were picked by a congressional caucus, through which members of Congress coordinated with state legislatures to select their party's nominee for president (Norrander 2010; Steger 2015). Following the demise of the congressional caucus system in 1824, presidential nominees were chosen via a caucus-convention system for the remainder of the nineteenth century, by which national convention delegates were picked through a series of local and state party meetings (Steger 2015). In the late 1800s and early 1900s, primaries emerged as a progressive solution to the corruption that existed in the caucus-convention system (Steger 2015). Although primaries became more important, this era was characterized by the mixed-caucus-primary-convention system because the nomination was still decided at a national convention (Steger 2015).[1]

Like most states, South Carolina explored a presidential primary in the wake of the tumultuous 1968 Democratic nomination (Steger 2015). As a result of the "backroom deals" on behalf of the eventual nominee, Hubert Humphrey, and as a consequence of the party's dissatisfaction with Nixon's victory in the general election, Democratic leaders created the Democratic Commission on Party Structure and Delegate Selection (Norrander 2010). Known as the McGovern-Fraser Commission, this group developed eighteen guidelines for the subsequent 1972 nomination contest, the most important of which focused on creating a more open and transparent delegate selection process (Norrander 2010). In an effort to comply with these guidelines, the party held more presidential primaries across the country over the next decade, and Republicans followed suit, ushering in the modern primary and caucus system (Norrander 2010; Steger 2015).

Although modern primaries and caucuses grew out of an effort to give a greater voice to citizens, political parties still play a powerful role in selecting presidential nominees. In one of the most influential books about presidential nominations, *The Party Decides,* Marty Cohen, David Karol, Hans Noel, and John Zaller (2008) argue against the conventional wisdom that voters—alone—are responsible for deciding which candidate secures the party's nomination. Cohen and his coauthors build on what journalist Arthur Hadley (1976) labeled the "invisible primary," when candidates work behind the scenes to secure the support of elites, activists, and party leaders (see also Bawn, Cohen, Karol, Masket, Noel, and Zaller 2012). In simple terms, these groups play a substantial role in who wins and loses because they contribute resources, including financial support, expertise, and endorsements (Cohen et al. 2008; Bawn et al. 2012).

The Importance of the South Carolina Primary

Being First Matters

As primaries became more frequent following the 1968 Democratic nomination, states predictably jockeyed for early calendar slots in a phenomenon dubbed "front-loading" (Mayer and Busch 2004). After all, early states like Iowa, New Hampshire, and South Carolina receive a number of advantages by being first. Citizens in states with early contests have greater power over naming the eventual nominee. While these states may not pick the eventual winner, given the sheer number of candidates on the ballot, they often help narrow the field by eliminating candidates their citizens oppose (Norrander 2006). Research has also shown that candidates who do well in the early states and are perceived to be "electorally viable" carry that momentum into subsequent states (Abramowitz 1989; Adkins and Dowdle 2001; Bartels 1988; Norrander 2006; Redlawsk, Tolbert, and Donovan 2011; Steger 2007). If a candidate does well in Iowa, New Hampshire, or South Carolina, voters infer that the candidate has a strong chance of winning, and thus the candidate is likely to do well in future contests.

Citizens in early states benefit in two other ways beyond their raw power to influence who wins or loses the nomination. First, voters have the opportunity to interact with candidates and ask questions (Moore and Smith 2015; Redlawsk, Tolbert, and Donovan 2011). Such interaction has "educative effects," namely, it generates a more knowledgeable, informed, and engaged citizenry (Redlawsk, Tolbert, and Donovan 2011). And second, participation in presidential nomination campaigns helps citizens mobilize in subsequent elections by fostering a stronger sense of civic duty (McCann, Partin, Rapoport, and Stone 1996).

Early states also receive economic benefits. From political advertising and rallies to the various travel expenditures associated with campaigning, primaries are known to stimulate state and local economies (Lessem and Urban 2015). In fact, one study estimated the direct economic impact of the New Hampshire primary campaign at about $350 million (Moore and Smith 2015). Yet there can be indirect economic benefits as well. For example, early states secure greater federal spending in the years after a competitive nomination contest (Taylor 2010), although some studies suggest such benefits hinge on whether the state was a political supporter of the newly elected president (Husted and Nickerson 2014; Kriner and Reeves 2015; Wood 2009).

Not surprisingly, there are critics of the current primary system featuring Iowa, New Hampshire, and South Carolina at the front. According to political scientists William Mayer and Andrew Busch (2004, 56), the main objection is that front-loading "greatly accelerates the voters' decision process and thus makes the whole system less deliberate, less rational, less flexible, and more chaotic." Some favor alternative schemes to address these limitations such as a national primary (Altschuler 2008). Others cite limitations with *any* system of primaries and caucuses. For example, Nelson Polsby (1983) has argued that the McGovern-Fraser reforms, which gave voters greater power over a party's nominee, limited the power of parties to properly vet candidates and select consensus nominees that could unite various factions within the parties. A number of political scientists come down somewhere in the middle. Barbara Norrander (2010) labels the current system "imperfect," arguing that it has both strengths and weaknesses. Resolving these debates is not the purpose of this book, and we sidestep normative questions about the "best" way to structure nomination contests. Rather, our interest lies with South Carolina's place in the current primary system and empirical questions about its consequences.

Being First in the South Matters

We are certainly not the first to argue that being an early state comes with certain advantages. Less commonly addressed, however, is that being first in a geographic region can matter as well. Being first in the *South* is uniquely important for three related reasons: southern states share much in common and tend to vote alike; southern states hold their primaries earlier than any other region; and a candidate who does well in South Carolina can quickly amass an insurmountable delegate advantage in the subsequent southern states.[2] For these reasons, South Carolina has been called a "New Hampshire of the South" (Graham 1998, 49) and a "New Hampshire below the Mason-Dixon line" (Cook 2000, 647).

A number of authors have shown that southern states in general, and southern politics in particular, share a range of characteristics and dynamics (Black and Black 1987; Black and Black 1992; Black and Black 2002; Key 1949; McKee 2018a; Woodard 2013). For example, southern states have been reliably Republican in presidential politics. The GOP has won a majority of southern states in each election since 1980 and swept the South in 1984, 1988, 2000, and 2004.[3] And while Democrats have shown signs of strength in parts of the region, most notably in Florida, Virginia, and North Carolina, Republicans continue to dominate the political landscape as a whole. Additionally, there is a shared culture and common identity in the American South that has an influence on the region's politics (Cobb 2005; Cooper and Knotts 2017; Reed 1983). Despite an influx of new residents from other regions over the past few decades (Mackun and Wilson 2011), recent research shows that the level of southern identity among people living in the South remains well above 70 percent (Cooper and Knotts 2017).

A natural consequence of the strong bonds of southern identity and shared political culture is that candidates who win South Carolina are likely to do well in other southern states. Aggregate election results validate this point, and presidential candidates, strategists, and political reporters share in this belief. Covering the first ever South Carolina primary, Bill Peterson and Jack Bass (1980a), reporters for the *Washington Post,* noted that the results would "have a psychological impact on the primaries in Alabama, Florida, and Georgia three days later." In 1996, South Carolina governor David Beasley called the South Carolina primary "the gateway to the South," and Bob Dole's campaign manager, Scott Reed, expressed a similar view, noting that the South Carolina primary "serves as a spring board for Super Tuesday" (Edsall 1996).[4]

All in all, candidates who do well in South Carolina and as a result do well in other southern states can quickly build an insurmountable delegate advantage given that nearly all of the southern primaries are early on the primary calendar. As Seth McKee (2018b, 24) aptly puts it: "The South punches above its weight in presidential nomination contests because most of its states vote early in the nomination calendar." For example, there were 2,472 GOP delegates at stake during the 2016 primary season (Real Clear Politics 2018b). To secure the nomination, a candidate needed 1,237 delegates, and there were 735 delegates available in the South (Real Clear Politics 2018b). Simply put, a candidate who can sweep the South has 59 percent of the delegates needed to secure the Republican nomination for president. The region also has considerable influence in the selection of the Democratic nominee. In 2016, Democrats awarded 4,051 delegates (with another 712 as superdelegates), and a candidate who swept the South would win 1,032 delegates, 51 percent of the delegates needed to win a majority of the awarded delegates (Real Clear Politics 2018a).

South Carolina Is a Different Test

Given South Carolina's strategically important position on the calendar, the Palmetto State often draws comparisons to Iowa and New Hampshire. In most instances since 1972, the Iowa caucuses have been the first nominating contest, followed about a week later by the New Hampshire primary (Moore and Smith 2015; Redlawsk, Tolbert, and Donovan 2011). Yet there are key demographic and institutional differences between South Carolina, Iowa, and New Hampshire. For these reasons, South Carolina affords a "different test" than Iowa and New Hampshire do, but it is no less important.

Demographically, South Carolina stands out from the other early primary states. In particular, Iowa and New Hampshire have demographic and political features that make these states *unrepresentative* of both parties' national nominating electorate. On the most basic level, Iowa and New Hampshire are both small, rural, and disproportionately white, making them "poor barometers for selecting presidential nominees" (Huffmon, Knotts, and McKee 2017, 10). South Carolina is much more racially diverse than Iowa or New Hampshire, and as

Citadel political scientists Laurence Moreland and Robert Steed argue, the state's large minority population provides "a different kind of test for presidential candidacies" (2012, 476). No doubt the state's racial diversity is more consequential on the Democratic side given the party's support from African Americans in contemporary politics. Yet many observers also note that South Carolina is demographically representative of the national Republican nominating electorate. According to the South Carolina Republican party itself, the state has "unique characteristics and demographics which are more reflective of the national electorate at large—and therefore a much stronger indicator than any of the other early primaries or caucuses" ("First in the South" 2018).

A number of commentators have suggested that South Carolina's demographic diversity explains the state's strong record when it comes to predicting which candidate secures the Republican nomination. The state's Republican voters supported their party's eventual nominee in six of the seven contests held since 1980.[5] Iowa and New Hampshire do not have the same predictive ability. South Carolina's lone "miss" was in 2012, when the state's GOP voters supported the former U.S. House Speaker from Georgia, Newt Gingrich, over Mitt Romney, the eventual nominee. Republicans got back on track in 2016, helping legitimize the candidacy of Donald Trump and to propel the billionaire businessman toward the Republican nomination and general election victory.

On the Democratic side, South Carolina has selected the party's nominee in three of six contests since 1980.[6] South Carolina's only modest predictive ability in Democratic contests is often blamed on the opposite feature: that the state's Democratic voters do *not* represent the party's national nominating electorate. Commentators frequently cite the state's high percentage of African Americans and a less liberal electorate. Bernie Sanders famously brought attention to this state of affairs in 2016 when he dismissed Democratic voters throughout the South, saying "we're out of the Deep South now. And we're moving up" (Newkirk 2016). With a host of multinational corporations in Greenville, Columbia, and Charleston, South Carolina is more diverse than it is thought to be, and the state's demographics are changing rapidly (Bowerman 2017; Slade 2018). Since 1992, when Democrats adopted a primary, the state has had a better track record and has correctly selected the eventual winner in contested primaries on three of four occasions. Additionally, the state serves as a counterweight to Iowa and New Hampshire on the Democratic side and thus adds representativeness in the aggregate. In fact, national Democrats have supported South Carolina's coveted position on the calendar for exactly this reason.

In addition to being more demographically diverse than Iowa and New Hampshire, South Carolina provides a different test owing to its open primaries. Notably, South Carolina is one of just eleven states with a fully open primary for presidential contests.[7] Unlike most states, voters do not register by political party in South Carolina, and registered voters can participate in either the Republican or the Democratic presidential primaries. By comparison, Iowa is classified as "partially" open because voters are required to register with a political party to participate in the caucuses (Redlawsk, Tolbert, and Donovan 2011). New Hampshire is categorized as "open to unaffiliated voters" for presidential nomination contests, as voters register by party but have the option of registering as "undeclared" and voting in either the Republican or Democratic primary (Moore and Smith 2015).

Why does the openness of a state's nominating contests matter? Simply put, research has shown that open primary states are more representative of the general election electorate than closed primary states (Kaufmann, Gimpel, and Hoffmann 2003). In this respect, open primaries help moderate what some see as a problematic feature of primaries writ large: that they magnify the influence of an ideologically extreme electorate. South Carolina is likely to be more representative than Iowa and New Hampshire—and thus supply a different test—because of the manner in which the state conducts its contests.

A final unique feature of the South Carolina primary is the fact that it is typically held on a Saturday. The GOP primary has taken place on a Saturday since the first one in 1980, setting it apart from Iowa and New Hampshire. The Iowa caucuses are typically scheduled on Monday, although they occurred on Thursday in 2008 and Tuesday in 2012. New Hampshire has always held its primary on Tuesday. On the Democratic side, the initial presidential primary in 1992 occurred on a Tuesday, but every subsequent Democratic contest has taken place on a Saturday. Holding elections on Saturday makes it easier to get volunteers, and it is more convenient for voters. Similarly, it is important to note that Democratic and Republican primaries in South Carolina have nearly always taken place on different dates, although Republicans have always gone first.[8] Since voters can only participate in one presidential nomination contest per cycle, going first gives Republicans a strategic advantage over Democrats in the Palmetto State. In Iowa and New Hampshire, Democrats and Republicans cast ballots on the same day.

South Carolina Deserves Greater Attention

Given both the importance and growth of the South Carolina primary since 1980, the Palmetto State ought to be receiving the attention of academics and journalists alike. Yet as we document here, most observers focus disproportionately on Iowa and New Hampshire. A range of statistics help us quantify the significance of the South Carolina primary. To begin with, the first GOP primary in 1980 exceeded turnout projections with 145,501 voters (Cook 2000). For context, consider that approximately thirty-five thousand people voted in the 1974 GOP primary for governor, even though the primary featured military hero General William C. Westmoreland (Cook 2000). Among the naysayers regarding the South Carolina primary was the South Carolina Democratic Party chair Don Fowler, who predicted between thirty and fifty thousand participants in the inaugural Republican presidential primary (United Press International 1979).

Figure 1.1 shows participation in contested South Carolina primaries for both Republicans and Democrats. As you can see, there has been a steady increase in Republican voter turnout since the first primary in 1980. There was a particularly strong surge in turnout in 2000 owing to a hotly contested primary encapsulated in the contentious battle between John McCain and George W. Bush, and the 2016 GOP contest had a record turnout with 743,667 voters.[9] Overall, the South Carolina Republican primary grew 411 percent between 1980 and 2016. As a point of comparison, South Carolina's population grew by only 48 percent during the same thirty-six-year period.[10]

As the primary grew, Republicans greatly expanded their base of support in the Palmetto State. According to political analyst Rhodes Cook (2000, 647), "The South Carolina GOP has expanded beyond white-collar professionals and well-heeled retirees to include Christian conservatives and converts from the Democratic Party." Looking back, South Carolina state senator John Courson pointed to two elements of success: that the primary was held on Saturday (allowing conservative, blue-collar Democrats to vote) and that it was the first southern contest (B. Smith 2012). In addition, the South Carolina GOP owes much of its present dominance to the open primary, and a shift to closed primaries would likely result in decreased participation.

Figure 1.1 shows that the number of participants in the Democratic primary has also increased. In 1992, the Democratic primary had 116,414 voters. Although this was a good start for South Carolina Democrats, the initial effort had fewer participants than any of the state's Republican contests, including the first GOP primary in 1980. Again, it is important to remember that the South Carolina GOP held a primary on the same day in 1992, which is unusual in the state, as we noted. Participation increased considerably between 1992 and 2004, growing by 152 percent. Again, there was no GOP primary in 2004 since George W. Bush was running for reelection. The peak in the number of Democratic primary voters was the historic 2008 contest between Hillary Clinton, Barack Obama, and John Edwards. In this election, 532,151 people participated in the Democratic primary. It also garnered the second largest voter turnout of any South Carolina primary up to that point, as only the 2000 GOP contest drew more voters. The number of Democrats who participated in the 2008 contest exceeded that of the of Republicans, who also voted in 2008, by 86,474 voters. Democratic turnout dipped in 2016 to 370,904—a 31 percent decrease from turnout in the 2008 Democratic primary.[11]

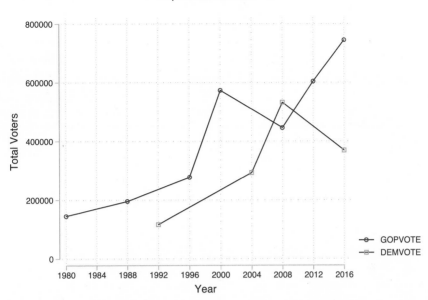

FIGURE 1.1. The Growth of the Republican and Democratic Presidential Primary (1980–2016)
Source: Cook 2000, Cook 2007, and uselectionatlas.org/RESULTS

Alongside increasing turnout, there has also been a growth in national news coverage of the South Carolina primary. We measured national news coverage by identifying stories about the South Carolina primary and the South Carolina caucuses printed in the *New York Times* between January 1 and December 31 in presidential election years between 1980 and 2016 (see also Redlawsk, Tolbert, and Donovan 2011). Figure 1.2 shows that coverage of the state's primaries and caucuses has grown considerably. Between 1980 and 1992, there were fewer than twenty stories per election cycle. While the lower number for 1992 may seem surprising, since both Democrats and Republicans held presidential primaries during this cycle, this was the year Georgia leapfrogged South Carolina to temporarily gain first-in-the South status. Despite there only being contested Republican elections in 1996 and 2000, coverage of the South Carolina primary increased considerably. Following a brief dip in 2004, when Democrats were the only party to hold a contest, coverage of the South Carolina primary grew considerably in 2008 with two contested primaries and the historic candidacy of Barack Obama. Even though there was only a GOP primary in 2012, coverage increased again between 2008 and 2012. Finally, coverage of the South Carolina primary exploded in 2016, with a record ninety-nine stories; this was likely because there were two contested early primaries and given the media fascination with Trump's candidacy.

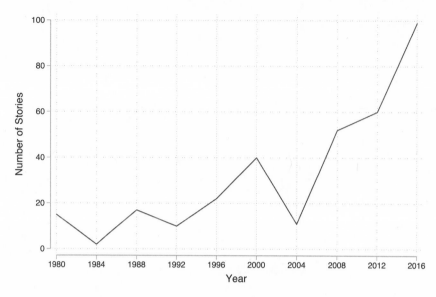

FIGURE 1.2. Print Media Coverage of the South Carolina Primary and Caucuses (1980–2016)

Source: *New York Times*

Another measure of the growth and significance of the primary is the increase in the filing fee for GOP participants since the first primary in 1980. Filing fees are intended to offset the costs of administering an election, as well as to discourage frivolous candidates from running. Ostensibly, as a primary grows, its filing fees should increase. Figure 1.3 shows the filing fee between 1980 and 2016. In 1980, the fee was just $1,500, but by 2016, it had increased to $40,000. This increase is not solely an effect of inflation. According to the Bureau of Labor Statistic's Consumer price index inflation calculator, $1,500 in January 1980 had the same buying power as $4,568 in January 2016 (data.bls.gov/cgi-bin/cpicalc.pl).

The expensive filing fee for South Carolina's GOP candidates is not the norm, however. More typically filing fees are in the $1,000 range, with some notable exceptions (Zurcher 2015). It costs $25,000 to get on the primary ballot in Arkansas and $15,000 to participate in the Kansas or Kentucky caucuses (Zurcher 2015). For Democrats in South Carolina, the filing fee has remained $2,500 since the first primary in 1992.

Despite both the importance and growth of South Carolina's first-in-the-South primary, the media focuses overwhelming on Iowa and New Hampshire, and evidence indicates that this disproportionate media attention further enhances the power of these two states (Adkins and Dowdle 2001). Figure 1.4 demonstrates this with data from the 2016 contest. On the y-axis is the volume of news articles that mention each state's primary or caucus from January 15,

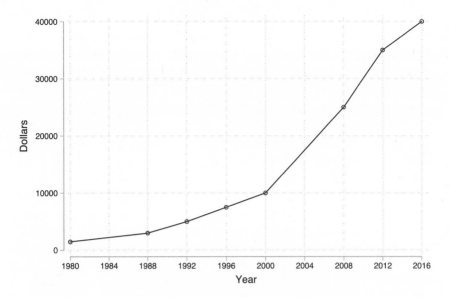

FIGURE 1.3. Increase in the GOP Filing Fee (1980–2016)
Source: various, compiled by authors

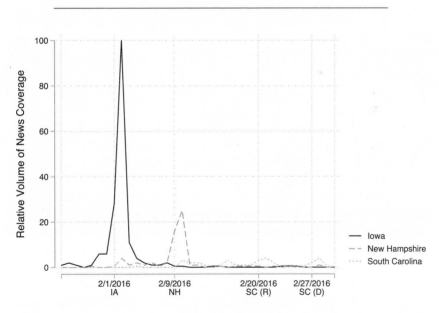

FIGURE 1.4. News Coverage of Iowa, New Hampshire, and South Carolina Contests (2016)
Source: Google trends

roughly two weeks before the Iowa caucus, to the end of February.[12] We denote the date of each contest on the x-axis. Notably, the greatest volume of media coverage is always the day *after* the state's contest. As is typical, South Carolina's Democratic and Republican primaries were held a week apart in 2016. But even the number of articles about the South Carolina Democratic and Republican contests combined is much smaller than that focused on Iowa and New Hampshire. Ultimately, the figure reveals that the peak in South Carolina media attention is barely noticeable relative to Iowa and New Hampshire. In particular, the data show that in 2016, South Carolina received 92 percent less media coverage than Iowa and 68 percent less media coverage than New Hampshire.

Of course, journalists are not alone in focusing overwhelmingly on Iowa and New Hampshire. Academics prioritize the two earliest states as well. Although many academic articles have explored nomination contests in Iowa and New Hampshire (e.g., Adkins and Dowdle 2001, Steger, Dowdle, and Adkins 2004, and Stone, Abramowitz, and Rapoport 1989), we are aware of just a few that focus specifically on the South Carolina primary (Craven, Ragusa, and Thevos 2017; Graham 1998; Huffmon, Knotts, and McKee 2017). Likewise, there are a number of books on the Iowa caucuses and New Hampshire primary, including *Why Iowa: How Caucuses and Sequential Elections Improve the Presidential Nominating Process* (Redlawsk, Tolbert, and Donovan 2011) and *The First Primary: New Hampshire's Outsize Role in Presidential Nominations* (Moore and Smith 2015), yet there is no comparable book-length study of the South Carolina primary.

Conclusion

Early states enjoy a range of advantages over states with later primaries and caucuses, the most obvious being their disproportionate power over which candidate secures a party's nomination. Yet not all states with early contests are created equal. Being first in the South is especially important given the region's strategic position in the delegate race and the tendency of southern states to vote alike. South Carolina also provides a different test than Iowa and New Hampshire do, most notably by adding much needed diversity to the early nomination states. For these reasons, and despite the overwhelming focus on Iowa and New Hampshire by journalists and academics alike, we believe South Carolina deserves more attention. In the remainder of the book, we examine the South Carolina primary in considerable detail, focusing on our primary research questions.

★ 2 ★
BECOMING FIRST
IN THE SOUTH

For South Carolina, becoming first in the South was a long and difficult struggle and keeping this coveted position has been equally difficult. As they sought to create the first southern primary in 1980, local GOP officials fought with each other, Democrats, and their national party leadership. Democrats experienced many of the same challenges when they held the first southern primary in 2004. Subsequently, there has been a near constant effort by other states to leapfrog South Carolina on the nomination calendar. As South Carolina gained attention, leaders in other states mounted campaigns to hold early primaries in an effort to capture the money and influence that comes with being in such a strategically important position.

How did South Carolina become first in the South? The story begins in the 1970s, a time when Democrats dominated South Carolina politics, one indicator of which is that following the 1978 state elections there were only 16 Republicans in the 120-member South Carolina House and just 4 Republicans in the 46-member Senate.[1] Republicans were working to build a competitive two-party system in the Palmetto State, and the presidential primary that they held in 1980 was part of the party's strategy to influence national politics and recruit new members. The GOP primary has served as an organizational tool and a public relations windfall for the South Carolina Republican Party. South Carolina Democrats had a number of starts and stops in their quest to be first in the South, eventually holding a presidential primary in 1992 before conducting the first southern primary twelve years later. Like Republicans, state Democrats fought with each other, the national party, and other states to secure and maintain first-in-the-South status. The early nomination contests for Democrats brought considerable attention to the party and elevated the role of African American voters both nationally and across the Palmetto State.[2]

The Birth of a Presidential Primary

Initially, there was not a lot of support for a Republican presidential primary. According to Dan Ross, state GOP chair from 1976 to 1980 and primary booster, "Jim Edwards hated it, didn't even want it. Strom Thurmond didn't want it. They didn't want to see a primary" (2001, 82). Edwards, the state's first Republican governor since Reconstruction, did not want to commit South Carolina's national convention delegates to the primary winners. As he explained, "If we go uncommitted, we would have a real hammer we could use to try to get some commitments out of the various candidates" (Cothran 1979, B1). Thurmond, the state's senior senator, backed Texas senator John Connally for president in 1980, and his objection to the primary appears to have been strategic—he worried that Ronald Reagan's acting background and charisma would give him an edge in a primary. According to Associated Press reporter Thomas Cothran (1979, B1), "Thurmond did not like the idea of a primary because someone who could act well would use television to sway the voters. The remark appeared to be against Reagan."

FIGURE 2.1. South Carolina GOP Chair Dan Ross

Source: Daniel Ross Papers, South Carolina Political Collections, the University of South Carolina

Primaries, particularly for South Carolina Republicans, were quite the novelty. In the 1976 presidential election, just over half of states held primaries (Kamarck 2016a). In South Carolina, the state GOP held primaries for governor in 1974 and 1978, but there had not been a presidential primary and there were no provisions in state law for holding this type of election.

In 1979, the South Carolina GOP announced the creation of a committee to study "the prospects of staging" a presidential primary ("S.C. Republicans to Study" 1979, 15A). Two decades later, Ross, recalling the creation of this committee, said that he appointed people to it who were favorably predisposed to the primary (2001, 82). After the committee had been established, GOP executive director Wayne Adams highlighted the benefits of the primary: it would bring presidential candidates to South Carolina, help the party raise money, and elevate Republican prospects in a solid Democratic state ("S.C. Republicans to Study" 1979). Committee chair Marshall Parker also stressed the positives of holding a primary—increased interest in the Republican Party from party regulars and independents and economic benefits that would come to South Carolina ("GOP Creates Committee" 1979, 4B).

Even though the committee was stacked with primary supporters, there was some opposition among party activists (D. Ross 2001). According to Ross, "The people in the boondocks and the precincts did not want the primary, in the beginning," because running an extra election would entail "too much effort on their part" (2001, 82). Ross anticipated the resistance from local officials: "They knew they were going to have to organize the precincts. That's hard work" (82). Ultimately, winning support from the GOP county chairs was key to getting the primary approved. Ross's typical pitch was "Hey, this is what it means, it gives us a mailing list, it means we're going to get publicity, national [publicity], it means that we're going to become a household word in South Carolina because we're having a presidential primary and the Democrats aren't" (83).

As support for the primary grew, the decision about when to schedule the primary was a key point of contention. Harry Dent, former chair of the South Carolina Republican Party, advocated an early primary, naming March 11 (Associated Press 1979e). Gene McCaskill, chair of the Kershaw County Republican Party, argued for an even earlier primary on March 1, suggesting this date to guarantee that the South Carolina contest would be the second primary in the nation and first primary in the South (Associated Press 1979e). On the other end of the spectrum, Ross supported holding the primary in June alongside contests for local and statewide officials (Associated Press 1979e). Ross cited the party-building advantages of having local and state primaries concurrent with a presidential primary as well as the cost savings of holding both on the same day (Lundgren 1979).

In the end, the committee voiced strong support for the Republican presidential primary and endorsed a date that would make South Carolina first in the South. Of those favoring a primary, 67 percent favored an early primary in February or March (South Carolina Republican Party 1979). Ultimately, the committee recommended March 8 because this date would be "more convenient than a later date" and argued that "preceding other Southern primaries by three days will allow candidates to concentrate efforts in the South" (South Carolina Republican Party 1979, 2). There was certainly a strategic component to the earlier date as well. According to the report, "being the very first Southern state to hold a primary will set us up as the bellwether of the South, focusing a great deal of attention on the people of South Carolina" (South Carolina Republican Party 1979, 2).

As we have already noted, the GOP primary was innovative in two other ways: it was to be held on a Saturday and was open to all registered voters. In 1980, each of the states with Republican contests ahead of South Carolina held their election on a Monday (Iowa) or Tuesday (New Hampshire, Massachusetts, and Vermont) (FrontloadingHQ 2009a). Likewise, several states held contests on Tuesday, March 11, including Alabama, Georgia, and Florida (FrontloadingHQ 2009a). As with the decision to make South Carolina the first southern primary, there was a rationale for the Saturday date. According to the report, "The selection of Saturday enables more people to participate, not only as voters but as workers" (South Carolina Republican Party 1979, 2). Ross echoed this sentiment but also highlighted the ability of a Saturday primary to bring blue-collar voters to the Republican side, calling it a "working man's primary" (2001, 86). The party was also open to all registered voters, which had the potential to further increase voter turnout and help build the party. According to the report, "The highly visible characteristics of the presidential primary will generate voter interest in the Republican Party and its candidates, therefore enhancing the public image of Republicans, not only from the standpoint of issues, but from the fact that this is yet another alterative offered by the real party of the people" (South Carolina Republican Party 1979, 1).

Following the successful committee vote, the state's GOP executive committee also voted to approve the study committee's recommendation of the March 8 date (Associated Press 1979c). Not long after the executive committee met, candidates from across the country committed to campaign in South Carolina. By the end of August, South Carolina Republicans had assurances from the leading GOP presidential candidates in 1980, including John Connally, Ronald Reagan, George Bush, and Philip Crane (Associated Press 1979d). If Republicans could take the final step of approving the primary at their October 1979 convention, the state's first-in-the South primary would become a reality.

Opposition to the Primary

As Republicans came together to support the primary, one of the state's lead-ing Democrats spoke out against it. South Carolina Democratic Party chair Don Fowler came just short of calling the primary illegal, saying it was "highly questionable," "extralegal," and "outside the law" (Associated Press 1979a, 8B). "Almost every step of the electoral processes is specific in law," he noted. "Yet, without the benefit of law, the Republicans jumped into this procedure" (Asso-ciated Press 1979a, 8B). Fowler even expressed doubt about whether the Repub-lican presidential primary results would be binding (Associated Press 1979a). Charleston County Republican Party chair, Glenn McConnell, who was also an attorney, countered Fowler's contention: "I have found nothing in the [South Carolina] election law that prohibits us from having a presidential primary" (Matthews 1979, 7B). Looking back, Ross said, "It was none of his business. This is a private primary, we are holding it. It has nothing to do with the state, so there is nothing illegal about it" (2001, 83).

During the heat of the debate over the 1980 primary, Ross fought back in the press, accusing Fowler of trying to "disrupt" the presidential primary and main-taining his remarks were a "smokescreen" to confuse voters (Adams 1979, 6B). Fowler, Ross further argued, showed that he "lack[ed] confidence in the people" by not holding a Democratic presidential primary (Adams 1979, 6B). In an effort at reassurance, Ross said, "I want him and the people of South Carolina to know that we consider our primary a very serious undertaking and that we mean busi-ness. We will conduct a legal primary. It will be fair. It will be honorable. And it will be open to all registered voters, regardless of where they live or how they have voted in the past" (Adams 1979, 6B).

The editorial boards of South Carolina newspapers also spoke out against the primary. The *State*'s editorial board questioned the motivation for the primary and echoed Fowler's predictions of a low turnout, saying "one would think, how-ever, that Republicans . . . would be as interested in a large voter turnout as they would be in an early spring circus" ("A GOP Primary" 1979, 2B). The response from the *News and Courier* was even less enthusiastic. An editorial entitled "The Bad Outweighs the Good" was critical of primaries in general, noting that "they tend to turn the presidential nominating process into a media 'event' in which the slickest-packaged, photogenic candidate with the most money captures the prize" ("The Bad Outweighs the Good" 1980, 12A). That such a process, the edi-torial continued, "puts the most competent man in the White House is hardly supported by the records of recent presidents who have won nomination and election by this process" ("The Bad Outweighs the Good" 1980, 12A).

Ross responded to the criticism about the motivation for switching to a primary in a letter to the editor published in the *State*: "Sure, we'd like the publicity that the party and our candidates would receive. It would provide an excellent forum to present the Republican philosophy. Publicity, however, is not the major reason for holding the primary" (1979). In the letter, he also cited two main objectives: opening up the nomination process to the public and party building: "As more people vote in our primary, the Republican party will grow. Therefore, the primary is an integral part of our expansion. With it, we provide yet another alternative to the present way of doing things" (2001, 14A).

Finalizing the GOP Primary

Despite resistance from Democrats and some in the media, South Carolina Republicans finalized the creation of the first-in-the South primary at their annual convention in October 1979 (Associated Press 1979b). At the convention, there were lingering disagreements about the primary among prominent South Carolina Republicans. Jim Edwards remained opposed to the primary, as did textile executive Roger Milliken and former South Carolina House member George Dean Johnson of Spartanburg County (Associated Press 1979b). Some of the opposition stemmed from fear that Democrats would "raid" the open primary, voting in the Republican presidential contest "with deliberate intention of trying to nominate a candidate they think would be easiest for the Democratic presidential candidate to defeat in the general election" (Lanier 1979, 10B). Although the convention could have bogged down in these disagreements, ultimately the six-month process to build support for the Republican presidential primary worked.

As most observers expected would happen, the March 8 primary date was approved and convention attendees agreed to assign presidential primary delegates based on a winner-take-all system (Associated Press 1979f). Even some of the Republican opposition came around to the idea of a primary in the end. After the vote, Edwards noted that "I think the Republican Party wants a primary. I had some concerns, and still have some concerns. . . . [But] I believe strongly in a primary, and I would not say so if I didn't" (Clements 1979, 1A and 12A). Thurmond urged unity: "I think we all need to come together and work together to make this primary a great success. Our state will be a bellwether, and I hope there will be no bickering." (Clements 1979, 1A and 12A).

Less than two months after the *State* published its editorial criticizing the primary, it published another editorial expressing support for the primary and praising the process employed by South Carolina Republicans: according to the piece, the primary "could attract a considerable amount of national attention and could have importance beyond the size of the state's 25-vote strength at the

1980 GOP national convention" ("Republican Primary Blueprint Is Sound" 1979, 8A). In addition, the editorial endorsed the March 8 date, arguing that holding the primary then would be beneficial to both the state and the region. Finally, the editorial struck a prophetic tone, arguing that South Carolina Republicans had "out-maneuvered their more muscular Democratic rivals and figure to get far, far more attention in the early going next year" (8A).

Gearing Up for the 1980 Primary

Winning approval of the primary at the GOP convention was only half the battle, as there were a number of critical issues to address before the day of the primary. On the most basic level, there were questions about who could actually vote in the first-in-the South primary. Since South Carolinians did not select a party when registering to vote, there was not an easy mechanism by which to determine who could and could not participate. State GOP executive director Wayne Adams said, "We are encouraging anyone interested in who gets the Republican presidential nomination, and would like to participate in the selection process, to vote. We don't expect them to do so facetiously" (Lanier 1979, 10B). Ed Craig, executive director of the South Carolina Democratic Party, expressed little worry about the primary syphoning off reliably Democratic voters (Lanier 1979). As the primary approached, there was general agreement that voters would be permitted to vote in the Republican presidential primary and still vote in the Democratic primary for federal, state, and local officials in June (Lanier 1979). In the end, the first South Carolina GOP presidential primary was open to registered voters in the state as long as they had not already participated in a presidential primary that same year, and all subsequent primaries have been as well (Associated Press 1979f).

Running the state's initial first-in-the-South presidential primary took an extensive volunteer effort. One challenge was finding volunteers in Fairfield and Chesterfield Counties, places without any GOP organization (United Press International 1979). To coordinate the endeavor, the South Carolina GOP put together a "Poll Managers Handbook," providing instructions on how to conduct the primary. The party emphasized the historical nature of holding the first southern primary on the calendar: "You are about to participate in the making of history in South Carolina. For the first time ever, a political party—the Republican Party—in South Carolina is opening its presidential nominating process to the people" (South Carolina Republican Party 1980b). Figure 2.2 is a picture of the sample ballot used in the first presidential primary. On Election Day, over sixteen hundred precincts were opened (Peterson and Bass 1980) and votes were cast in all forty-six South Carolina counties (South Carolina Republican Party 1980a). Greenville County had the largest number of voters with

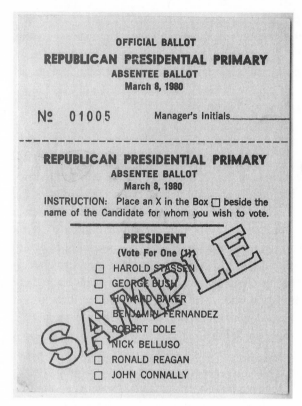

FIGURE 2.2. First GOP
Presidential Primary Ballot
in South Carolina

Source: Republican Party
of South Carolina Papers,
South Carolina Political
Collections, the University
of South Carolina

19,741, while McCormick County had just 170 (South Carolina Republican Party 1980a).

As the primary approached, the feud between the state's Democratic chair, Don Fowler, and Republican chair, Dan Ross, continued. Fowler repeated his assertion that the primary was being held "without any legislative foundation" and argued that "it is irresponsible on their part to seek to nominate a president in such an extralegal manner" (United Press International 1979, 16B). Ross shot back: "The fact of the matter is that just because there isn't a law doesn't mean you can't do it" (United Press International 1979, 16B). Ross pledged to open all precincts, saying that the GOP was "promoting the idea that every cotton pickin' precinct will be manned," but Fowler was skeptical, warning Republicans that if all the precincts were not open, "the whole process" would be opened up to fraud and predicting that people in areas with closed polling places would vote in multiple locations (United Press International 1979, 16B). The *State* even published a tongue-in-cheek editorial entitled "The Don and Dan Show" that took shots at both men (1979, 16A).

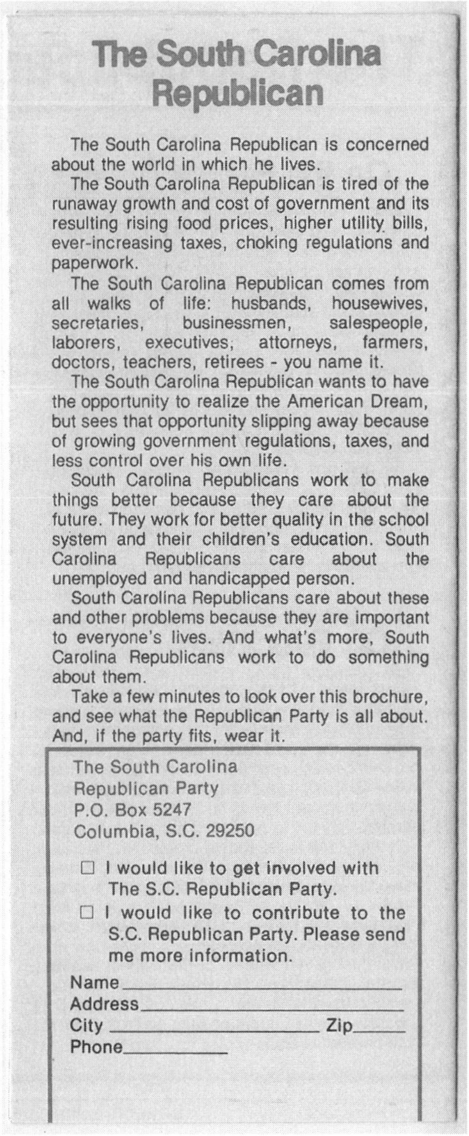

The South Carolina Republican

The South Carolina Republican is concerned about the world in which he lives.

The South Carolina Republican is tired of the runaway growth and cost of government and its resulting rising food prices, higher utility bills, ever-increasing taxes, choking regulations and paperwork.

The South Carolina Republican comes from all walks of life: husbands, housewives, secretaries, businessmen, salespeople, laborers, executives; attorneys, farmers, doctors, teachers, retirees - you name it.

The South Carolina Republican wants to have the opportunity to realize the American Dream, but sees that opportunity slipping away because of growing government regulations, taxes, and less control over his own life.

South Carolina Republicans work to make things better because they care about the future. They work for better quality in the school system and their children's education. South Carolina Republicans care about the unemployed and handicapped person.

South Carolina Republicans care about these and other problems because they are important to everyone's lives. And what's more, South Carolina Republicans work to do something about them.

Take a few minutes to look over this brochure, and see what the Republican Party is all about. And, if the party fits, wear it.

The South Carolina
Republican Party
P.O. Box 5247
Columbia, S.C. 29250

☐ I would like to get involved with The S.C. Republican Party.
☐ I would like to contribute to the S.C. Republican Party. Please send me more information.

Name_____
Address_____
City _____ Zip_____
Phone_____

FIGURE 2.3. GOP Recruitment Brochure from 1980

Source: Republican Party of South Carolina Papers, South Carolina Political Collections, the University of South Carolina

There were also calls for the South Carolina GOP to keep the party's momentum going once the primary concluded. For Republicans, this was an ideal opportunity to reverse the Democratic stranglehold on state power and make the GOP the state's majority party. The South Carolina GOP created a brochure (see figure 2.3) to help grow the party. In addition, South Carolina House minority leader Moffatt Burriss distributed a white paper the day before the primary about the future of the South Carolina Republican Party. Burriss wrote that "if

SOUTH CAROLINA

REPUBLICAN

PARTY

A SPECIAL THANK YOU

Dear Friend,

On behalf of the South Carolina Republican Party, I want to personally thank you for participating in **your** Republican Presidential Primary. By taking the time and interest to cast your vote, you have demonstrated your commitment to responsible government.

In South Carolina, we believe the Republican Party has emerged as the party of the working people. That's the chief reason we scheduled the primary on a Saturday — to encourage maximum participation from working people like you and me.

Every registered voter in South Carolina is welcome to participate in the Republican Presidential Primary, and we welcome new members into the Republican Party.

We actively seek your participation in the Republican Party and your input into local, state, and federal government; a detachable list of Republican elected officials and our state party headquarters is provided on the back of this letter for your convenience.

Once again, my sincere thanks for taking the time to make your voice heard in government.

Sincerely,

Van

Van D. Hipp, Jr.

FIGURE 2.4. GOP Thank You Postcard from 1988 Primary

Source: Republican Party of South Carolina Papers, South Carolina
Political Collections, the University of South Carolina

this rare opportunity is capitalized upon and pursued vigorously as suggested herein, the present dispersal of political power and influence in South Carolina could be altered dramatically" (1980). Burris talked specifically about the excitement surrounding the primary, noting that "newspapers and news broadcasts have been filled with coverage of the contending Republicans" (1980).

The GOP held another successful primary in 1988. Once again, the party used the primary to build support for the Republican brand. Dan Ross worked with party chair Van Hipp to create a thank you postcard that was sent to all voters (see figure 2.4). Since the primary was conducted by local Republican Party organizations, the state South Carolina GOP provided guidance for placing newspapers ads (see figure 2.5) and encouraging turnout.

Democrats Debate A Primary

From the Reconstruction period through the mid-1960s, South Carolina was a core part of the "solid South," a region dominated by one-party Democratic politics (Grantham 1992). Though Democrats talked about holding a presidential primary as far back as the late 1960s (Surratt 1988a), party leaders continued to hold caucuses in an effort to maintain control over the eventual nominee (Surratt 1988b). For example, one reason the Democrats did not hold a primary in 1976 is that party leaders were concerned that George Wallace, the segregationist Alabama governor and frequent presidential candidate, would win in a

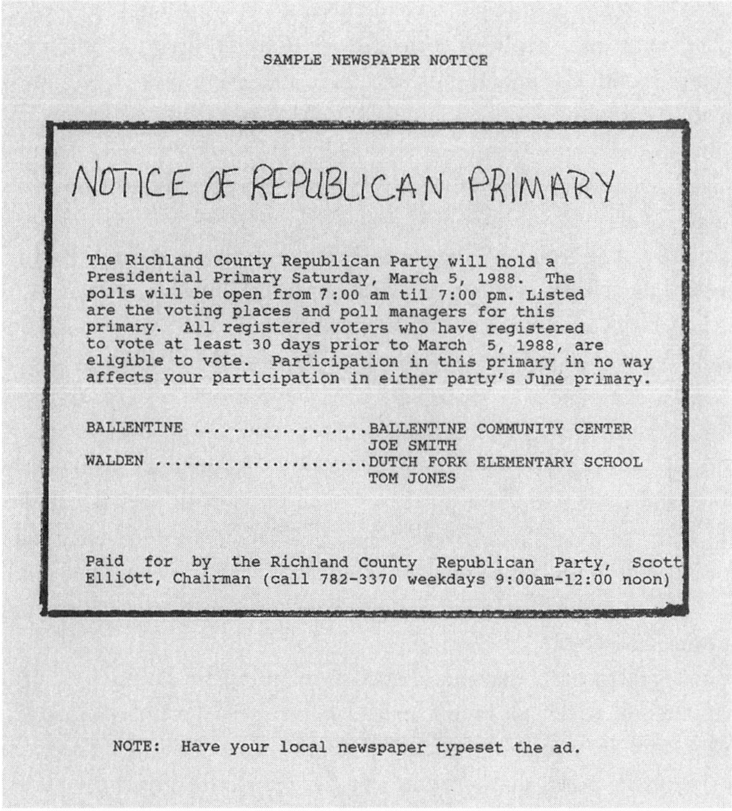

SAMPLE NEWSPAPER NOTICE

NOTICE OF REPUBLICAN PRIMARY

The Richland County Republican Party will hold a
Presidential Primary Saturday, March 5, 1988. The
polls will be open from 7:00 am til 7:00 pm. Listed
are the voting places and poll managers for this
primary. All registered voters who have registered
to vote at least 30 days prior to March 5, 1988, are
eligible to vote. Participation in this primary in no way
affects your participation in either party's June primary.

BALLENTINE ....BALLENTINE COMMUNITY CENTER
                           JOE SMITH
WALDEN ....DUTCH FORK ELEMENTARY SCHOOL
                           TOM JONES

Paid for by the Richland County Republican Party, Scott
Elliott, Chairman (call 782-3370 weekdays 9:00am-12:00 noon)

NOTE: Have your local newspaper typeset the ad.

FIGURE 2.5. Sample GOP Newspaper Ad for 1988 Primary

Source: Republican Party of South Carolina Papers, South Carolina
Political Collections, the University of South Carolina

landslide and that his victory would embarrass the South Carolina Democratic
Party (Surratt 1988a).

Following the GOP's successful first-in-the-South primary in 1980, some
South Carolina Democrats advocated for a presidential primary at the 1982 state
convention (Surratt 1982b). Advocates cited the excitement over the Republican primary and expressed worry over the possibility that voters might shift
allegiances to the GOP after participating in the open primary (Surratt 1982b).
In an effort to address the call for a primary, the South Carolina Democratic
Party followed the lead of the state's GOP by forming a committee to study the
issue. However, there was not strong support for a presidential primary among
the state's Democratic leadership. According to the committee's report, a 1984
primary was an "impossibility." The report emphasized many of the themes
Fowler had stressed in his public comments about the 1980 GOP primary and

referenced the early planning that would need to occur, noting that April 1, 1983, was the date the national Democratic Party required delegate selection plans to be in place (South Carolina Democratic Party 1984, 1).

In addition to the concerns outlined in the report, there were political reasons for not holding a Democratic presidential primary in 1984. Democratic Party leaders cited the potential negative impact of a primary on the presidential candidacy of the state's junior U.S. Senator Fritz Hollings (Surratt 1982a). According to South Carolina's Democratic Party chair Bryan Dorn, "Sen. Hollings is running, and a primary in his own state could cost him some money. He needs to use his energy in other states. A primary in South Carolina would slow him down. We're all for backing him as a favorite son" (Surratt 1982a). There was also a racial component to opposing a Democratic primary in 1984, since African American civil rights activist Jesse Jackson was running for the Democratic nomination. According to one report, "Some Democrats whispered privately that they didn't want to have a primary with Jackson as possibly the leading candidate in the state" (Surratt 1988c). All in all, Democrats decided not to hold a primary prior to 1992 for largely the same overarching reason the Republicans chose to hold a primary in 1980: strategic considerations about the party's electoral future in the state.

In 1988, Democrats once again took steps toward a Democratic primary. Some of the state's African American leaders preferred a primary to the existing caucus system of voting for presidential nominees. State senator Theo Mitchell from Greenville noted that a primary would reduce the pressure of a caucus: "There are people who'd like to support Jesse, but when they come down to the caucuses they feel pressure. There's no question that people would like to keep their ballots secret, and that's what you would have in a primary, not to mention broader participation" (Bandy 1987). South Carolina Republicans even reached out to Democrats, offering to hold a primary or caucuses on the same day in 1988, but national party rules prevented Democrats from holding a nominating contest before March 8 (Shurr 1988; Williams 1987). Some pointed to an ulterior motive by Republicans: aiding Jesse Jackson's candidacy. According to South Carolina political reporter Lee Bandy (1987), "Republicans, wanting nothing better than to embarrass Democrats with Jackson, have challenged their counterparts to hold a primary to demonstrate that they are not a closed party controlled by a few bosses." As they did in 1984, South Carolina Democrats passed on holding a presidential primary in 1988. Following the record turnout in South Carolina's 1988 Republican presidential primary, state GOP Chair Van Hipp said, "I think they're kicking themselves in the rear end right now" (Shurr 1988).

Even though Democrats stuck with caucuses in 1988, grassroots support for a Democratic presidential primary was building in South Carolina. Based on a survey of Democratic county chairs reported in the *State* on March 11, the day before the 1988 Democratic caucuses and six days after the GOP primary, the party's chairpersons supported a primary by a two-to-one margin (Surratt 1988a). John Ruoff, Fairfield County Democratic chair, said, "Primaries involve more people and are fundamentally more democratic. Caucuses are confusing and in-timidating" (Surratt 1988a). Spartanburg County chair Jack Lawrence shared his frustration: "It's the most confusing system we've ever come up with. It's crazy to do it this way" (Surratt 1988a). Yet some Democratic leaders defended the caucus system. Mary Jean Byrd, Democratic chair in York County, argued that "the caucus is a much better method to pick the best candidates" (Surratt 1988a). Other leaders emphasized the grassroots involvement caucuses fostered and the ability to conduct party business at them (Surratt 1988b). After the state's 1988 Democratic caucuses concluded, debates about a primary continued. Demo-cratic fund-raiser Sam Tennebaum and Richland County councilmember Bob Coble urged the party to move to a primary. Coble said, "I'm not concerned about Republicans' publicity, but our process is not open; it discourages people" (Bryant 1988).

Momentum for a Democratic first-in-the-South presidential primary con-tinued to build. At the national level, nearly three-fourths of the states held primaries in the 1988 contest (Kamarck 2016a). Additionally, Democrats lost a third presidential election in a row when George H.W. Bush defeated Michael Dukakis in November. On top of that, Carroll Campbell, South Carolina's popu-lar Republican governor, was reelected in a landslide two years later. In an effort to create a more democratic process, change the party's fortunes, and compete directly with the state's GOP, South Carolina Democrats "took a page directly from the Republicans' book" by scheduling the first primary in a southern state, three days before the 1992 Super Tuesday contests on March 7 (Surratt 1991, 5B). The *State's* editorial board praised the decision, saying that state Democrats had "finally decided to play it smart. . . . By opting for a Presidential primary, the Democrats wisely concluded—as the Republicans did 11 years ago—they can best serve their political ends by opening up the nominating process and making it as accessible as possible to the greatest number of South Carolinians" ("Democrats Wisely Opt to Open Up Process" 1991). While this primary was billed as the first Democratic presidential primary in the South, Georgia moved in front of both the Democratic and Republican primaries in South Carolina in 1992, momentarily stealing away the coveted first-in-the-South designation.

Republicans Struggle to Stay First in the South

Maintaining first-in-the-South status was a constant struggle for the South Caro-lina Republican Party. In 1992, Georgia leapfrogged South Carolina, moving its primary to March 3, the Tuesday before South Carolina's March 7 Democratic and Republican contests. It is important to note that this was not a conscious attempt by Georgia Republicans to move in front of South Carolina but instead something instigated by Georgia's Democratic governor Zell Miller (Associated Press 1991). Miller, a moderate southern Democrat, urged the Georgia state legislature to move the primary up to help his friend, Arkansas governor and 1992 presidential candidate, Bill Clinton (Clark and Haynes 2002). The bill to reschedule the Georgia primary was fast-tracked through the legislature during the first three days of the 1992 session and signed by Miller on January 15 (Associated Press 1992).

No doubt, the rescheduling of the Georgia primary was a direct assault on South Carolina's first-in-the-South designation. One of the key Georgia legislators involved in moving the primary up said, "We will be the bellwether for the Southeast on presidential politics" (Bandy 1992b, 5B). There was also a recognition that Georgia had a big media advantage over South Carolina, particularly with the presence of CNN in Atlanta (Bandy 1992b). Journalists and political pundits in South Carolina conceded the coup. Lee Bandy wrote, "The bloom is off the South Carolina presidential primary, thanks to neighboring Georgia" (Bandy 1992b, 5B). Similarly, Clemson University political scientist David Woodard remarked that South Carolina's new placement on the electoral calendar meant that "South Carolina will become just another Southern state" (Bandy 1992b, 5B).

Soon after being upstaged by Georgia, South Carolina Republicans vowed to regain their first-in-the-South position. A month before the 1992 primary, and four years before the 1996 election, South Carolina GOP executive director Mike Burton, said "We will have a primary in February next time. We want to be the first primary in the South, the New Hampshire in the South. It is important to be first in the region" (Bandy 1992b, 5B). As the 1996 cycle approached, state GOP leaders once again battled for first-in the-South status. Republican officials in Louisiana voted to hold caucuses on February 6, almost a month before the date the South Carolina Republican presidential primary had been scheduled for (Bandy 1995). Mike Francis, chair of the Louisiana Republican Party, said, "Why shouldn't we get some of the attention?" (Bandy 1995, D4). South Carolina GOP chair Henry McMaster shot back that "we're still the first-in-the-South primary. Their's is just a caucus" and put South Carolina's GOP primary in historical context: "More battles were fought in South Carolina during the Revolutionary War than any other state. . . . So, it's only fitting that this state will be the battleground for the conservative revolution" (Bandy 1995, D4). South Carolina was able to combat Louisiana's late move with support from Republican presidential candidates (with the exception of Phil Gramm and Pat Buchanan), who signed pledges not to campaign in the Pelican State (Bandy 1995, D4).

During the 2000 cycle, the threat against the South Carolina primary did not come from other southern states but instead from two large midwestern states. South Carolina Republicans planned to hold their primary on the first Saturday in March, three days before Super Tuesday, but Michigan and Ohio considered moving their primaries to the same day (Bandy 1999e). Trey Walker, the state's GOP executive director, observed that "if Michigan and Ohio move up to the day we traditionally hold our primary, South Carolina is not significant anymore," adding that "if I were a candidate, I would play up to those two Rust Belt states because there are more convention delegates there." He pledged to maintain the first-in-the-South position, noting "we're going to nip that one in the bud" (Bandy 1999e, B1). The party initially voted to schedule the South Carolina primary for February 26 (Bandy 1999e) but later moved it to February 19, thus distancing the state from Michigan and Ohio (Bandy 1999b).

Although Republicans did not hold a primary in 2004, because George W. Bush was seeking reelection as president, securing first-in-the-South status was once again a high priority for the South Carolina GOP in 2008. South Carolina Republicans set the primary date for February 2 but were put in a difficult position when the Florida legislature moved its primary to January 29 (Sheinin 2007c). In 2006, South Carolina GOP party chair Katon Dawson, said, "We're solidly committed to being the first in the South primary, regardless of the date" (Bandy 2006b, B3). He was even willing to go against RNC rules prohibiting a primary before February 2. Responding to the prospect of being stripped of delegates and assigned less desirable hotel rooms at the national convention for breaking the rule, Dawson said, "I would rather stay in my hotel room and watch the proceedings on television . . . than surrender our position" (Bandy 2006b, B3). By this time, South Carolina was working to coordinate its primary date with New Hampshire (Sheinin 2007c). In a response to Florida's move, Dawson traveled to Concord, New Hampshire, to meet with New Hampshire secretary of state Bill Gardner, ultimately announcing a new date of January 19, the earliest South Carolina GOP primary in history. Dawson proclaimed, "There's no Southern state ahead of the 19th, and we're fairly sure it remains that way" (Sheinin 2007c, B1). In 2008, Florida, Michigan, New Hampshire, South Carolina, and Wyoming were stripped of half of their convention delegates by the Republican National Committee for holding primaries before the approved date (Hendin, Pinto, and Salvanto 2011).

In 2012, Florida once again threatened South Carolina's first-in-the-South position by moving its primary to January 31 (G. Smith 2011a). This action violated RNC rules and led the early primary states of Iowa, New Hampshire, Nevada, and South Carolina to once again change their primary date (G. Smith 2011a). As they had done in previous years, South Carolina Republicans moved the date back, setting their 2012 primary for January 21 (G. Smith 2011a). Responding to the Florida decision, South Carolina GOP chair Chad Connelly said, "Last Friday, a nine-person committee brought chaos to the 2012 calendar. Today, South Carolina is making things right," adding that "South Carolina Republicans have a 30-year track record of picking the eventual Republican presidential nominee. We will continue that historic tradition on Jan. 21, 2012" (G. Smith 2011a, A1). The Republican Party yet again penalized Arizona, Florida, Michigan, New Hampshire, and South Carolina for scheduling early contests in 2012 (Helfand 2012).

Democrats Struggle to Stay First in the South

South Carolina Democrats likewise wanted to secure and maintain the coveted first-in-the-South primary slot. Although Democrats immediately lost first-in-the-South status for their initial primary in 1992 because of Georgia's successful bid to move ahead of South Carolina on the nomination calendar, the biggest opposition to state Democrats' bid to be first in the South came from the Democratic National Committee (DNC). In fact, South Carolina Democrats and the DNC engaged in an epic battle over the date of the 2000 contest. Responding to the South Carolina GOP's efforts to move the Republican primary to February, the state Democratic Party's executive committee voted in April 1999 to hold a primary on the same day (Bandy 1999d). Notably, DNC rules prohibited any primaries or caucuses before the first Tuesday in March, with waivers for just two states, Iowa and New Hampshire (Bandy 1999d). Although a waiver for South Carolina seemed unlikely, the state's newly elected Democratic governor, Jim Hodges, backed the February date, as did South Carolina Democratic Party chair Dick Harpootlian (Bandy 1999d). Anticipating the waiver denial, Harpootlian said, "The national party folks are more concerned about their interest than about building the party in South Carolina. We've been ignored, timewise and moneywise by the DNC. So we have to go our own route" (Bandy 1999d, A1). GOP executive director Trey Walker tried to stoke the flames of the divisions among his rivals, saying "It's only natural for the Democrats to copy our successes. We'd love for them to bring their freak show to South Carolina, because what a tremendous contrast we'd have to Al Gore and Bill Bradley, slugging it out over who is the most liberal" (Bandy 1999d, A1).

South Carolina Democrats debated the 2000 presidential primary date at their annual convention (Bandy 1999c). Fowler, who was now a DNC committee member, proposed a resolution asking the state executive committee to "reconsider plans" to move the primary to February (Bandy 1999a). Emphasizing the DNC rule about no primaries before the first Tuesday in March, Fowler told delegates, "It's a rule of law. . . . I don't think the Democratic Party needs to do

anything because the Republicans are doing it" (Bandy 1999a, B1). Fowler esca-
lated the rhetoric when he compared the executive committee move to the 1948
Dixiecrat revolt led by South Carolina's Strom Thurmond (Bandy 1999a, B1).
Harpootlian responded in the media that "this is not 1948. And I'm not Strom
Thurmond. And this is not about civil rights. It's about winning elections in
South Carolina in the year 2000" (Bandy 1999a, B1).

Despite the resolution to reconsider, South Carolina Democratic leaders
voted to request a waiver from the DNC so that they could hold the state's Democratic presidential primary on February 19. Harpootlian said, "The governor and
I believe this to be an effective party-building tool" (Bandy 1999b, B1), adding
that "we don't want to be a one-team state" (Strope 1999). Scott Anderson, executive director of the South Carolina Democratic Party, presented the state's
waiver request to the DNC, emphasizing the cost of holding separate contests
(between $500,000 and $750,000) and the confusion that can arise from separate primaries (Davis 1999). However, and as expected, the waiver was unani-
mously denied (Davis 1999). Fowler, who didn't vote, said that there was "a good
and sufficient reason" for the DNC rules preventing states from scheduling primaries before the first Tuesday in March, noting that the long primary season
led to lower participation rates among voters in some states (Davis 1999, B1).
In the end, Democrats opted for March 9 caucuses in the 2000 cycle, two days
after over a dozen states held their contests on March 7. Because of the caucus
format, turnout was much lower than it would have been if a primary were held:
only 9,657 voters cast ballots compared to 116,413 that participated in the state's
Democratic presidential primary eight years earlier (Cook 2000).[3]

While South Carolina Democrats' attempt to host the first southern primary
in 2000 ended in disappointment, they continued to pursue first-in-the-South
status in the lead up to the 2004 nomination contest. In early 2002, the DNC
announced that states would be permitted to hold primaries in February, much
earlier than in previous cycles (Bandy 2002). As a result of the rule change,
South Carolina Democrats scheduled their presidential primary on February
3. According to Carol Khare, who in 2004 was the co-chair of the DNC's Rules
and Bylaws Committee, "We want to send a message to candidates that we're
going to be first in the South" (Bandy 2003b, B3). Reflecting on South Carolina's
first-in-the-South placement, Democratic consultant Kevin Geddings emphasized the state's ethnic diversity and the affordability of its media markets, while
Harpootlian remarked that "if you can't win in South Carolina, you can't win
nationally" (Bandy 2003b).

To celebrate having secured the early primary, South Carolina Democrats
hosted a kickoff weekend for 2004 presidential contenders titled "The Road to
a Democratic White House Starts in South Carolina." Harpootlian boldly predicted that "whoever wins this primary will be the nominee" (Bandy 2003b, A1).

Party leaders also discussed what it would take for Democratic hopefuls to succeed in the South Carolina primary. While the African American vote would be key, state representative Gilda Cobb-Hunter emphasized that "you can't win the presidency by focusing just on black folks" (Bandy 2003b, A1). Winthrop University's Scott Huffmon said, "The candidate who can attract the independent white vote is the kind of candidate who can carry a Southern state or two, and that's what Democrats need in order to win" (Bandy 2003b, A1). Enthusiasm among South Carolina Democrats was palpable in 2004. Delegate Isaac Williams from

SEVEN DAYS TO SOUTH CAROLINA VICTORY:

KEY FACTS ABOUT THE SC PRIMARY

First-In-The-South

The February 3rd South Carolina Primary plays a critical role as the gateway to the South. It will be the first time candidates are exposed to the voters they will need to win over and inspire and the issues they will need to lead on in order to win the general election in 2004. Democrats must be ready to run on their message of hope and leadership across the nation – from North to South to take back the White House.

The First and Most Significant Test of Support With African American Voters

Between 30 to 40 percent of the South Caroline Primary electorate is African American. This is the first state where candidates will be forced to confront issues critically important to African American voters. Without significant African American support in the fall, Democrats cannot take back the White House.

A True Presidential Primary – All Precincts Will Be Opening

Unlike other some of the other states holding primaries and caucuses on the 3rd, the South Carolina Democratic Party is running a true Presidential Primary. All polling places will be open and staffed from 7:00 AM to 7:00 PM

First With Results – South Carolina Democratic Party Chair has brought the Iowa reporting system to South Carolina Primary

South Carolina is the biggest state in the Eastern Time Zone which has an election on February 3rd. We will have an automated reporting system to get results. Our Presidential preference question is the only thing on our ballot so we expect rapid results. As precincts finish their counts, results will be phoned into headquarters.

FIGURE 2.6. Democratic Talking Points for Initial First-in-the-South Primary in 2004 (Part 1)
Source: Democratic Party of South Carolina Records, South Carolina
Political Collections, the University of South Carolina

Columbia remarked, "I haven't seen this much excitement in 20 years" (Bandy 2003a, A10). According to Bandy (2003a, A10), "Everyone attributed the new enthusiasm to the earlier primary—the first the party has held since 1992, when 114,000 voters went to the polls."

Seven days before the contest the South Carolina Democratic Party issued a press release entitled "Key Facts about the SC Primary" (see figures 2.6 and 2.7) that emphasized a few main points. First, state Democrats highlighted the fact that it was to be the region's first primary, noting that it would play "a critical

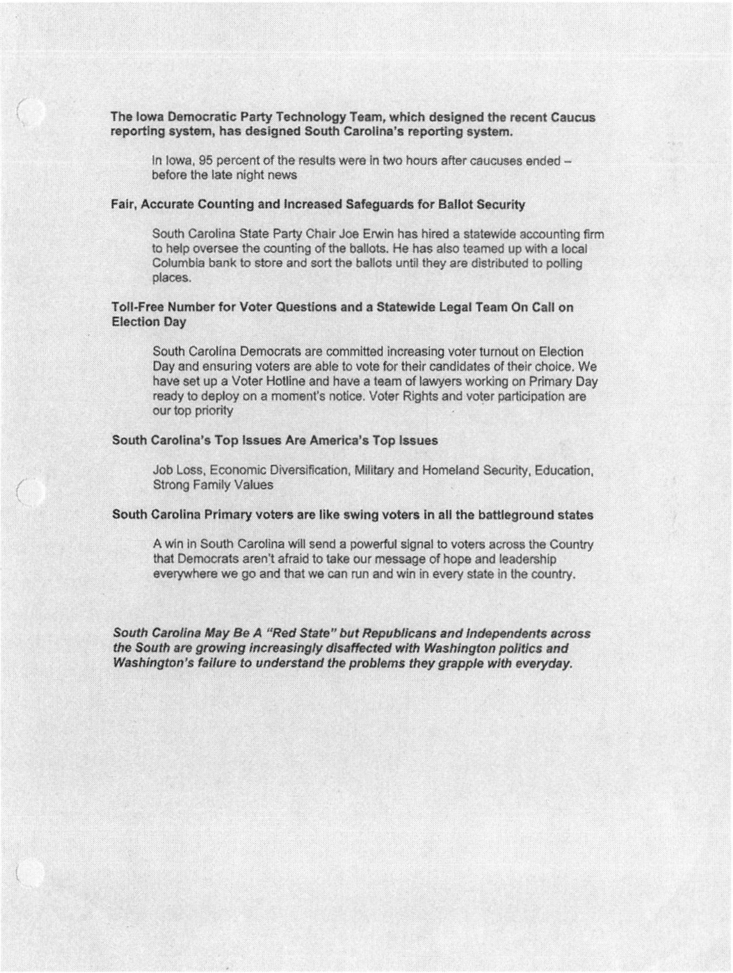

The Iowa Democratic Party Technology Team, which designed the recent Caucus reporting system, has designed South Carolina's reporting system.

In Iowa, 95 percent of the results were in two hours after caucuses ended – before the late night news

Fair, Accurate Counting and Increased Safeguards for Ballot Security

South Carolina State Party Chair Joe Erwin has hired a statewide accounting firm to help oversee the counting of the ballots. He has also teamed up with a local Columbia bank to store and sort the ballots until they are distributed to polling places.

Toll-Free Number for Voter Questions and a Statewide Legal Team On Call on Election Day

South Carolina Democrats are committed increasing voter turnout on Election Day and ensuring voters are able to vote for their candidates of their choice. We have set up a Voter Hotline and have a team of lawyers working on Primary Day ready to deploy on a moment's notice. Voter Rights and voter participation are our top priority

South Carolina's Top Issues Are America's Top Issues

Job Loss, Economic Diversification, Military and Homeland Security, Education, Strong Family Values

South Carolina Primary voters are like swing voters in all the battleground states

A win in South Carolina will send a powerful signal to voters across the Country that Democrats aren't afraid to take our message of hope and leadership everywhere we go and that we can run and win in every state in the country.

South Carolina May Be A "Red State" but Republicans and Independents across the South are growing increasingly disaffected with Washington politics and Washington's failure to understand the problems they grapple with everyday.

FIGURE 2.7. Democratic Talking Points for Initial First-in-the-South Primary in 2004 (Part 2)
Source: Democratic Party of South Carolina Records, South Carolina Political Collections, the University of South Carolina

role as the gateway to the South." Second, Democrats stressed that the South Carolina contest was "the first and most significant test of support with African American voters." And third, the party took a shot at the South Carolina GOP, calling the Democratic primary "a true presidential primary" and noting that "all precincts" would be open (South Carolina Democratic Party 2004).

The 2004 Democratic contest, the initial first-in-the-South election for Democrats, included a large, experienced, and diverse roster. In addition to U.S. senators John Edwards, John Kerry, and Joe Lieberman, the field included two African American candidates, Carol Mosely Braun and Al Sharpton. The full list of candidates can be seen on the sample ballot in figure 2.8.

OFFICIAL STATEWIDE ABSENTEE BALLOT

SOUTH CAROLINA DEMOCRATIC PARTY
PRESIDENTIAL PRIMARY

FEBRUARY 3, 2004

No.

_____
Initials of Issuing Officer

- -

OFFICIAL STATEWIDE ABSENTEE BALLOT

SOUTH CAROLINA DEMOCRATIC PARTY
PRESIDENTIAL PRIMARY

FEBRUARY 3, 2004

INSTRUCTIONS: To vote this ballot make a cross (X) in the voting square (☐) opposite the name of the candidate on the ballot for whom you wish to vote. Before leaving the booth, fold the ballot so that the initials of the manager will be seen on the outside.

Vote for no more than one.

☒ CAROL MOSELEY BRAUN

☐ WESLEY K. CLARK

☐ HOWARD DEAN

☐ JOHN EDWARDS

☐ DICK GEPHARDT

☐ JOHN F. KERRY

☐ DENNIS J. KUCINICH

☐ JOE LIEBERMAN

☐ AL SHARPTON

FIGURE 2.8. Ballot for Democrat's Initial First-in-the-South Presidential Primary
Source: Democratic Party of South Carolina Records, South Carolina Political Collections, the University of South Carolina

In 2008 there were no obvious threats to the state's Democratic first-in-the-South position. After battling with the DNC for many years, South Carolina Democrats received good news from the national party in 2006 when the DNC approved rules allowing four states, one from each region, to hold contests before February 5 (Clark 2009). Since Iowa, located in the Midwest, and New Hampshire, part of the Northeast region, would remain in place, the DNC looked to add a state from the South and a state from the West. With the goal of creating demographic balance, there was a particular focus on selecting states that represented African Americans, Hispanics, and labor unions (Kamarck 2016a). South Carolina also had two members on the Rules and Bylaws committee, Carol Khare and Don Fowler, to advocate for the Palmetto State (Bandy 2006a). Khare emphasized South Carolina Democrats' commitment to ensuring that they held the first southern primary: "It's very important to us that we remain the first-in-the-South primary because of the natural benefits we get" (Bandy 2006a, B1). She also emphasized the strategic considerations behind holding an early primary: "When the South Carolina Republicans have an early primary," she asserted, it was important that "we do also" (Bandy 2006a, B1). In the end, the DNC selected South Carolina because of its substantial African American population and Nevada because of its Hispanic population and because it had labor unions (Kamarck 2016a). The DNC also agreed to penalize states if they held contests before February 5 (Clark 2009). Khare circulated a letter asking Democratic presidential candidates not to campaign in states other than Iowa, New Hampshire, South Carolina, and Nevada before February 5 (Kamarck 2016a).

The 2008 version of the state's Democratic presidential primary was originally set for January 29, but there were two problems with this date. South Carolina Republicans had scheduled their primary on January 19, and Florida, another southern state, had a primary scheduled on January 29. Khare was not only concerned about South Carolina losing its position as first in the South but also about the date for the GOP contest: "I'm not comfortable being 10 days after the Republicans. This is a South Carolina thing, not a Florida thing" (Sheinin 2007b, A1). However, although she was not able to schedule the Democratic primary to coincide with the Republican primary, she was able to move the primary from January 29 to January 26 (Sheinin 2007a).

Other Threats to the South Carolina Primary

South Carolina's first-in-the-South status was also put in jeopardy when, as South Carolina Republicans planned for the 2000 edition of the primary, Democratic state representative Todd Rutherford filed a complaint with the U.S. Justice Department alleging racial bias by the GOP for not opening up polling places in many predominantly African American precincts (Bandy 2000c). From the beginning, state GOP leaders questioned the impetus for the lawsuit. South Carolina Republican Party chair Henry McMaster noted that "their motivation is not to increase the participation in the Republican Party but to score cheap, petty, partisan points by further inflaming racial tensions" (Bandy 2000c) and said that this was "an attempt by Harpootlian to attack the credibility and success of the Republican primary because the Democratic primary is demonstrably a flat, abject failure" (Bandy 2000d). Just five days before the GOP's scheduled primary in 2000, a three-judge panel, appointed by the Fourth Circuit Court of Appeals in Richmond, heard the complaint (LeBlanc 2000a). The South Carolina Republican Party agreed to open "all available polling places," estimated to be about 1,600 of the 1,752 in the state (LeBlanc 2000b). Following the settlement, Rutherford took a parting shot: "It is shameful that the Republican Party had to be dragged into the 21st century, to make a federal court point a gun at their head to allow African-Americans access to polling places" (LeBlanc 2000b). Despite the legal challenge, the GOP's first-in-the-South primary took place as scheduled in 2000, with the highest level of participation of any South Carolina presidential primary up to that point.

Another challenge to the first-in-the-South primary was finding a way to pay for the event. The state political parties were responsible for conducting primaries before the passage of a 2007 law requiring that the state election commission oversee presidential primaries in South Carolina ("S.C. Politics Today" 2007; B. Smith 2012). The legislation allowed the South Carolina GOP and South Carolina Democratic Party to set the dates and filing requirements but changed the ways the elections are conducted and funded ("Presidential or Advisory Primaries Act" 2007). The legislation, introduced by Democratic state senator Vincent Sheheen, was initially vetoed by Governor Mark Sanford on the grounds that it would cost more to hold Republican and Democratic primaries on separate days ("S.C. Politics Today" 2007). In his veto message, he wrote that "if the parties were able to come together on a single election, I could support the legislation ("Same-Day Presidential Primaries" 2007). However, the veto was overridden near the end of the 2007 legislative session ("S.C. Politics Today" 2007).

Disputes about financing the first-in-the-South primaries continued during the 2012 cycle. Though the state election commission was now in charge of the state's presidential primaries and was required to pay for the elections, the state legislature did not allocate enough money to cover all election expenses (G. Smith 2011b). Greenville County election officials reported over $20,000 in unreimbursed costs from 2008 (G. Smith 2011b). In the period leading up to the 2012 contest, the state legislature had authorized $680,000, but the state election commission estimated that the primary would cost about $1.5 million (Beam 2011). In October 2011, four counties (Beaufort, Chester, Greenville, and Spartanburg) filed suit against the commission, arguing that it was not authorized to conduct the 2012 presidential primaries and that the general assembly had not provided sufficient funds to administer the elections (G. Smith 2011b). The legal wrangling threatened to delay or perhaps even lead to the cancelation of the 2012 primary (Beam 2011). In *Beaufort County v. SC Election Commission,* the South Carolina Supreme Court rejected the petition by the counties in a three to two decision, ruling that the commission must conduct the presidential primary but declining to wade into the issue of payment (Associated Press 2011). Ultimately, the state and counties would be required to cover the costs of the primaries.

Conclusion

In this chapter, we have addressed the book's first research question: how did South Carolina become first in the South? For the state's GOP, the decision to schedule the first southern primary was part of a strategic calculation; Republicans hoped to influence national politics, strengthen the state party, get more people to consider Republican candidates, and bring publicity and notoriety to the state. Although there was considerable opposition to the 1980 GOP primary from local party leaders, as well as former governor Jim Edwards and Senator Strom Thurmond, the party's presidential primary committee worked to build consensus for the primary throughout the summer of 1979. Winning support from the party's county chairs was particularly important given the logistical challenges of holding an early primary with higher voter participation and more frequent campaign events. When the Republican state convention gathered in the fall, the primary passed with near unanimous approval, and South Carolina's first-in-the-South primary was born.

No doubt the success of the GOP primary strengthened the Republican Party in South Carolina. Party building was one of the most frequent justifications for holding the first presidential primary in 1980. Republican officials and prominent journalists cited a range of benefits to holding a primary: increased voter turnout in Republican contests, greater visibility for the party at both the state and national levels, and, of course, greater power over who became the GOP's presidential nominee. Although the primary was certainly not the main cause of the Republican realignment in South Carolina, as the realignment occurred in every other southern state, the primary likely accelerated GOP growth in South Carolina and was one factor, among a few, in the strong Republican tide that swept the Palmetto State in the subsequent decades.

For South Carolina Democrats, the path to first-in-the-South status was much longer and far more difficult. Democratic Party chair Don Fowler was a strong supporter of the caucus format, and the state's Democratic leadership blocked efforts to create a presidential primary in 1984 and 1988. Owing to mounting pressure from within the party and a growing perception that the GOP presidential primary was a resounding success, the South Carolina Democratic Party changed course in 1992, shifting to a primary format and securing, albeit temporarily, the coveted first-in-the-South calendar slot. In early 1992, Georgia moved ahead of South Carolina, making the Palmetto State the second southern state on the nomination calendar. Disputes with the Democratic National Committee prevented South Carolina Democrats from holding the first southern primary in 2000, but South Carolina Democrats finally secured first-in-the-South status in 2004 due, in part, to the state's racial diversity, and they have maintained that distinction in all subsequent elections.

Although the main focus of this chapter is the story of how the South Carolina primary became first in the South, another topic we have covered is the strategic considerations that party leaders confronted when deciding whether to shift from a caucus to a primary. Party leaders on both sides of the aisle weighed the pros and cons of moving to primaries, with proponents working hard to convince recalcitrant members of their party of the virtues of a primary format. Notably, Democrats decided not to hold a primary prior to 1992 for the same reason Republicans decided to hold a primary in 1980: strategic considerations about the party's electoral future. Ultimately, the story of the first-in-the-South GOP presidential primary is one of a minority party looking for a way to attract attention, raise money, and enhance its fortunes. It is also a tale of entrepreneurial party leaders and activists and a relentless fight for legitimacy and respect in a state and region that had been dominated by Democrats for over a century. For Democrats, sticking with caucuses until 1992 helped the party maintain stricter control over state politics, while holding the first-in-the-South primary represented a chance to recapture ground that had been lost to Republicans. It was also an opportunity for a more conservative state, and a state with a high percentage of African American voters, to diversity the slate of early states and have an influence on the party's presidential nominee.

★ 3 ★

SOUTH CAROLINA'S
PRIMARY ELECTORATE

While the Iowa caucuses and New Hampshire primary receive the lion's share of attention from both journalists and academics, we have argued that South Carolina's first-in-the-South primary is equally, and in some ways *more,* deserving of investigation. One of the main reasons South Carolina deserves greater attention is that it has an impressive track record in correctly predicting the eventual nominee, particularly in Republican nomination contests, and adds much needed diversity to the slate of early states.

Since South Carolina's initial Republican presidential primary in 1980, the state's winner has secured the GOP nomination in six of seven contested primaries, an 86 percent success rate.[1] Iowa and New Hampshire correctly selected the winner 29 and 71 percent of the time, respectively. South Carolina's only miss on the Republican side was when a neighboring state candidate, Newt Gingrich of Georgia, won in 2012. A number of commentators have claimed that South Carolina's predictive ability hinges on the state's unique blend of different GOP voting blocs, a feature that distinguishes the Palmetto State from Iowa and New Hampshire.

South Carolina has correctly selected the winner in three of six contested Democratic elections since 1980, a 50 percent success rate.[2] By comparison, Iowa and New Hampshire predicted the Democratic winner 67 and 33 percent of the time, respectively. According to most observers, South Carolina's Democratic primary electorate is not a microcosm of the party's national electorate, even though most commentators agree the state provides critical demographic balance, unlike Iowa and New Hampshire.

We begin this chapter by addressing our book's second research question: does South Carolina have a special ability to predict who secures each party's nomination? To address this question, we conduct an analysis of the predictive accuracy of all fifty states to try to determine whether South Carolina's track record is truly notable. Then, we turn to our third primary research question: is South Carolina representative of each party's national nominating electorate? In an effort to answer this question, we develop a measure of South Carolina's representativeness using responses to demographic and attitudinal questions from nationwide exit poll data. Our analysis allows us to investigate South Carolina's primary electorate in detail while also enabling us to make direct comparisons with the primary electorates in other states. In the final section of this chapter, we use the first two analyses to examine whether representative states better predict the eventual nominee, as many have claimed. Although no one state is able to fully reflect the nation as a whole, and no state, alone, shapes the entire nominating process, some states are certainly more representative and more impactful than others.

Predictive Ability Matters

It may be tempting to dismiss a state's predictive ability in nomination contests as a trivial matter, one that concerns mere bragging rights. Yet there are very real political and economic consequences when a state gets it wrong in a primary or caucus. First, a state's political clout suffers when it consistently supports losing candidates. For example, former New Hampshire governor John Sununu famously dismissed the Iowa caucus, saying the "Iowa picks corn, New Hampshire picks presidents" (Redlawsk, Tolbert, and Donovan 2011, 27). One consequence of Iowa's low predictive ability is the fact that some candidates skip the state entirely. Not only does this reduce Iowa's political clout but it denies its citizens the opportunity to interact with prominent national figures and even hurts the state economically (McCann, Partin, Rapoport, and Stone 1996; Moore and Smith 2015; Redlawsk, Tolbert, and Donovan 2011). Second, states that support losing candidates are likely to have higher number of elected officials that did not endorse their party's standard bearer. An incorrect endorsement can, in turn, hurt that official's reputation in subsequent elections and make her or him less likely to garner a spot in a president's administration or other prominent positions. And third, a state that votes incorrectly could be harmed by executive branch policy decisions. As just one example, a number of studies in political science and economics have found that the allocation of federal disaster assistance is affected, in part, by whether a state is a supporter or opponent of the president in the general election (Husted and Nickerson 2014; Kriner and Reeves 2015; Wood 2009).

The most serious consequence of a state backing a losing candidate, especially when that state holds an *early* contest, is its potential to undermine the legitimacy of the nomination process itself. Because they wield disproportionate power over who becomes the eventual nominee, many commentators argue that the early states should reflect the social, political, and economic characteristics of the nation as whole. As Elaine Kamarck (2009) notes, the main criticism of old nominating system is that it was undemocratic. The current primary system has also been criticized as having undemocratic elements. Iowa and New Hampshire are the subject of frequent criticism among reform advocates given the perception that outlying demographic and attitudinal characteristics on one side of the aisle or the other determine who wins.

Predictive Ability and Representativeness

Journalists cite three features that distinguish the Iowa caucuses, from the primaries of most states. Iowa is sparsely populated and rural, and 91 percent of its population is white.[3] Given these features, "Why," as Andrew Prokop puts it, "do we care so much about who wins?" On the Republican side, a large evangelical and socially conservative bloc in the western part of the state distinguishes Iowa as well. Political journalist Benjamin Wallace-Wade (2016) calls the state's Republican electorate "stringently evangelical" and cites this as a reason for the recent streak of socially conservative winners in Iowa—Cruz in 2016, Santorum in 2012, and Huckabee in 2008—that often lose the GOP nomination. On the Democratic side, observers cite the state's urban centers with younger and more educated voters as an outlying feature in Democratic contests (Cohn 2016). Yet not everyone agrees that Iowa's voters are as far outside the mainstream as is often claimed. Writing for the *Wall Street Journal,* Randy Yeip, Max Rust, and Jessia Ma (2016) say the state "isn't a monolith" while Nate Cohn (2016) notes that "Iowa's demographic homogeneity obscures considerable political diversity."

Journalists note that the same three features make New Hampshire an outlier in its primaries: it is small and rural, and its population is 94 percent white.[4] Despite these similarities, the two states have a penchant for selecting different candidates. Since 1980, no Republican nonincumbent has won both states, and John Kerry in 2004 is the only Democrat with victories in both Iowa and New Hampshire. For Republicans, New Hampshire has fewer evangelicals and has a higher concentration of Catholics than the national average (Cook 2016). Moreover, the Democratic primary electorate is wealthier than in most other states according to many observers (Gaudiano 2016). But perhaps the most frequently cited characteristic is the state's number of self-declared independents and moderates. According to National Public Radio's Brakkton Booker and Domenico Montanaro (2016), "a lot of those voters are independents or undeclared—roughly 44 percent. Not surprising for a place whose state motto is 'Live Free or Die.'" Not everyone agrees with this characterization, however. Andrew Smith and David Moore (2016) argue that this "myth" stems from confusing undeclared voters with independents; "no candidate has won the New Hampshire primary," they point out, "without winning a plurality of his or her party's registered voters."

The conventional wisdom among journalists and other observers regarding South Carolina is that it is, in contrast to Iowa and New Hampshire, representative of the national Republican primary electorate. If there is any disagreement, it lies in the wide range of factors that are often cited to explain the state's demographic balance. Scottie Nell Hughes of the Tea Party News Network observes that the Palmetto State combines the notable elements of both Iowa and New Hampshire—evangelicals and ideological moderates—and is thus "a real test of what America wants" (Hatuqa 2016). Similarly, Henry Olsen (2015), a senior fellow at the Ethics and Public Policy Center, says the state is "neatly balanced between the GOP's four factions," citing blocs of "moderates," "somewhat conservatives," "very conservative evangelicals," and "very conservative seculars." Noting a different type of balance, Clemson University political scientist David Woodard points out that in South Carolina "the economy drives the elections, but we are also interested in foreign policy because we have many military retirees" (Hatuqa 2016). Another South Carolina political scientist, Furman University's Danielle Vinson, claims that the state has a diverse array of Republicans, citing "a military contingent, a strong business establishment, and evangelicals who don't always vote in a bloc" (Rosen 2015).

On the other side, there is less consensus on whether South Carolina accurately reflects the Democratic Party's national primary electorate. Yet virtually all observers agree that the state *adds* critical demographic balance missing from Iowa and New Hampshire. As we discuss in chapter 2, the Democratic National Committee granted South Carolina an early primary slot in order to increase the representativeness of one key Democratic voting bloc: African Americans. No doubt, the black vote in South Carolina's Democratic primaries is a "proven portion of any winning Democrat's coalition" (J. Ross 2016). However, a number of commentators have said the state *over*represents African Americans, and this alleged overrepresentation is often cited to explain South Carolina's misses in the 1988 caucuses when Jesse Jackson won the state but lost the nomination. Likewise, the power of black voters may, in turn, lead to the overrepresentation of both women and religious adherents. Jaime Harrison, former chair of the South Carolina Democratic Party, has said that African American women are the "absolute heart of the party" (Allen 2016). And while white evangelicals are important in South Carolina Republican politics, blacks attend church at higher rates than whites in the Palmetto State (Monkovic 2016). Lastly, some believe South Carolina's Democratic primary voters are too conservative relative to the national party to be considered representative of the national electorate. While the South as a whole may be conservative, as Bernie Sanders claimed in explaining his losses on Super Tuesday in 2016, it has also been argued that the Democratic primaries reflect the region's ideological balance and speak to "what the Democratic Party ostensibly seeks to be and represent moving forward" (Newkirk 2016).

Although the popular wisdom cited by journalists and other observers offers valuable insights into South Carolina's key demographic blocs, academics have mostly ignored the topic of a state's representativeness in primary elections.[5] Moreover, neither journalists nor academics have sufficiently addressed the states' predictive ability in nomination contests. Instead, the academic literature often focuses on the candidates who win their party's nomination. A key finding is the existence of momentum effects, where candidates who exceed expectations in early states increase their chances in later states due their perceived viability (Abramowitz 1989; Adkins and Dowdle 2001; Bartels 1988; Norrander 2006; Redlawsk, Tolbert, and Donovan 2011; Steger 2007). Another frequent topic in the literature is the critical role of endorsements. In nomination contests, where voters cannot rely on simple cues like party identification, endorsements have powerful effects on who wins and loses (Cohen et. al. 2008; Dominguez 2011; Steger 2007). An additional group of studies examines the characteristics of winning candidates, focusing on their race, religion, gender, quality as a candidate, and level of campaign spending, among other factors (Adkins and Dowdle 2000; Dolan 2004; Heldman, Carroll, and Olson 2005; Pomper 1996; Steger 2000). We examine how each of these factors influences performance in the South Carolina primary in the next chapter.

A second area of the literature explores primary campaigns. For example, a number of authors have studied whether campaign stops mobilize voters, finding that visits to a state do indeed increase turnout and thus shape election outcomes (Herrnson and Morris 2007; Holbrook and McClurg 2005; Jones 1998; Moran and Fenster 1982; Norrander 1991; Shaw 1999a; Shaw 1999b). Related work indicates that a state's delegate allocation method impacts campaign spending decisions (Ridout, Rottinghaus, and Hosey 2009). Finally, researchers have examined the way the timing of a state primary, the amount of media coverage, and a state's delegate size affects a campaign's strategic use of resources (Buell 1987).

Although scholars have ignored the topic of state representativeness, researchers have examined related topics. For example, a handful of studies look at whether primary outcomes are shaped by the ideological compatibility of a candidate and voters in that state. John Aldrich and Michael Alvarez (1994) find evidence of ideological matching in primaries, while Fred Cutler (2002), Joshua Stockley (2008), and David Gopoian (1982) do not. In perhaps the most comparable research to ours in this chapter, a group of authors asks whether primary voters are representative of the *general* election electorate. In the 1950s, V. O. Key famously concluded that primary voters do not resemble the party's general election electorate, arguing that "those who vote in the primaries do not make up miniatures of the party membership" (1956, 145; see also Geer 1988). However, subsequent research has found little demographic and ideological differences between primary and general election electorates (Norrander 1989; Ranney 1968).

Calculating a State's Predictive Ability

In an effort to assess South Carolina' success rate in nomination contests, we draw explicit comparisons with the Iowa caucuses and New Hampshire primary. We also compare the predictive ability of these three states to all fifty states. But first, we need to establish a baseline for what counts as high or low accuracy, as aggregate statistics provide an incomplete picture of a state's predictive track record.

To assess each state's predictive ability, we compiled data on the outcome of every primary and caucus in contested elections from 1980 to 2016.[6] According to the raw data, the average state correctly predicted the winner a whopping 73 percent of the time. When compared to this baseline, South Carolina's 86 percent record in Republican primaries since 1980 (six of seven) does not seem remarkable. On the other side, the state's 50 percent record in Democratic primaries since 1980 (three of six) is below average. Yet even casual observers know these aggregate statistics ignore a key factor: a state's place on the primary calendar. Simply put, while Iowa, New Hampshire, and South Carolina are in an enviable position, being one of the first contests comes at the expense of predictive ability. Late primary states are often highly predictive of which candidate secures the nomination since fewer candidates are on the ballot and a delegate leader usually emerges.

Figure 3.1 presents a visual for this point, showing the average state success rate by month. Looking at the figure, we can see that states holding their contest in January—five months before the last primary, with many candidates still in the race—fare only slightly better than 50 percent in the aggregate. In each of the next three months, the average predictive ability increases roughly 10 percent: to 61 percent in February, 71 percent in March, and 84 percent in April. By June, a state can be expected to predict the winner 89 percent of the time.

Given the clear relationship between calendar placement and a state's predictive ability, we would expect South Carolina to be less accurate compared to most states given that the average date of the South Carolina primary since 1980 has been February 18. Of course, this is also true for Iowa and New Hampshire. For these reasons, it is critical that we figure out a state's likelihood of picking the winner taking into account its calendar placement. Sports fans will recognize this logic: it is akin to a handicap in golf or a point spread when betting on a

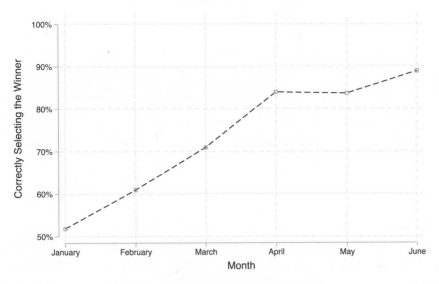

FIGURE 3.1. State Predictive Accuracy by Month
Source: various, compiled by authors

football game. Once we estimate a state's likelihood of picking the winner given its calendar placement, we can then say whether that state has overperformed or underperformed against its baseline.

We began by estimating a statistical model that predicts whether the state will correctly select the winner in its primary or caucus.[7] Our main explanatory factor in this model is the state's competitiveness, which we measured with data recording the number of days between the state's contest and the last election and the number of competitive candidates who were still in the race by the date of a state's election.[8] This analysis allows us to assess the extent to which competitiveness hurts a state's predictive ability and to compute each state's performance against this baseline. Additional details, including a table with the statistical results, are available in appendix B.

In brief, the analysis confirms what is plainly evident in figure 3.1: the more competitive a state, the lower the chance the state will select the eventual winner. Once again, states like Iowa, New Hampshire, and South Carolina are at a disadvantage in this respect. States with late contests and those with fewer candidates remaining in the race have a higher chance of picking the winner, by comparison. For example, since 1980 New Mexico has correctly predicted the Republican winner 100 percent of the time. However, the state's primary has always been in June. Given this fact, just how notable is the state's 100 percent record in Republican contests? Likewise, is the state's 67 percent in Democratic contests high, low, or in line with expectations?

In figure 3.2, we present the expected success rate from 1980 to 2016 for South Carolina, Iowa, and New Hampshire in both Republican and Democratic contests from our analysis. In the figure, the grey box is our estimate of how often the state should correctly select the winner given its competitiveness. A confidence interval reveals the amount of variation in the model's prediction. We also include a black dot that is the actual percentage of the time the state correctly selected the winner. As we note in a moment, the difference between *actual* success rate and the *estimated* success rate is the state's *performance* given its competitiveness.

Figure 3.2 shows that Iowa should correctly select the winner in Republican primaries just 36 percent of the time. Viewed in this context, Iowa's 29 percent record does not seem all that low.[9] However, both New Hampshire and South Carolina beat expectations by a large margin in Republican contests. New Hampshire outperforms the model's prediction by 29 percent, having successfully selected the winner 71 percent of the time rather than the 42 percent that the

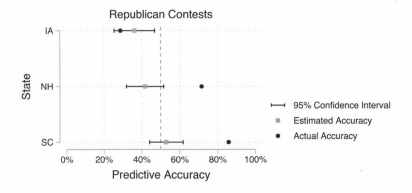

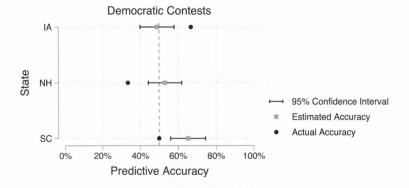

FIGURE 3.2. Estimated Accuracy in Light of State Competitiveness
Source: various, compiled by authors

model estimates. South Carolina outperforms expectations by 33 percent, beating New Hampshire by 3 percent on the Republican side. As the figure shows, South Carolina should select the winner just 53 percent of the time given its competitiveness, whereas its actual record is 86 percent.[10] Simply put, our analysis reveals that in Republican contests, South Carolina has a greater ability to correctly select the eventual nominee than its two early state brethren.

The model expects Democrats in the Iowa caucuses to correctly select the winner 49 percent of the time.[11] Unlike on the Republican side, Iowa therefore beats expectations by 18 percent given its 67 percent record. Figure 3.2 shows that New Hampshire underperforms on the Democratic side by 20 percent, correctly selecting the winner just 33 percent of the time compared to the model's prediction of 53 percent. South Carolina performs worse relative to exceptions as well, though less so than New Hampshire. Our model predicts the Palmetto State should select the winner 65 percent of the time in Democratic contests, whereas its actual success rate is 50 percent, and thus it underperforms by 15 percent.

As a whole, our analysis confirms the conventional wisdom in some ways, refutes it in others, and raises a host of questions. First, Iowa's poor record when it comes to predicting the winner in Republican contests is not that unusual given that the state is in the difficult position of being first. Furthermore, on the Democratic side, the state beats the odds by a wide margin. New Hampshire and South Carolina exceed expectations by a wide margin in Republican contests, consistent with the conventional wisdom. Notably for our purposes, the data indicate that South Carolina edges New Hampshire. Yet in Democratic contests, both New Hampshire and South Carolina underperform relative to expectations, although South Carolina performs better than New Hampshire on the Democratic side as well.

Needless to say, these patterns suggest that an important factor beyond the race's competitiveness is lurking in the background. Furthermore, we can see that a state's predictive ability hinges on party dynamics: the same state can over- and underperform depending on which party is choosing a nominee. In a subsequent section, we explore whether a state's representativeness is this missing factor.

Lastly, we computed *every* state's performance relative to expectations. While it is important to isolate Iowa, New Hampshire, and South Carolina given their pivotal positions on the nomination calendar, the predictive ability of all fifty states provides a broader comparison. For example, while New Hampshire and South Carolina were shown to be quite accurate in Republican contests, just like Iowa on the Democratic side, perhaps there are other states that have a special ability to get it right. Figures 3.3 and 3.4 present each state's relative performance in Republican and Democratic contests. On the x-axis is a state's performance, which is simply a state's actual success rate minus its estimated success rate given its competitiveness. Values greater than zero indicate the state has over-performed against its baseline, while values less than zero indicate the state has underperformed.

Figure 3.3 shows that South Carolina and New Hampshire do quite well in Republican primaries even when compared to all fifty states, coming in third and sixth, respectively. In short, the Palmetto and Granite States possess a special ability to correctly select the winner of Republican contests, but South Carolina

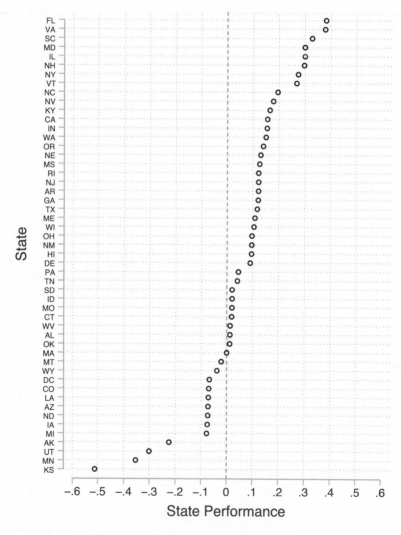

FIGURE 3.3. State Performance in Republican Contests

Source: various, compiled by authors

beats New Hampshire on this metric. Only Florida and Virginia, both with perfect track records since 1980, were ranked higher than South Carolina, while Maryland and Illinois ranked above New Hampshire. At the other end, Kansas, Minnesota, Utah, and Alaska stand out for having exceptionally low predictive abilities in Republican contests. Iowa ranks near the bottom as well, coming in sixth from last.

Figure 3.4 shows that Georgia takes the top spot for Democrats, having overperformed expectations by the largest margin, while Iowa comes in second.

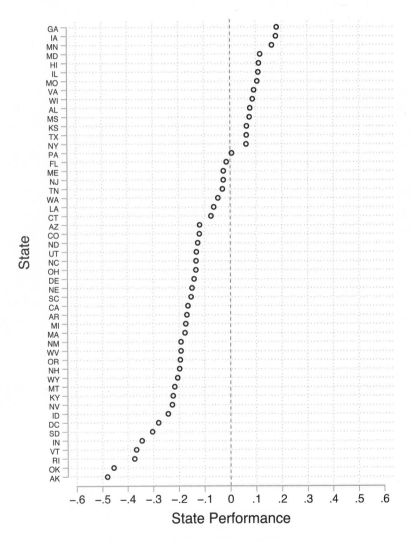

FIGURE 3.4. State Performance in Democratic Contests
Source: various, compiled by authors

According to the data, Georgia has correctly picked the winner in Democratic contests in five of six elections despite being fairly early on the calendar, while Iowa's four-of-six record is good for second given its first-in-the-nation status. Minnesota comes in a close third in Democratic contests. At the other end, Alaska and Oklahoma stand out for having exceptionally low predicative abilities in Democratic contests. Finally, both South Carolina and New Hampshire rank in the bottom one-third of the distribution, with fairly low predictive abilities, although South Carolina beats New Hampshire by eight spots.

State Representativeness

In this section, we switch our focus from each state's predictive accuracy to each state's representativeness. We are interested in state representativeness for two reasons. First, it is often hypothesized that a key factor in a state's ability to correctly select the winner of a party's nomination contest is whether voters in that state resemble a party's national primary electorate. Before we can answer that question, however, we need to know the key characteristics of each state's primary electorate. We also need to know what South Carolina's Republican and Democratic primary electorates look like in a descriptive sense and to compare the Palmetto State to New Hampshire and Iowa. As noted at the outset of this chapter, while a state's place on the calendar is significant, the makeup of the electorate gets at the heart of a state's importance in nomination contests.

Data and Analysis

In an effort to compare South Carolina's primary voters to other states' voters, we obtained data on each state's Republican and Democratic electorate in primaries and caucuses conducted since 2000 from the National Election Pool (NEP) exit polls.[12] The NEP, a consortium of the major media outlets, provides a large-n, nationwide source of information about who voted in state elections, their demographics, and what factors were relevant to their decision. Unfortunately, the NEP exit polls were not conducted in all fifty states, with states holding their contests in May and June often excluded. Another challenge we face is the fact that common questions were not used in each state (see also Kaufmann, Gimpel, and Hoffman 2003). On the Republican side we have thirty-seven states with useable data and on the Democratic side we have forty-one states with useable data.

We culled through the roughly two hundred exit polls and identified questions that were asked consistently across states and years by the NEP. Our analysis below is based on seven demographic items (sex, race, age, education, income, religion, military service) and four attitudinal items (a respondent's self-reported ideology and answers to questions about the importance of three issues to voters). Complete details can be found in appendix B.

After identifying the exit poll questions, we created a profile of the typical national Republican and Democratic primary or caucus voter, which shows what each party's primary electorate looks like in a demographic and attitudinal sense and provides a baseline for our state-by-state comparison.[13] For example, 51 percent of Republican primary and caucus voters are male, while 45 percent nationally describe themselves as born-again Christians. For Democrats, 48 percent of national primary and caucus voters report having a college degree, while 18 percent consider health care the most important political issue.

Our second step is to compare each state's average response on the individual items to the national average. Once again, our goal is to discern which states most closely resemble the national Republican and Democratic electorates.[14] Simply put, larger values on this measure indicate how far a state deviates from the national average while a value of exactly 0 indicates a perfectly representative state. Lastly, to create a single score for each state, we compute the mean deviation across the various items, where higher values indicate states that are unrepresentative while lower values indicate more representative states.

State Representativeness in Republican Contests

Figure 3.5 presents the estimates for the thirty-seven states with exit poll data on Republican contests. In the left part of the horizontal, x-axis, the vertical line at zero is where a perfectly representative state would lie. No state is perfectly representative, however, as every state deviates from the national average on at least a few items. On the vertical, y-axis, we ordered the states from top to bottom based on their representativeness, placing the least representative states at the top and the most representative states at the bottom.[15]

Looking at the top of figure 3.5, we see that two states stand out for being the most deviant from the national Republican primary electorate. West Virginia's primary electorate is the least representative of all states, according to our data, followed closely by Rhode Island. According to the exit poll data we compiled, West Virginia's Republican primary voters are far more concerned about economic issues and far less concerned about foreign policy issues. Rhode Island's two biggest deviations in Republican primaries are in its greater percentage of college graduates and voters' higher-than-average incomes. Notably, Iowa is the fourth least representative state, while New Hampshire is the tenth least representative state. Given their pivotal spot on the primary calendar, it is perhaps surprising to see the degree to which these two important states are outliers. We discuss the specific demographic and attitudinal features of Iowa and New Hampshire in a moment.

Looking at the bottom of figure 3.5, we see that the two most representative states in Republican contests are Missouri and Ohio. According to our data, Missouri is the most representative of all states in its ratio of males to females

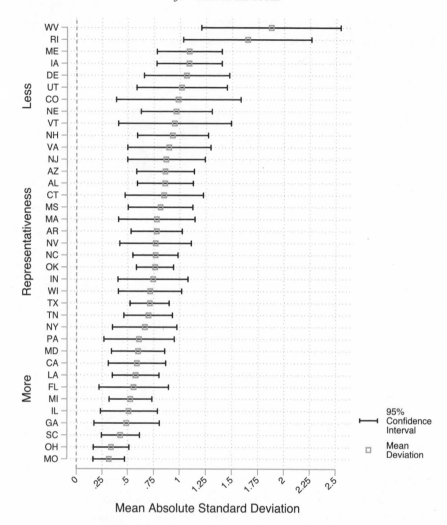

FIGURE 3.5. Index of Republican Representativeness by State
Source: NEP Exit Polls

and income in addition to being in the top ten in five other categories. Ohio is the most representative of all states on one item, its percentage of born-again Christians, but is in the top ten in five other categories. Rounding out the top five most representative states in Republican contests are South Carolina, Georgia, and Illinois, in that order.

Of course, we are most interested in South Carolina's representativeness, with our main hypothesis being that South Carolina's predictive ability in GOP primaries is a function of the state's balanced mix of key voting blocs. As noted, figure 3.5 reveals that South Carolina is the third most representative state of the thirty-seven we were able examine. By this metric, South Carolina is about twice as representative of the national Republican primary electorate as Iowa and New Hampshire.[16] In this respect, the exit poll data support our argument that the South Carolina primary is important.

Figure 3.6 digs deeper into the data, presenting each individual item in the three early states.[17] In the figure, the vertical reference line at zero indicates the position of the typical Republican primary voter on that item. All statistical

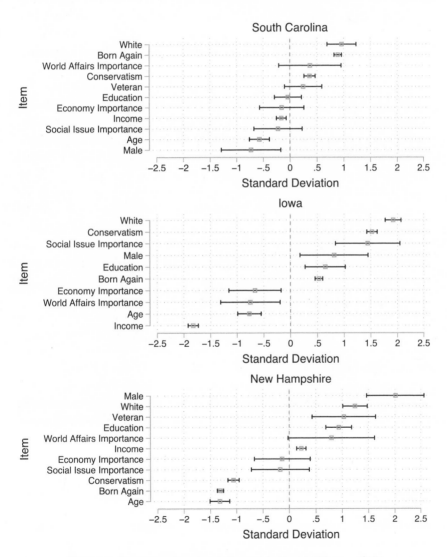

FIGURE 3.6. Republican Representativeness by Item in SC, IA, and NH

Source: NEP Exit Polls

items are the same as in figure 3.5, expect that in this figure we do not take the absolute value of each deviation; this is so we can see whether the state is above or below the national average. Values to the left of zero indicate less of that characteristic compared to the national Republican primary electorate, while values above zero indicate more of that characteristic compared to the national Republican primary electorate.

We can see visually in figure 3.6 what we concluded based on the aggregate statistic shown in figure 3.5: South Carolina's demographic and attitudinal items are much close to the national average, while Iowa and New Hampshire have outliers spread out on both sides of the reference line. On the positive end of the spectrum, indicating overrepresentation in Republican contests, South Carolina's two biggest deviations are its percentage of whites and born-again Christians. In statistical terms, both are approximately 1.0 deviation above the national mean. Yet Iowa and New Hampshire have larger deviations—in some cases *much* larger—on three items each. Iowa's Republican caucus voters are disproportionately white, conservative, and concerned about social issues compared to the national average, while New Hampshire's Republican primary voters are more likely to be male, white, and veterans. On the negative end of the spectrum, indicating underrepresentation, South Carolina's biggest deviation is its percentage of males. However, this deviation is rather small in magnitude, only about 0.75 below the national mean. Iowa and New Hampshire each have three noteworthy negative deviations that are as big or larger. Iowa's Republican caucus voters have lower incomes, are younger, and are less concerned with foreign affairs, while New Hampshire GOP primary voters are younger, less likely to be born-again Christians, and are less conservative.

Looking at just South Carolina, we conclude that the state is representative of the national Republican primary electorate on five items: the percentage of voters who are veterans, the percentage with a college education, and the importance of world affairs, the economy, and social issues to voters. Simply put, these are the items that provide the state with its notable balance in Republican contests. Conversely, New Hampshire mirrors the national electorate on just three items—voters' concern with world affairs, economic issues, and social issues—while Iowa is representative on zero items.

State Representativeness in Democratic Contests

We now report the same findings for Democratic contests. Figure 3.7 is the same as figure 3.5. In the aggregate, three states stand out for being the most unrepresentative of the national Democratic primary electorate. Kentucky is the least representative of all states, based on the exit poll data, followed by Mississippi and West Virginia. According to our analysis, Kentucky's Democratic primary voters are far more concerned about the economy, less concerned about health care, and less liberal than the typical Democratic primary voter. Mississippi has two large deviations: the percentage of whites and income, both which are below the national Democratic primary average. Finally, West Virginia's Democratic primary electorate is far more concerned about economic issues and modestly outlying in a number of other categories. Rounding out the top five most deviant states in Democratic contests are Oregon and Vermont.

Looking at the bottom of figure 3.7, we can see that a number of states are in a close contest for the most representative in Democratic elections. In order, the

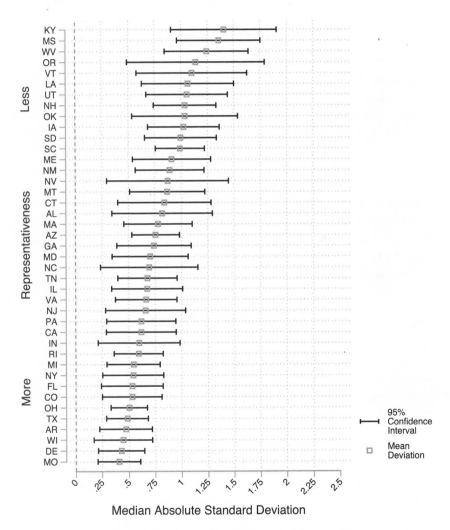

FIGURE 3.7. Index of Democratic Representativeness by State
Source: NEP Exit Polls

top five states are Missouri, Delaware, Wisconsin, Arkansas, Texas, and Ohio. According to the exit poll data the most representative features of each state are as follows: liberalism in Missouri, the percent with a college education in Delaware, the percentage of nonreligious voters in Wisconsin, those citing the importance of economic issues in Arkansas, and self-reported income in Texas.

We find that unlike in Republican contests the Palmetto State is not representative of the national Democratic primary electorate. Figure 3.7 shows that South Carolina ranks thirtieth out of forty-one states, placing it in the bottom one-third of the scale, albeit one of the most representative states in the bottom group. South Carolina's representativeness score indicates that on the mean indicator, the state is roughly 1.0 deviation away from the national mean. By this metric, South Carolina's Republican primary electorate is twice as representative of its party's national electorate than the state's Democratic primary electorate. Despite the Palmetto State's low score in Democratic contests, it is notable that South Carolina is more representative than either Iowa or New Hampshire. Nonetheless, we caution that these differences are small in magnitude.

Figure 3.8 presents each individual item in the three early states of Iowa, New Hampshire, and South Carolina for Democratic contests. We can see that Iowa, New Hampshire, and South Carolina have an equivalent number of outlying characteristics, albeit on different items per state. South Carolina's four largest deviations—in either direction—are in the state's lower percentage of whites, males, high-income earners, and voters with no religious affiliation. To put this in opposite terms, Democratic primary voters in South Carolina are disproportionately black and female and have lower incomes and stronger religious attachments. By comparison, Iowa has three equivalently sized outlying features in either direction in Democratic contests: its voters' lower average income, greater concern for health care, and lower concern with economic issues. Interestingly, New Hampshire's Democratic primary electorate shares Iowa's greater concern with health care and lower concern with economic issues. However, Democratic voters in the Granite State are also far younger than the national primary electorate.

Looking at just South Carolina, we conclude that the state is not representative of the national Democratic primary electorate in any single category. Indeed, South Carolina's confidence intervals never overlap with the reference line at zero, which indicates the national average on that item. Iowa is statistically average on just one item, its ratio of males to females, and New Hampshire is statistically average on just two items, its voters' concern with world affairs and the ratio of males to females. Once again, none of the three early states are representative of the national Democratic primary electorate, according to the exit poll data.

South Carolina balances Iowa and New Hampshire in the aggregate, however, serving as a critical counterweight. South Carolina is disproportionately black, while Iowa and New Hampshire are both disproportionately white. As noted elsewhere, the state's regional and racial balance is the main reason why South Carolina was made a carve-out state by the Democratic National Committee prior to the 2008 contest. In addition, South Carolina's Democratic primary voters are more concerned about economic issues and less educated and liberal on average, while Iowa and New Hampshire's voters are less concerned about economic issues and more educated and liberal. Finally, South Carolina

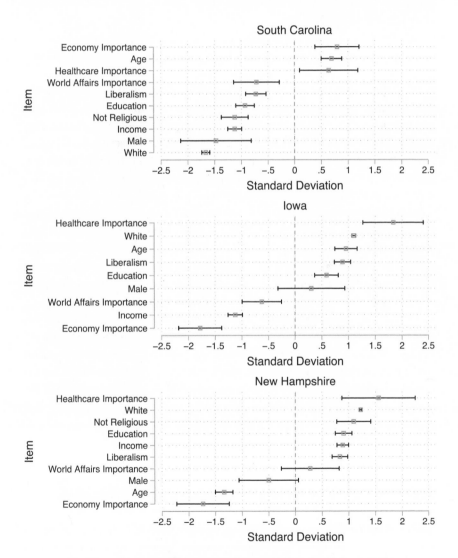

FIGURE 3.8. Democratic Representativeness by Item in SC, IA, and NH

Source: NEP Exit Polls

balances New Hampshire in two additional ways: South Carolina's Democratic primary voter is older and more religious than the typical Democratic primary voter while New Hampshire's primary voter is younger and less religious.

All in all, our finding that South Carolina is not representative of the national Democratic nominating electorate does *not* undermine our book's claim about the importance of the South Carolina primary. The Palmetto State serves as a critical counterweight to Iowa and New Hampshire and helps make the group of early states representative in the aggregate.

Representativeness and Predictive Accuracy

Do representative states have a superior ability to correctly select the winner of a party's nomination contest? Although a number of commentators have claimed that they do, to our knowledge we are the first to test this proposition. We are most interested in whether it is fair to conclude that South Carolina's ability in selecting the winner in Republican contests is due to its representativeness. Similarly, we want to know if its lower predictive accuracy with respect to Democratic primaries is a consequence of the state's lack of representativeness. Furthermore, we investigate whether representativeness matters once we control for a state's competitiveness, presumably the best predictor of whether a state gets it right in a caucus or primary. After all, it is possible that competitiveness explains so much of a state's predictive accuracy that its demographic and attitudinal representativeness matters little in the end. If this is the case, it would undermine, albeit only partly, our argument for why South Carolina's first-in-the-South primary is so important for Republicans.

Fortunately, it is easy to answer these questions by simply combining the data used in the prior two sections. For the analysis here, we return to the model of predictive accuracy reported in the first analysis. Our key explanatory factor in the first model was the state's competitiveness, which remains in the second model reported here. In this section, we simply add to the first model a predictor that records each state's representativeness from the prior analysis. The raw statistical results appear in appendix B.

Consistent with expectations, the results indicate that states that mirror their party's national electorate indeed have a higher chance of correctly predicting the winner of a party's nomination contest. Conceptually, this indicates that South Carolina's representativeness in Republican contests is indeed a key reason for the state's ability to correctly select the candidate that eventually wins the nomination. By the same logic, the state's poor record in Democratic contests can be attributed to its multiple outlying features (though it is worth reiterating that these outlying features balance Iowa and New Hampshire in the aggregate). In the model, a state's competitiveness remains an important factor in correctly predicting the winner. In other words, a state's representativeness is not the only factor that matters. In fact, our analysis indicates that competitiveness matters about four times as much as representativeness when it comes to a state's predictive ability. Because competitiveness is presumably the strongest predictor of whether a state gets it right in a nomination contest, this is not entirely surprising.

Conclusion

Iowa and New Hampshire are the most frequent focus of attention by academics and nonacademics alike given their positions as first and second on the primary calendar, yet as we have argued in this chapter, a state's predictive ability and representativeness are important factors in nomination contests as well. In the first analysis, we used data on primary and caucus results from 1980 to 2016 to estimate each state's ability to get it right when selecting a nominee. Doing this allowed us to say how much each state has over- and underperformed relative to the timing of the state's primary or caucus. In the second analysis, we used exit poll data from 2000 to 2016 to identify what each state's nominating electorate looks like in a demographic and attitudinal sense. We then compared each state to the national electorate to identify the most representative states. And in the third part, we examined whether representative states have a better ability to correctly select the winner in primaries and caucuses.

Does South Carolina have a special ability to predict who secures each party's nomination? Our data show that it does in the case of Republican contests. Not only does South Carolina beat both Iowa and New Hampshire, but the Palmetto State comes in third out of all fifty states. It should be noted, however, that New Hampshire also has a strong ability to correctly select the winner and that Iowa's poor record is not that low given the state's competitiveness. Our key findings therefore reinforce the point about the importance of South Carolina's first-in-the South primary. South Carolina is one of the best barometers of who wins the Republican nomination in the entire country and the best predictor among the early states.

On the Democratic side, South Carolina has less predictive ability than most states. South Carolina has underperformed relative to expectations by 15 percent, a result that is due, in part, to the fact that the state's Democratic primary voters are disproportionately black and female with lower incomes and stronger religious attachments compared to the party's national nominating electorate. Notably, Iowa has the second greatest predictive ability of all fifty states, while South Carolina edges New Hampshire by eight spots in Democratic contests.

Is South Carolina representative of each party's national nominating electorate? In Republican contests, South Carolina ranks third with respect to representativeness. By comparison, Iowa and New Hampshire rank toward the bottom of the thirty-seven states with usable exit poll data. We find that South Carolina's strength comes from a balanced mix of issue priorities (from the economy and social issues to world affairs) as well as its parity in the percentage of veterans and college graduates. In this respect South Carolina is one of the best in the country at reflecting the national Republican nominating electorate. South Carolina's Republican electorate does have a few outlying features, however. According to our data, voters in GOP primaries are disproportionately white, born-again Christian, and female compared to the Republican national average.

At the same time, the state's Democratic primary voters are much less representative of the national Democratic electorate Although this may seem to diminish the case for the Palmetto State's importance, there are two things to keep in mind. First, South Carolina is more representative of the national Democratic nominating electorate—albeit only slightly—than either New Hampshire or Iowa. Second, South Carolina serves as a critical counterweight to Iowa and New Hampshire and helps make the three early states representative of the national Democratic nominating electorate in the aggregate. In addition to balancing out Iowa and New Hampshire's disproportionately white population, South Carolina's provides much needed balance with respect to the percentage of voters concerned with economic issues and level of education and ideology.

An important issue we do not address in this chapter is the question of whether South Carolina's demographics are in flux and whether the state's predictive accuracy or representativeness might decrease in the future. It is no secret that South Carolina's population is increasing. Between 2000 and 2010, the population grew by 15.3 percent, the tenth biggest percentage increase of all states.[18] Most observers expect this trend to continue—or even accelerate— as South Carolina is projected be one of the ten fastest growing states through 2040.[19] Moreover, many of these in-migrants are non-Hispanic whites (Slade 2018), and a sizable portion are moving from the Northeast, demographic trends that can change state politics in a myriad of ways. On the Democratic side, these changes could make the state more representative by bringing the black percentage of the electorate in line with the party's national averages, while on the Republican side, these changes could make South Carolina more of an outlier as the state's GOP primary voters are already disproportionately white.

Another factor that could affect who votes in the Republican primary has to do with whether it remains open or is closed. A number of Republican reformers have fought to make South Carolina a closed primary state, which would mean that only registered partisans could vote in the party's primary. Notably, the June 12, 2018, GOP primary had an advisory question on this matter that had 82 percent support for the move to close the state's primaries.[20] Research has shown that closed states are less representative of the general election electorate

(Kaufmann, Gimpel, and Hoffmann 2003) because the restrictions imposed by a closed primary constrain voter participation. Both Iowa and New Hampshire are more restrictive than South Carolina under the current system. Ultimately, a move to a closed primary would likely threaten South Carolina's predictive ability and representativeness in Republican contests.

★ 4 ★
WINNERS
AND LOSERS OF
THE SOUTH CAROLINA
PRIMARY

What does it take to win in South Carolina? In this chapter, we address this question by expanding on an earlier analysis (Craven, Ragusa, Thevos 2017), explaining who wins and loses the South Carolina Republican and Democratic presidential nomination contests. While picking winners and losers in American elections is a risky proposition, there are a number of techniques to both forecast and make sense of election outcomes. On the most basic level, we know the results of previous elections, allowing for the opportunity to see what types of individual characteristics and contest-specific conditions are most often associated with candidate success. Our model is developed using data for the sixty-three candidates who ran in South Carolina from 1988 to 2016. We compiled data on a range of factors—including a candidate's characteristics, features of the campaign, and the candidate's performance in earlier states—and estimated a statistical model predicting a candidate's vote share in the Palmetto State. Our goal is to understand past election outcomes and predict future winners and losers in the South Carolina primary.

In the succeeding pages, we address a host of issues raised throughout the book. For example, we look more closely at the relationship between outcomes in Iowa, New Hampshire, and South Carolina. We also examine just how important is it that prospective nominees receive endorsements from prominent political officials. In addition, we investigate whether southern and evangelical candidates have an advantage in South Carolina's contests. And finally, we address the two instances since the state switched to a primary format in which South Carolina voters did not selected the party's eventual nominee—when Newt Gingrich won the 2012 Republican primary and John Edwards won the 2004 Democratic primary.

Forecasting Nomination Contest Results

When it comes to general elections, a cottage industry of academics and jour-nalists focus on the factors that predict who wins and who loses. For example, every two years, an entire volume of a political science journal is dedicated to forecasting presidential and congressional election results.[1] Yet when it comes to primary elections, academics and journalists have spent far less time trying to understand the dynamics of a candidate's performance.

To be fair, the greater focus on general rather than primary outcomes is un-derstandable. First, the fundamentals that correlate with general election results are often poor predictors in primaries. For example, it is well known that there is a robust relationship between national economic conditions and the fate of the president's party in general elections (Abramowitz 1988; Fiorina 1981; Nadeau and Lewis-Beck 2001). Indeed, macroeconomic conditions and a handful of other factors (like the president's approval rating and an incumbency advantage) are reliable predictors of presidential election results (see Abramowitz 2012). Yet these factors can have little to no predictive power in nomination contests when the candidates belong to the same party and are all nonincumbents. Second, primaries occur in a highly volatile and uncertain environment. Voter turnout in nomination contests is often far lower than in general elections, and primary outcomes often depend on state- and election-specific dynamics that are idio-syncratic in the aggregate and create a host of forecasting challenges (Adkins and Dowdle 2000; Steger 2009).

Although the focus on general election outcomes is understandable, primary outcomes are nonetheless important. First, a candidate must win his or her par-ty's nomination before competing in a general election. Candidates typically appeal to their base in a primary and pivot to the center in a general election. Second, presidential nomination contests often represent voters' first exposure to the candidates and therefore serve an important informational purpose. Such an effect is especially important in early and small states, where citizens have a better chance of interacting with one or more of the candidates. And third, whoever wins a party's nomination becomes the standard bearer and thus plays a major role in the party's future. Even nominees who failed to win the general election have reshaped their party's platform.

Winners and Losers in South Carolina Primaries

A number of political scientists have isolated factors that predict winners and losers in nomination contests. One key finding, noted in the last chapter, is the existence of momentum effects: candidates who beat expectations in early states do well in later states because they are regarded by voters as electorally viable (Abramowitz 1989; Adkins and Dowdle 2001; Bartels 1988; Norrander 2006; Redlawsk, Tolbert, and Donovan 2011; Steger 2007).

Based on this research, the winners of Iowa and New Hampshire should perform better in South Carolina as a general rule. However, chapter 3 also shows key similarities and differences in each state's nominating electorates. According to our findings from that chapter, there are greater similarities between all three states in Republican contests than there are in Democratic contests. Focusing on the Republican side, Iowa and South Carolina are similar in terms of the percentage of born-again Christians, the conservatism of voters, the average age of voters, and the percentage with a college degree. South Carolina and New Hampshire differ by wider margins on each of these items in Republican contests. Among Democrats, however, the differences between all three states are large across the board and evenly spread across items. We therefore expect a strong connection between a candidate's performances in Iowa and South Carolina in Republican contests and a weak but positive relationship in all other state/party contests.

We have also noted the critical role of endorsements in nomination contests. Researchers have shown that because voters cannot rely on easy cues like party identification, endorsements play a key role in nomination contests (Cohen et. al. 2008; Bawn et al. 2012; Dominguez 2011; Steger 2007). We expect the same results in our analysis, as endorsements have often played a key role in a candidate's performance in South Carolina. For example, Governor Carroll Campbell's endorsement of George Bush in 1988 is often cited as a key reason for his twenty-eight-percentage point victory over Bob Dole (Miller 1988b). Likewise, Governor Dick Riley's endorsement of Bill Clinton in 1992 was seen as key to his victory (Ifill 1992b). Yet there are examples of failed endorsements as well: Senator Strom Thurmond backed John Connally in 1980 and Dole in 1988, Governor Nikki Haley endorsed Romney in 2012 and Rubio in 2016, and Riley endorsed Gephardt in 1988. Nonetheless, these cases may be exceptions or easily explained by other factors.

An additional set of studies find that a candidate's sociodemographic features are important in primaries and caucuses. A candidate's age, race, and gender are often predictors of success, as people tend to support primary candidates from groups to which they also belong (Cutler 2002; Gopoian 1982; Stockley 2008). These kinds of demographic attributes are often the easiest way for voters to distinguish between candidates in a primary or caucus when all candidates are members of the same party. Related research finds that high-quality candidates, usually defined as those who have held prior elective office, perform better than low-quality candidates in both congressional elections (Green and Krasno 1988) and presidential primaries (Dominguez 2011). Conceptually, voters may view high-quality candidates as possessing the experience needed to both win a presidential campaign and perform well if elected president.

Two sociodemographic candidate groups are thought to be critically important in South Carolina: evangelicals on the Republican side and African Americans in Democratic contests. As noted in chapter 3, white evangelicals comprise a large percentage of the GOP primary electorate—roughly 70 percent in 2016—while black voters are about 60 percent of the Democratic primary electorate. Yet the two most recent Republican winners—Trump in 2016 and Gingrich in 2012—have caused some to question the conventional wisdom that a candidate's religion matters in South Carolina's Republican primaries. Scott Huffmon, Winthrop University political scientist and director of the Winthrop Poll, notes that "evangelicals here behave as voters and not church-goers" (McCormick and Niquette 2016). Few dispute the conventional wisdom about importance of black voters in Democratic contests, and as we discuss in chapter 6, African Americans played a pivotal role in Barack Obama's 2008 and Hillary Clinton's 2016 primary victories.

Another frequently discussed demographic feature is a candidate's home state, with some wondering whether candidates from southern states have an advantage in South Carolina. Although southern identity is sometimes cited to explain primary victories by Gingrich in 2012 and Edwards in 2004, a number of southern candidates have underperformed in the Palmetto State: Jeb Bush in 2016, Ron Paul in 2008, Al Gore in 1988, and Howard Baker in 1980. Both Gingrich and Edwards were from the neighboring states of Georgia and North Carolina, respectively, so perhaps the advantages of name recognition and greater familiarity with South Carolina politics that come with being from a neighboring state trump the value of being a southerner writ large.

And finally researchers have found that characteristics of a candidate's campaign, including their spending (Adkins and Dowdle 2000; Steger 2007) and the extent of the media attention they receive (Patterson 1980), are important in explaining nomination contest outcomes. However, how much a candidate spends on a campaign often has an inconsistent effect on outcomes (Steger 2007), and that effect can depend on factors such as momentum and name recognition (Gurian 1990; Haynes, Gurian, and Nichols 1997). There is evidence of this inconsistent effect in the 2016 contest in South Carolina: while Jeb Bush came in fourth despite $130 million in spending, Hillary Clinton outspent Bernie Sanders by a wide margin and won. In contrast, the 2016 campaign provides clear evidence of the power of media attention, as Donald Trump and Hillary Clinton dominated national and state media coverage in the weeks prior to the election. We therefore expect media attention to be a reliable predictor of a candidate's performance in South Carolina's nominating contests but take an agnostic view of the effect of campaign spending.

Predicting Election Outcomes

We explore these issues using data on the candidates who ran in South Carolina from 1988 to 2016. We focus on explaining a candidate's vote share in our model. Guided by the academic and journalistic claims we have outlined, we examine predictors in three general categories: campaign effects, candidate resources, and candidate characteristics. Additional details of our modeling strategy and the data used in our analysis are included in appendix B.

We examine the impact of two key campaign effects: the percentage of the vote a candidate received in Iowa and the percentage of the vote received in New Hampshire. We have noted that candidates who do well in earlier states may do well in South Carolina due to momentum effects and a perception that they are electorally viable. Simply put, we want to know which state better predicts results in South Carolina in light of the discussion about demographic similarities by party and state in the previous chapter. We test the impact of two additional campaign factors. First, we have a variable for the number of candidates in the race, a key factor in the prior chapter's analysis.[2] We expect that when there are more competitive candidates on the ballot, each will receive fewer votes because the candidates will split the vote. Second, we explore the effect of a candidate's experience in South Carolina using data on vote share in a previous nomination contest. It stands to reason that candidates who campaigned previously in the state—and thus have advantages like name recognition, knowledge of the state's demographics, and relationships with key statewide officials—will do better than first-time candidates.

Our analysis of a candidate's performance also includes three measures of a candidate's resources. First, we have a measure for the candidate's volume of endorsements from prominent South Carolina figures. Our specific measure weights gubernatorial endorsements-as-most-important, the endorsement of state legislators as least important, and the endorsement of members of Congress as the middle category.[3] As we have noted, research indicates that endorsements play a critical role in nomination contests. Second, we explore the value of media coverage using data that combines the volume of state and national coverage for the candidate in the week prior to the election.[4] We expect media coverage to affect who wins and losses that the public is less attentive to primary campaigns. And third, we test the effect of a candidate's campaign expenditures.[5] As we have noted, while some research shows that campaign spending is an important factor in nomination contests, other research reveals the effect of spending is mixed.

Lastly, we have five indicators that account for a candidate's sociodemographic characteristics. We test whether candidates from the South outperform candidates from other regions.[6] Although we think it is intuitive that regional identity plays a key role in South Carolina contests, southern candidates have a mixed record. A related factor in our analysis explores whether candidates from the neighboring states of Georgia and North Carolina have an advantage in South Carolina. Given that candidates from these states are likely to have a range of advantages, we suspect they perform better, all else being equal. We also test the extent to which candidate quality is a factor in the state's contests. As we have observed, research shows that high-quality candidates—defined here as current or former governors, senators, and representatives—tend to perform better than candidates without prior federal or gubernatorial electoral experience. Lastly, two additional factors test the importance of black candidates in Democratic contests and evangelical candidates in Republican contests. According to the conventional wisdom, because there are large percentages of African American Democratic primary voters and evangelical Republican primary voters in South Carolina, candidates with these attributes may have an advantage over white and nonevangelical candidates.

Findings

Table 4.1 shows which factors matter and which do not for voters picking winners and losers in the South Carolina primary. In the table we also include information about each factor's effect size, which is simply a numerical representation of how much that item positively or negatively affects a candidate's vote share in the South Carolina primary. We discuss each of these quantities in what follows. Once again, additional details of our analysis can be found in appendix B.

TABLE 4.1 Candidate Vote Share in
South Carolina Nomination Contests (1988–2016)

Significant Factors	Effect Size	Insignificant Factors	Effect Size
Competitive Contests	-3.4%	Previous Vote	—
Iowa % (Democrats)	-1.1%	Campaign Receipts	—
Iowa % (Republicans)	16.0%	Evangelical Candidate	—
New Hampshire % (Democrats)	6.3%	Quality Candidate	—
New Hampshire % (Republicans)	6.4%		
Media Attention	5.9%		
Endorsements	4.7%		
Southern Candidate	7.5%		
Neighboring State Candidate	14.4%		
Black Democrat Candidate	19.7%		

Notes: Effect sizes reported here summarize the complete results found in appendix B. See the appendix for additional details.

A key question in this chapter is whether a candidate performs the same in South Carolina as in Iowa and New Hampshire. One of our main findings in the analysis is that Republican candidates who do well in Iowa do very well in the South Carolina.[7] In particular, table 4.1 shows that a Republican candidate who garners 34 percent of the vote in the Iowa caucus—a standard deviation above the mean—is predicted by our model to earn an additional 16 percent in the South Carolina primary, controlling for all else. This effect is consistent with our findings from the last chapter, revealing a few key demographic similarities in the Republican nominating electorates in these two states (namely, that both states have a high percentage of born-again Christians and strong conservatives). By comparison, Democrats who perform similarly well in Iowa are predicted to earn 1.2 percent less in South Carolina, which is the opposite of expectations. It is important to note that this reduced vote share is insignificant in the model and thus not an important factor in explaining election outcomes in South Carolina presidential primaries.

In the analysis we find that both Republican and Democratic candidates who do well in New Hampshire do better in South Carolina, as one would expect, yet the effect size for both parties is only modest. Our results indicate that candidates who win 33 percent of the vote in New Hampshire—a standard deviation above the mean—receive an additional 6.3 percent in South Carolina if they are a Democrat and 6.4 percent if they are a Republican. Both effects are statistically significant. Our analysis therefore indicates that only Iowa on the Republican side is strongly predictive of a candidate's performance in the South Carolina primary, whereas the New Hampshire primary has a modest predictive ability for both parties' candidates.

An important note about these results is that the winner of one of the two earlier states does not necessarily win the South Carolina primary. Given the amount of competition in the early states, it is difficult to win all three contests. It is no surprise, therefore, that table 4.1 shows that competitive contests in South Carolina decrease a candidate's vote share. Since 1980, only one candidate has won all three early states, Al Gore in 2000, and as the sitting vice president, he faced very little competition. In coverage of primaries and caucuses most political observers focus on a candidate's ability to outperform expectations in the early states and survive as he or she heads into subsequent states. For this reason, our analysis focuses on a candidate's vote share, not whether he or she won or lost the South Carolina primary. Candidates who do well in Iowa or New Hampshire may be advantaged in the South Carolina primary yet lose due to other factors.

In our analysis of candidate performance, we find that two of the candidate resource measures are important predictors of vote share in the South Carolina primary. A candidate's volume of media coverage and their endorsements from state officials both increase that candidate's vote share. Looking at table 4.1, we can see that these two effects matter roughly the same amount in terms of how much they increase a candidate's vote share. In particular, a large volume of media attention in the week leading up the South Carolina primary results in an additional 5.9 percent of the vote, while a large number of endorsements adds 4.7 percent to a candidate's vote share.[8] Examples include Bill and Hillary Clinton securing the bulk of statewide endorsements in 1992 and 2016 on their way to victory, and Newt Gingrich's and Donald Trump's dominance in preelection media coverage in their 2012 and 2016 victories.

Interestingly, two other candidate resource measures in our analysis, the volume of campaign receipts and the candidate's previous vote in the state in a primary, are not significant predictors of how one performs in South Carolina. Campaign money has a mixed effect, the best example of which is perhaps the fact that Hillary Clinton had sizable money advantages in both her 2008 and 2016 bids but lost in the first case and won in the second. Likewise, although it makes sense that candidates with prior experience in a South Carolina primary would have an advantage the second time around, there are many examples of first timers who did quite well: Bill Clinton, George W. Bush, Barack Obama, and Donald Trump were all newcomers the years they won the South Carolina primary, secured their party's nomination, and became president.

Finally, our analysis includes six factors that reflect a candidate's sociodemographic characteristics. A number of studies, as we have already pointed out, find that these factors are important in a state's nomination contest because voters cannot fall back on party identification as they can in a general election. As table 4.1 reveals, candidates from the neighboring states of Georgia and North Carolina have an advantage in the South Carolina primary as do candidates from the eleven former Confederate states. We also find that African American candidates perform well in Democratic contests in South Carolina. Surprisingly, however, evangelical and high-quality candidates do not have an advantage in the South Carolina primary. We discuss each of these factors in more detail in what follows.

Candidates from a neighboring state perform 14.4 percent better than candidates from the other forty-eight states. This effect may stem, as we have suggested, from greater name recognition, greater familiarity with South Carolina politics, or both and helps explain why John Edwards, of North Carolina, and Newt Gingrich, of Georgia, won South Carolina in 2004 and 2012, respectively, the only instances where the state's voters selected the wrong candidate since the switch to a primary format. Although not in our analysis, it is also notable that Jimmy Carter—from Georgia—performed about 10 percent better in South Carolina than he did nationally in 1980.

Being from one of the former eleven Confederate states yields an additional advantage in South Carolina beyond that of being from neighboring Georgia or

North Carolina. The estimates in table 4.1 reveal that candidates from the South perform 7.5 percent better than candidates from other regions of the country. Although this is about half the value of being from a neighboring state, it is sizable compared to other significant predictors in the analysis. While there are certainly southerners who performed poorly in the South Carolina primary, a fact that explains the smaller effect size, there are also a number of southern candidates who did exceptionally well: Bill Clinton, Al Gore, George H. W. Bush, and George Bush. An argument can be made that our estimate of 7.5 percent is conservative given that it does not include Jesse Jackson's 1988 victory or Hillary Clinton's win in 2016. Although both have credible claims to being southern, by birth and marriage, respectively, our measure prioritizes where a candidate spent the most recognizable part of their political career.

A final key factor in our analysis is the importance of race in Democratic contests. African Americans make up 27.9 percent of the state's population and roughly 60 percent of the state's Democratic primary electorate.[9] For these reasons, it is no surprise that African American candidates are predicted by our model to perform 19.7 percent better in Democratic primaries in South Carolina. Notably, this is the largest single effect in our analysis. No doubt the best example is Barack Obama in 2008, who solidified his position at the top of the Democratic field with a strong performance in South Carolina, winning the Palmetto State by a far larger margins than he did in either Iowa or New Hampshire. Jesse Jackson won the Palmetto State outright in 1988, and the Reverend Al Sharpton performed better in South Carolina in 2004 than in any other state.[10] Our analysis indicates that race is a critical factor in Democratic primaries in South Carolina, consistent with the conventional wisdom.

Although our analysis confirms the importance of race in Democratic contests, it disconfirms the popular belief that evangelical candidates have an advantage in South Carolina. Although we do not dispute the pivotal role of evangelical *voters* in the state, we find no advantage for evangelical *candidates* in our model. As Oran Smith and James Guth (2018, 174) aptly put it, the state's Christian conservatives are not a "'disciplined army,' but always a loose alliance of religious groups, sometimes competing, sometimes cooperating." The historical record shows that a number of evangelical candidates underperformed in South Carolina relative to their performance in the Iowa caucus: Dick Gephardt in 1988 and 2004, Mike Huckabee in 2008, and Ted Cruz in 2016.

Likewise, our analysis refutes the academic finding that high-quality candidates—defined in our analysis former governors, senators, and representatives—are advantaged in the South Carolina primary. We offer the caveats that most of these academic studies focus on congressional elections rather than presidential contests and on general elections rather than primaries. In addition, some studies adopt a broader definition of quality than we do in our analysis. Nonetheless, there are plenty of examples of high-quality candidates who performed poorly in South Carolina—Joe Lieberman in 2004 and Jeb Bush in 2016—and a handful without prior federal or gubernatorial experience who did quite well—Donald Trump in 2016 and Jesse Jackson in 1988.

Conclusion

What does it take to win in South Carolina? In this chapter, we have presented an analysis that predicts a candidate's performance in South Carolina's nomination contests. We tested a range of factors mentioned in both journalistic and scholarly sources as being key to winning primaries in general and South Carolina contests in particular. Our results confirm the conventional wisdom in a number of respects but also reveal a few surprises.

We find that three factors are uniquely strong predictors of a candidate's vote share in South Carolina and thus key to winning the state's primary. First, in Democratic primaries, black candidates have a sizable advantage owing to the large percentage of African Americans in the Democratic primary electorate. Second, we find that being from the neighboring states of Georgia and North Carolina yield significant advantages in South Carolina. It is perhaps notable that these two effects—among the three most consequential—derive from factors beyond the candidate's control. And third, in Republican contests, there is a strong link between a candidate's performance in Iowa and South Carolina. We suspect this has to do with the large percentages of born-again Christians and strong conservatives in the Republican electorates in both states.

A handful of other factors are reliable predictors of a candidate's performance as well. Candidates from southern states perform better than candidates from other regions of the country, all else being equal. Southern identity is an important construct in many academic studies, and journalists often speculate about the value of being from a southern state, but our analysis quantifies just how much being from the South matters in the South Carolina primary. We also find that a candidate's performance in New Hampshire predicts his or her vote share in South Carolina on both sides of the aisle, though less than does the performance of a candidate in Iowa in Republican contests. Thus while it is always advantageous to do well in one of the earlier states, there is substantial variability in which state and party best predicts performance in South Carolina. And finally, a candidate's volume of state endorsements and media attention are both notable predictors of success in South Carolina. In the months leading up to the primary, the candidates vie for the backing of key state figures, and in the final weeks they hold rallies and debates that garner critical media coverage. Our analysis confirms that these are indeed pivotal moments in the campaign.

Our analysis also reveals a few surprises. First, candidates with the largest sums of campaign money do not perform better in South Carolina. Underfunded candidates have just as good a chance of winning South Carolina, according to our analysis. Second, high-quality candidates with gubernatorial or federal electoral experience do not have an advantage over candidates with no such experiences. Third, we found no advantage for candidates who previously campaigned in a South Carolina nomination contest. Given the last two findings, we conclude that political experience is not a litmus test in the state's nominating contests. And fourth, evangelical candidates do not outperform candidates of other faiths. Although evangelical voters are certainly a powerful voting bloc in the state, they do not seem to vote in unison for candidates who share their religious views.

While our findings provide a view of the South Carolina primary in the aggregate, they do not address the unique features of specific election cycles. In other words, no statistical model can fully capture the nuance of any given contest. Therefore, we provide an in-depth examination of four Republican contests (1988, 2000, 2012, and 2016) and four Democratic contests (1992, 2004, 2008, and 2016) in chapters 5 and 6. We selected these cases because they are historically notable elections and thus yield key insights about the South Carolina primary. We intentionally picked the two instances where South Carolina primary voters did not select the eventual nominee, 2012 for Republicans and 2004 for Democrats. Ultimately, chapters 5 and 6 allow us to expand on our key findings from this chapter and explore particular instances where these findings do not hold up.

★ 5 ★
LESSONS FROM KEY REPUBLICAN CONTESTS

In this chapter, we focus on the winners and losers in four key Republican primaries. We picked primaries that were historically significant and ones that allow us to better understand the predictors of success identified in chapter 4. In addition to telling the story of these pivotal contests, we continue to address our fourth research question: what does it take to win in South Carolina?

Our first case is the 1988 Republican presidential primary. In 1988, South Carolina voters backed Vice President George H. W. Bush over a strong field of candidates that included Kansas senator Bob Dole, U.S. representative Jack Kemp, and televangelist Pat Robertson. Next, we move to the 2000 Republican primary, an epic and contentious battle between Texas governor George W. Bush and Arizona senator John McCain. Bush's triumph in South Carolina propelled him to success in other southern states and, ultimately, helped him win the White House that year. We then investigate the 2012 GOP primary, a deviant case in that it is the sole instance where South Carolina's Republican primary voters did not select the party's eventual nominee. We explore why former U.S. House Speaker Newt Gingrich beat the establishment favorite, former Massachusetts governor Mitt Romney. Finally, we investigate the case of the 2016 GOP primary, a contest that surprised many observers when New York billionaire and reality television star Donald Trump won the South Carolina primary. Trump's victory helped legitimize his candidacy and propel him toward the Republican nomination and ultimately the presidency.

Following the Reagan Playbook

South Carolina's 1988 presidential primary highlights many of the last chapter's predictors of what it takes to be successful in the first-in-the-South primary. Perhaps most obvious, George H. W. Bush's victory demonstrates both the importance of securing key statewide endorsements and the value of media attention. Bush also had the advantages of being a southerner and winning New Hampshire, both key factors in our analysis. Finally, 1988 is an interesting case because it includes the campaign of Pat Robertson, the first, but certainly not the last, evangelical candidate that struggled to win votes in the South Carolina Republican primary despite shared religious affiliation with a key GOP voting bloc.

In the 1988 contest, President Ronald Reagan's second term was up, so a strong field of Republicans jockeyed for the nomination that year. With the first-in-the-South primary on March 5, the South Carolina GOP once again dominated headlines as the national media turned its attention to the Palmetto State. As is often the case, there was not a clear frontrunner coming out of Iowa and New Hampshire. Dole won Iowa with 37.3 percent support, followed by Robertson (24.6 percent), and Bush (18.6 percent) (Cook 2000). However, Bush won New Hampshire with 37.6 percent of the vote, with Dole coming in second (28.4 percent), Kemp third (12.8 percent), and former Delaware governor Pete DuPont fourth (10.1 percent) (Cook 2000). South Carolina's primary assumed what ended up becoming a familiar tie-breaking function.

Given Bush's third place finish in Iowa, one might have expected him to perform poorly in South Carolina given our results in the prior chapter. However, a candidate's performance in Iowa is just one of seven factors that predict who wins and loses the South Carolina primary. Simply put, Bush's advantages with respect to the other factors helped propel him past Bob Dole and Pat Robertson despite Iowa. Second, though Bush's 19 percent in Iowa was only good for third place, it is above average for Republican candidates in our analysis. In this respect, Bush still performed well in Iowa, and our model therefore predicts that he would have had a strong showing in South Carolina. In fact, Bush's performance in Iowa is predicted by our model to contribute about 9 percent to his vote share in South Carolina, controlling for all else.

Most experts viewed Bush as the frontrunner in South Carolina in 1988. Bush was familiar to Palmetto State voters, had contacts from the 1980 campaign, and benefited from Reagan's popularity in the region. According to a survey of fourteen southern states in January 1988, Reagan had an 82 percent approval rating (Dionne 1988). Perhaps most importantly, Bush had the support of two key individuals from Reagan's successful 1980 campaign, Governor Carroll Campbell, who was the former state chair of the 1980 Reagan campaign, and Lee Atwater, Reagan's state director in 1980, who ran Bush's campaign. Atwater grew up in South Carolina, becoming interested in politics after interning with South Carolina senator Strom Thurmond, and was known for running modern campaigns with voter lists and aggressive get-out-the-vote efforts (Lovler 1980). Atwater was also known for his hardball campaign tactics, most notably, the infamous 1988 Willie Horton ad that featured an African American man who raped a white woman when he was out of prison on a weekend furlough when Michael Duka-kis was governor of Massachusetts. Nonetheless, by most accounts, Bush's 1988 campaign was considered the best run and most well organized of all Republican operations (Ifill 1988).

While Bush had the advantage of endorsements and campaign resources, there were reasons to expect Robertson to do well in South Carolina. Southern candidates, as we have seen, have an advantage in the state's presidential prima-ries, and Robertson, from Virginia, was one of two southern candidates com-peting for the 1988 Republican nomination. Yet Bush was also from a southern state, having spent most of his professional career in Texas, thus negating one of Robertson's key advantages. However, there were questions about Bush's southern identity: he was born in Massachusetts and went to college at Yale Uni-versity. By most accounts, Robertson was better positioned to benefit from his connections to the region than was Bush.

In an effort to garner votes, Robertson played up his southern heritage while campaigning in South Carolina. During a swing through the state's Piedmont re-gion, Robertson told voters, "I'm the only candidate who was born at Stonewall Jackson Hospital . . . [and] the only candidate who went to college where Robert E. Lee was president" (Reid 1988), referring to Washington and Lee University, a liberal arts college in Lexington, Virginia (Christian Broadcasting Network 2018). Robertson also called the South "my backyard" and predicted victory in the South Carolina primary (Dionne 1988).

Robertson, the founder of the Christian Broadcasting Network and host of *The 700 Club*, also hoped to win the support of South Carolina's white evangeli-cal voters. By one measure, South Carolina ranks as the fifth most religious state in the country (O. Smith and Guth 2018). Yet our model does not indicate any measurable advantage for evangelical candidates in South Carolina, a finding we attribute to the fact that the state's Christian conservatives consist of several dif-ferent factions. As the GOP gained strength in South Carolina during the 1950s and 1960s, the party was made up of "upper-status mainliners such as Episcopa-lians, Presbyterians, Methodists, and some 'First Church' Southern Baptists" (O. Smith and Guth 2018, 163). However, Barry Goldwater's 1964 candidacy brought a more conservative religious faction into the Republican Party. Many of these newcomers were associated with Bob Jones University, a Christian liberal arts university in Greenville (Guth and Smith 1997; O. Smith and Guth 2018). By 1987, the Carolina Conservative Coalition, a third group of Christian conserva-tives, was participating in large numbers at precinct meetings and gained con-trol of the Charleston County Republican Party and nearly won a majority in Richland County (Moreland, Steed, and Baker 1991). Robertson could count on support from many, though certainly not all, of these groups that made up South Carolina's Christian conservative voters.

Bush also courted the state's Christian conservatives. Speaking to a group of evangelical ministers during the final week of the campaign, Bush remarked that "Jesus Christ is my personal savior" and added that if elected president he would "not be afraid to ask for God's help" (Germond and Witcover 1988, 14A). In addition, in a play to persuade some of the Robertson's supporters to move to his camp, Bush told the group of religious leaders that he believed South Carolina's Christian conservatives were not "monolithic" (Germond and Witcover 1988).

After disappointing showings in earlier contests, Jack Kemp, a former professional football quarterback and U.S. representative from New York, made South Carolina a priority. According to Kemp, "South Carolina is going to be the battleground around which the future of the Republican Party, not just in the South but in the whole country, is going to be decided" (Miller 1988c, 1C). Even though Reagan's vice president was also on the ballot in South Carolina, Kemp closely aligned himself with the policies of Reagan: "I have a good voting record, I helped start the Reagan revolution, I think there's a lot of things that Reagan years have left behind, and I believe—of all the conservatives in the race—I can best bring it to completion" (Associated Press 1988, 1A). Kemp often infused his speeches with heavy doses of economic theory, turning off some voters. Ellen Warren (1988, 1A), a political reporter for the *State,* said, "His standard stump speech, larded as it is with references to Keynesian theory, Malthus and Bretton Woods—almost always, Bretton Woods—is probably the most information-packed of the 10 presidential contenders. It is, to put it mildly, heavy going."

Bush spent considerable time and money campaigning in South Carolina. He was often flanked by a cadre of high-profile backers, including Governor Carroll Campbell and Tommy Hartnett, Bush's state chair and a former U.S. representative. Barry Goldwater even visited South Carolina to campaign for Bush (Miller 1988a). In an appearance during the final week of campaigning, Goldwater noted that he had "a great affection for South Carolina," adding that "I did pretty good in the South when I ran and if some of it can rub off on George, fine," referencing his 1964 presidential campaign ("Riley and McNair" 1988, 1A). Later in the week, Bush spoke about the national significance of the South Carolina primary at a campaign stop in Sumter, telling prospective voters "South Carolina will be on the national radar screen and on every TV set. South Carolina will be the forerunner of the most significant event of the modern-day nomination process" (Pope 1988b, 1A).

Kemp and Robertson also campaigned heavily in South Carolina, while Dole did not. Despite securing the endorsement of his U.S. Senate colleague Strom Thurmond (Rudin 2008), Dole did not mount a serious challenge in South Carolina (Edsall 1988), although his wife, Elizabeth Dole, a North Carolina native, campaigned extensively in the Palmetto State, visiting 39 of the state's 46 counties (Miller 1988c). In a last-minute push at the South Carolina State House,

Kemp attacked his opponents as unfaithful to the Reagan revolution, arguing that "Republicans in South Carolina recognize that there is somebody who understands the Reagan revolution and understands how to take it forward and bring it to completion and mend the flaws" (Pope 1988a, 1C). Robertson seemed to lose momentum in the final weeks. During a two-day bus tour of the state's coastal region, the crowds were described as "extremely small" and "subdued" (Pope 1988b, 1A). At the same time, a chorus of political analysts talked about the stakes for Robertson. Clemson University political scientist Charles Dunn said, "If Robertson can't win here, he can't win anywhere" (Boyd 1988, 1A). University of South Carolina political scientist Earl Black agreed: "If he can't do it here, it's hard to see where he can do it" (Bandy 1988a, 2C).

The candidates made their case to South Carolina voters not only through stump speeches and rallies but also political advertisements. As the frontrunner, Bush played it safe, emphasizing his experience, close ties to Reagan, and commitment to a strong military (Apple 1988). Kemp's ads focused on keeping the Panama Canal as long as that country's military leader, Manuel Noriega, was in power (Apple 1988). Dole ran ads criticizing Bush on taxes and the Iran-contra affair (Apple 1988). Robertson purchased full-page advertisements in South Carolina newspapers that were highly critical of Bush. One ad asked "Who Hijacked the Reagan Revolution?" answering the question by referencing "Eastern Republicans" like Bush who would not "let Reagan be Reagan" (Moreland, Steed, and Baker 1991, 126). The ad concluded by urging voters to elect "solid conservatives from the beginning," not "wimps" (Moreland, Steed, and Baker 1991, 126).

As many observers know, the South Carolina primary has a history of bareknuckle politics and dirty tricks. The 1988 contest was no exception. During the 1988 cycle, Bush operatives leaked information about a scandal involving televangelist Jimmy Swaggart, a friend of Roberson (Reid 1988). Swaggart confessed to hiring a prostitute, and Robertson placed the blame for the hard-ball campaign maneuver squarely on Atwater (Reid 1988). Not mentioning him by name, Robertson told the media, "I wouldn't tolerate someone like that. I'd fire him in a minute" (Bandy 1988b, 1A).

Polling showed Bush with a sizable lead prior to voting in the primary. Based on a survey of one thousand probable voters conducted just before the election by the *Washington Post,* Bush was ahead with 49 percent of the vote, followed by Dole at 26 percent, Robertson at 14 percent, and Kemp at 7 percent (Apple 1988). Bush indeed ended up securing an impressive victory in the 1988 South Carolina primary. He received a plurality of the vote, with 48.5 percent (Cook 2000). Dole placed second (20.6 percent), while Robertson was a close third (19.1 percent) (Cook 2000). Kemp was fourth (11.5 percent) (Cook 2000). In a postmortem article appearing in the *State,* political reporter Jeff Miller (1988a,

1A) explained why South Carolina was a "cakewalk" for Bush: "The vice president came in with the strongest organization, the most endorsements, the energetic backing of the governor, and a national campaign manager native to the state who had covered the territory for President Reagan in 1980." Needless to say, our analysis in the prior chapter identifies these as important factors. The Christian conservative vote was split in 1988, as "Robertson failed to expand his base much beyond his Pentecostal and charismatic constituency" (Guth 1995, 136). In addition, the state's Bob Jones University activists were divided among the GOP contenders, while Southern Baptists and mainline Protestants strongly supported Bush (Guth 1995).

In 1988, South Carolina was also a barometer for subsequent southern contests. Ten southern states (Alabama, Arkansas, Florida, Georgia, Louisiana, Mississippi, North Carolina, Tennessee, Texas, and Virginia) held Republican primaries just three days after South Carolina in 1988. Bush continued his success, winning all ten contests. He did particularly well in Mississippi (66.1 percent), Alabama (64.5 percent), Texas (63.9 percent), Florida (62.1 percent), and Tennessee (60 percent) (Cook 2000). As we argue in the first chapter, one of the reasons being first in the South is uniquely important is that candidates who do well in South Carolina can quickly amass an insurmountable delegate advantage in the subsequent southern states.

In summary, the 1988 GOP primary reinforces many of our key findings about what it takes to win in South Carolina. Perhaps most importantly, Bush had an overwhelming advantage in state endorsements and dominated preelection media coverage. And as a southern candidate, he benefited from his regional appeal. Though Robertson also hailed from the South, he was not able to turn his southern heritage to his political advantage. Finally, the 1988 contest is the first, though not the last, case where evangelical candidates have struggled to gain traction in South Carolina given the tendency of evangelical voters to split their ballots.

The "Old Guard" versus the "Young Turks"

Like the 1988 contest, the 2000 GOP primary illustrates many of the key predictors we have identified for what it takes to win in South Carolina. Namely, the 2000 election shows the advantage of being a southern candidate, the positive impact of key state endorsements, and the strong link between Iowa and South Carolina in Republican contests. In addition, the 2000 contest reveals that although evangelical candidates do not have an advantage in South Carolina, Christian conservatives play an important role in picking winner and losers in the Palmetto State's GOP primary. Finally, the 2000 GOP contest is often remembered as the nastiest presidential primary in South Carolina history.

After eight years of Democratic control of the White House, a number of Republican candidates lined up to secure the GOP nomination. In the primary, the leading Republican contenders were Texas governor George W. Bush and Arizona senator John McCain (Cook 2007). Steve Forbes, Gary Bauer, Orrin Hatch, and Alan Keyes competed for the 2000 Republican nomination as well but were never serious challengers (Cook 2007). In line with the pattern we have noted, voters in Iowa and New Hampshire backed different candidates in 2000. Bush won Iowa with 41 percent of the vote, followed by Forbes (30.5 percent), Keyes (14.2 percent), Bauer (8.5 percent), McCain (4.7 percent), and Hatch (1 percent) (Cook 2007). It is important to note that McCain did not complete in Iowa but instead focused on New Hampshire. McCain's strategy went according to plan, and he won the New Hampshire primary with 48.5 percent of vote (Cook 2007). Bush came in second (30.4 percent) in New Hampshire, Forbes was third (12.7 percent), and Keyes was fourth (6.4 percent) (Cook 2007). South Carolina would again play a crucial tie-breaking role.

Despite McCain's momentum coming out of New Hampshire, the South Carolina primary was "ready-made for Bush's candidacy" (Clark and Haynes 2002, 27). Polls taken near the time of the New Hampshire primary showed Bush with a comfortable fifteen- to twenty-point lead in the Palmetto State (Bandy 2000h). Likewise, we have identified a strong connection between Iowa and South Carolina in Republican contests—welcome news for Bush—and a comparatively weak effect of the New Hampshire outcome—bad news for McCain. In addition, South Carolina had been a firewall for his father—George H. W. Bush in 1988 and 1992—and the younger Bush hoped it would be for him too in 2000 (Walsh and Edsall 2000). Like his father, George W. Bush had the organization and the backing of most of the Republican Party establishment (Clark and Haynes 2002). Conversely, McCain ran as a self-styled "maverick" in 2000, hoping to win support from South Carolina's Democrats and independent-minded voters, since these voters were permitted to vote in the Republican primary, and from the state's veterans (Clark and Haynes 2002). And since there was no competitive Democratic contest in South Carolina, the chance to court the crossover voters was certainly an option in 2000.[1]

As is always the case in South Carolina Republican primaries, support from Christian conservatives was important to a winning electoral strategy. Given the fledgling campaigns of Bauer, Forbes, and Keyes, Christian conservatives faced a choice between Bush and McCain. According to Lee Bandy (2000f), "the choice was a no-brainer," and though far from a unified group, many of state's Christian conservatives lined up behind Bush. Bush often talked about his faith on the campaign trail and even said that Jesus Christ was his favorite political philosopher during a debate in Iowa (Bandy 2000f). In addition, although Pat Robertson, the 1988 presidential candidate, did not endorse a primary candidate, he did say Bush was "worthy of support" (Sobieraj 1999, A4) and expressed doubts about McCain (Bandy 2000b). Likewise, former Christian Coalition Executive director Ralph Reed openly vouched for the Texas governor (Bandy 2000b).

A memorable feature of the 2000 Republican primary was the January 7 debate in Columbia. Six candidates participated in the debate: Bauer, Bush, Forbes, Hatch, Keyes, and McCain. Even though this was a presidential debate, it was a state issue, the Confederate battle flag, which dominated the postdebate headlines. At issue was the fact that the flag was hoisted on top of the statehouse in 1962 to commemorate the civil war and protest against the civil rights movement (Prince 2004). When Bush was asked about the flag he responded, "I don't believe it's the role of someone from outside South Carolina and someone running for president to come into this state and tell the people of South Carolina what to do with their business when it comes to the flag" (Neal 2000a). No doubt this answer played well with the state's social conservatives. McCain, by comparison, struggled answering questions about the Confederate flag. Less than a week after the debate, McCain appeared on "Face the Nation," saying the flag was "offensive" and labeling it a "symbol of racism and slavery" (Firestone 2000). He flip-flopped a day later, distributing a statement to South Carolina reporters saying the flag was "a symbol of heritage" (Firestone 2000). Political scientists John Clark and Audrey Haynes (2002, 29) called it a misstep, arguing that "the senator who claimed to be a 'straight talker' waffled on the Confederate battle flag." By most accounts, these shifting positions on the flag likely damaged McCain's candidacy, and Bush's status as the governor of a southern state no doubt helped him in the minds of voters.

Despite the flag controversy, polling in early February indicated that the race was tightening (Neal and Edsall 2000). A Rasmussen Research poll had McCain at 41 percent and Bush at 40 percent, while a Zogby International poll had McCain leading Bush 44 percent to 39 percent (Bandy 2000h). It surprised many observers that an outsider like McCain, known for his straight talk and propensity to reach across the aisle, could be tied in South Carolina with a southerner named Bush. Perhaps one reason for McCain's resilience was his favorable press coverage. In fact, McCain's rivals disparaged his strong media coverage.

The back-and-forth between Bush and McCain became "legendary for its nastiness, branding the Palmetto State as perhaps the leader in dirty presidential politics" (Huffmon, Knotts, and McKee 2017, 13). McCain released a commercial saying that Bush's ad "twists the truth like Bill Clinton" (Bruni 2000). For GOP primary voters, this was one of the worst things you could say about a rival candidate. Clinton, who was impeached during his second term, was very unpopular with the state's Republican voters. After hearing about the ad, former Governor Carroll Campbell said, "I'm going to work about 10 times harder to make damn sure he doesn't win," and a statement issued by Senator Thurmond's office said that McCain's ads "reflect poorly on my friend from Arizona" (Davis 2000b, A1). McCain countered, accusing the Bush campaign of conducting push polls (Mitchell and Bruni 2000), a tactic used by pollsters to influence respondents' opinions. According to one account, the push polls asked respondents "if they are aware that McCain was reprimanded by the Senate in the 'Keating Five' savings-and-loan scandal" (Stensland 2000, B3). The push polling took an even more sinister turn when voters were asked, "Would you be more or less likely to vote for John McCain . . . if you knew he had fathered an illegitimate black child?" (Banks 2008). McCain and his wife, Cindy, had adopted their daughter, Bridget, from Bangladesh (Banks 2008; Bumiller 2008). Many attributed these objectionable tactics to Karl Rove, director of the Bush operation and a protégé of Atwater (Gooding 2004). Rove denies the allegations (Barr 2010).

Part of the McCain strategy was to win support from the state's moderates: "The McCain formula for victory is this: He must attract a large number of the 400,000-plus veterans, get a sizable response among the reform-minded independents and gain the backing of moderate-to-conservative Democrats" (Bandy (2000c, A1). McCain made overt appeals to crossover voters. Speaking to a crowd of five hundred at a rally in Greenwood, he said, "I ask you, I beg you, whether you're a Republican, Democrat, Libertarian or vegetarian, get out and get your friends out. We've got to get the greatest turnout in this state's history so that I can serve my country once more" (Ayers and Bruni 2000). While McCain highlighted his independent streak, Bush also made a play for the state's moderates. Rove explained that "our objective is to maximize our vote among independents in South Carolina. We're going out of our way with phone calls and postcards to invite these people to our events" (Berke 2000).

Candidates began dropping out of the race—Bauer on February 4 (United Press International 2000) and Forbes on February 10 (Bandy 2000e)—and so Alan Keyes became the lone alternative to Bush and McCain. For Keyes, the 2000 GOP primary represented a return trip to South Carolina, having finished fifth with 2.1 percent of the vote in 1996 (Cook 2000), and no doubt he hoped his having been a South Carolina primary contestant once before would help him now. However, as we note in the previous chapter, past experience in the South Carolina primary is not positively related to future performance in the Palmetto State. While Keyes's South Carolina campaign lacked money and organization, he hoped to capitalize on South Carolina's open primary by specifically targeting crossover and African American voters (Carroll 2000). Keyes also articulated a consistent campaign theme—the moral decline of the United States ("Keyes' Focus Too Narrow" 2000). Associated Press political reporter Tom Stuckey (2000, D4) summarized Keyes's message: "Abortion is at the heart of the moral decay; God is the only answer to the nation's problems; any Republican willing to compromise on moral issues is worthy only of scorn." Keyes often riled the party establishment by speaking out against his GOP opponents, particularly Bush. In response to Bush's inability to name the leaders of Pakistan, India, and Chechnya during an interview with a Boston television station, Keyes told the Lexington County Republican Party that Bush "has no knowledge of foreign affairs" and called him "a light-weight on foreign policy" (Root 1999, A4).

A second debate took place on February 15, just a couple days before the primary. There were only three participants at this point in the campaign: Bush, Keyes, and McCain. Keyes was positioned between the two top contenders, and the debate was heated at times. McCain criticized Bush for his negative tone and shady campaign tactics, telling his rival that he "should be ashamed" (Broder and Balz 2000). The candidates also battled over who would bring the most reform to Washington and who was the biggest outsider (Davis 2000c). Lastly, they discussed abortion policy, confirming their pro-life stances and committing to sign a ban on partial-birth abortions, though Bush refused to answer a question about what he would do if his daughter became pregnant out of wedlock, saying that he would not "drag his daughter into discussions" (Davis 2000c, A1).

In addition to its organizational prowess, the Bush campaign had a sizable fund-raising advantage in South Carolina. Campaign finance expert Fred Wertheimer said, "If there is a Bush fire wall in this presidential election, it turns out to be money, not South Carolina or any other individual state. Bush's financial flooding of South Carolina is the first on-the-ground, concrete example of just what his huge money advantage really means in this election" (Van Natta and Broder 2000). Although we do not dispute that financial resources are needed to run a successful campaign, our analysis in the last chapter shows that the candidate with the greatest money advantage does not automatically win the South Carolina primary. This point is illustrated by the loss of Bush's brother, Jeb, in the 2016 South Carolina primary. Simply put, we believe Bush's 2000 victory is best explained by other factors.

Bush also led in endorsements, securing the backing of Senator Strom Thurmond and U.S. representatives Floyd Spence and Jim DeMint (Davis 2000e). Perhaps most importantly, Bush had the endorsement of Campbell, the influential former governor. McCain had endorsements from U.S. representatives Lindsey Graham and Mark Sanford (Davis 2000e). Cast as a battle between the "old guard" and the "young Turks," the 2000 campaign also had a subplot, according to Francis Marion political scientist Neal Thigpen, namely, "a struggle to see who leads the Republican Party into the decades ahead" (Davis 2000a, A1). McCain framed the race in a similar way: "It's a generational contest between the older Carroll Campbell, David Beasley establishment and the younger Lindsey Graham and Mark Sanford establishment" (Bandy and Stensland 2000b, A1). In the final days of the campaign, McCain picked up an endorsement from Gary Bauer, his former rival (Bandy and Stensland 2000a). On balance, however, Bush had the edge in terms of the quality of his endorsements.

Another unique feature of the 2000 contest was the amount of time between the New Hampshire primary and the South Carolina primary. With eighteen days between the two primaries, the 2000 contest provided a lot of time to campaign in the Palmetto State. State GOP chair Henry McMaster said that "this primary has 10 times the intensity of the 1996 contest," and Clemson University political scientist David Woodard remarked, "I don't know of any time since 1980 that we've ever had anything this fierce" (Bandy 2000f, A1).

Once the votes were tallied, Bush had won the 2000 South Carolina primary by double digits. He received 53.4 percent of vote to McCain's 41.9 percent (Cook 2007). Given the recent polling that showed the race a statistical dead heat, this was a welcome and unexpectedly comfortable victory for the Texas governor. Keyes finished a distant third with just 4.5 percent (Cook 2007). Bush won substantial support from white evangelicals, and according to Woodard this was the result of a lack of trust in McCain by Christian conservatives: "They just thought he was real soft on their social issues—fetal-tissue research, homosexual rights, and abortion" (Stroud 2000, A1). The Bush victory also led to calls for the "Campbell machine" to reach out to McCain supporters to heal the state Republican Party after such a divisive primary. According to Woodard, "A large group of independents brought into the party by McCain can be had by some other leader if Bush supporters don't show some humility" (Bandy 2000a, A1). But Woodard also said that "Lindsey Graham and Mark Sanford are going to have a lot of fence-mending to do. They're going to have to explain to a lot of people exactly why they abandoned the 'establishment' for this candidate. There are a lot of people who want an explanation" (Davis 2000d, A1).

Bush's triumph in South Carolina helped propel him to success in other southern states and served as a springboard to his nomination. As we note throughout, one of the reasons why being first in the South is so important is the state's influence in subsequent southern primaries and the ability of candidates to quickly amass a sizable delegate lead. The Virginia primary was ten days after South Carolina's, and Bush won with 52.8 percent (Cook 2007). Georgia held a primary a week later, and again, Bush was victorious. In Georgia, Bush received an even higher vote total, 66.9 percent, prompting McCain to suspend his campaign just two days later (Cook 2007). With McCain on the sidelines, Bush won all five southern states (Florida, Louisiana, Mississippi, Tennessee, and Texas) holding contests on Super Tuesday, March 14 (Cook 2007).

Overall, there are a number of lessons from the 2000 GOP contest. First, it demonstrates the power of media coverage—often driven by a strong debate performance—and the pivotal effect of key endorsements. Second, the campaign highlights the vitally important role played by the state's Christian conservatives, even though they may not rally behind evangelical candidates in unison. Third, it demonstrates the power of a candidate's demographic characteristics, as once again a southern candidate bested a competitor from outside the region. Fourth, it shows the strong link between South Carolina and Iowa and the comparatively weak relationship between South Carolina and New Hampshire. And finally, the 2000 contest once again foreshadowed the results in subsequent southern states, continuing to serve as a springboard for the GOP presidential nomination. Additional lessons from the 2000 Republican contest come from factors that did *not* seem to affect the election results. First, it is notable that Alan Keyes, an African American Republican, won just 4.5 percent of the vote. Although we were unable to test the effect of race in Republican contests due to the lack of data points, it is interesting that the sizable advantage that black Democrats enjoy in South Carolina does not seem to translate to their Republican counterparts even though the state has open primaries. Second, one of our conclusions in the prior chapter is that campaign experience in the Palmetto State does not seem to confer any advantage. A number of contests exemplify this point, including the 2000 GOP primary. George W. Bush was a political newcomer to the South Carolina primary, but two of his opponents, Steve Forbes and Alan Keyes, had campaigned in the state's 1996 Republican contest.

A final interesting aspect of the 2000 election were the postelection apologies from Bush and McCain. Though not addressing the specific allegations of dirty tricks against McCain, Bush apologized for some of his actions in the South Carolina primary. During the campaign, Bush appeared at Bob Jones University, a school that in 2000 prohibited interracial dating. The trip to Bob Jones University "proved more controversial outside the state than within it" (Clark and Audrey 2002, 29), but, nevertheless, after the South Carolina primary was over, on February 28, Bush apologized for not "disassociating myself from [the] anti-Catholic sentiments and racial prejudice" (Broder and Allen 2000). McCain also offered a postprimary apology for actions he took in the heated 2000 contest. Specifically, he reversed the stance he took about the Confederate battle flag during the South Carolina debate. On April 19, he gave a speech at the conservative South Carolina Policy council explaining how he regretted his flip-flopping with respect to his views on the Confederate flag. He noted that he should have given an honest answer the question of his views about the flag but that he "did not do so for one reason alone. I feared that if I answered honestly, I could not win the South Carolina primary. So I chose to compromise my principles. I broke my promise to always tell the truth" (Neal 2000b).

GOP Voters Miss the Mark

Our next case is the 2012 GOP primary election. One of the main reasons we picked this contest is because it is a deviant case, the only time in South Carolina history when the GOP primary winner was not the party's eventual nominee. Yet the election also highlights a number of our key predictors of success in South Carolina. Most notably, the race once again demonstrates the advantage enjoyed by southern candidates and the added benefit of being from a neighboring state. Further, the 2012 election is another case that highlights our finding that evangelical candidates do not have an electoral advantage in the South Carolina primary.

With President Obama seeking reelection, Republicans had the spotlight to themselves in 2012. A large number of Republican candidates vied for the chance to face Obama in the general election because the perception was that he was beatable after Democrats' stinging defeat in the 2010 midterm. In total, nine Republican candidates appeared on the January 21 ballot in South Carolina.[2] According to most observers, the leading candidates were former Speaker of the House Newt Gingrich from Georgia, former Massachusetts governor Mitt Romney, former Pennsylvania senator Rick Santorum, and Texas representative Ron Paul. Also appearing on the ballot were U.S. representative Michele Bachmann from Minnesota, business executive Herman Cain, former Utah governor Jon Huntsman, former Nevada governor Gary Johnson, and Texas governor Rick Perry.

When examining the 2012 presidential election, it is important to consider the changes in campaign fund-raising prior to this cycle (Clark 2014). Individual contributors were permitted to spend unlimited amounts of money, often through super PACs, in an effort to influence election outcomes. These super PACs were allowed to spend money as long as they did not coordinate their activities with one of the campaigns. In addition, the 2010 *Citizens United v. Federal Election Commission* Supreme Court decision permitted corporations to be treated as individuals for the purposes of campaign spending (Clark 2014).

Once again, different candidates won Iowa and New Hampshire. Securing the substantial white evangelical vote in Hawkeye State, Santorum, known for his social conservatism, won a narrow, thirty-four vote victory over Romney, with both candidates receiving 24.5 percent of the total votes cast. Paul finished third in Iowa (21.4 percent), followed by Gingrich (13.3 percent), and Perry (10.3 percent). Romney won the New Hampshire primary with 39.3 percent of the vote. Paul was second in New Hampshire (22.9 percent), followed by Huntsman (16.9 percent), Santorum (9.4 percent), and Gingrich (also at 9.4 percent). Santorum finished just eleven votes ahead of Gingrich.[3]

In the 2012 GOP contest, Romney was the establishment pick, and South Carolina Republicans had a history of backing establishment candidates. This pattern is most evident in the Bush victories in 1988 and 1992, as well as wins by Dole in 1996, Bush in 2000, and McCain in 2008. But there were signs in 2012 that Palmetto State Republicans might veer from their establishment leanings. Back in 2008, Mike Huckabee finished a strong second in the South Carolina primary, a sign that establishment candidates might not be as safe as they once had been (G. Smith 2012e). In addition, Nikki Haley, a backbencher in the South Carolina House of Representatives, beat three "better known, more established rivals"—attorney general Henry McMaster, U.S. representative Gresham Barrett, and Lieutenant Governor Andre Bauer—winning the 2010 GOP nomination for governor (G. Smith 2012e, 19). Challenges to the Republican establishment were occurring nationally as well. The 2012 cycle was the first presidential election following the Tea Party revolution in 2010, an election cycle that exacerbated Republican cleavages (Ragusa and Gaspar 2016).

Not only was the environment tough for GOP establishment candidates, but South Carolina's social conservatives were leery of Romney, the establishment favorite, owing to his Mormon faith and shifting position on abortion. Yet as had often been the case in the past, social conservatives were spilt between Santorum, Gingrich, and Perry (Balz 2012). Perry and Gingrich did not do very well in Iowa or New Hampshire, so South Carolina became even more important to their campaigns (Balz 2012). Perry skipped New Hampshire to focus on South Carolina, and Santorum hoped to replicate the success of his Iowa strategy in South Carolina, courting the evangelical vote and spending considerable time in the Palmetto State (Beam 2012a).

While South Carolina GOP voters had a track record of supporting establishment candidates, the state was always expected to be a challenge for Romney. Not only had Romney performed poorly in the 2008 South Carolina primary, finishing in fourth place with 15.3 percent of the vote, but the states' electorate was "everything that Romney was not: southern, very conservative, and evangelical" (Balz 2013, 185).[4] Polling data indicated that Romney's support in South Carolina had a ceiling. According to three versions of the Clemson University Palmetto Poll, Romney hovered around 20 percent in November 2011, December 2011, and January 2012 (Graham and Buchanan 2014). By comparison, Gingrich had just 10 percent support in November but surged to 38 percent in December before falling slightly to 32 percent in January (Graham and Buchanan 2014).

Romney also faced intense political attacks from his rivals, particularly from Gingrich and Perry. In the heat of the campaign, Perry called Romney a "vulture capitalist," and Gingrich called Romney a "Massachusetts moderate" (Beam, Smith, and Phillips 2012). In addition, the Gingrich super PAC purchased the documentary *King of Bain* and put it on its website (Balz 2013). The twenty-seven-minute documentary was highly critical of Romney's time in private equity, showing how Bain Capital purchased companies, fired employees, and made huge profits for its partners (Balz 2013). The Gingrich team also ran negative advertisements against Romney, pointing out that Romney flip-flopped on the issue of abortion, supporting a woman's right to choose before becoming pro-life ("Elections 2012" 2012).

One of Newt Gingrich's main strategies as a candidate was to unite social conservatives behind his candidacy and convince voters he had the best chance to stop Romney. While campaigning in Florence, Gingrich said, "Any vote for Santorum or Perry is, in effect, a vote to help Romney become the nominee. The only reason Governor Romney is ahead at this moment is that the conservatives are spilt three ways" (Helderman and Tumulty 2012). Santorum also made his case to voters: "We have Governor Romney, who's timid and isn't what the country needs. Then you have Newt, who's bold but all over the place. Attacking capitalism, supporting capitalism. Against global warming, for global warming. We need someone who's bold and consistent" (Helderman and Tumulty 2012). Perry argued that "the tea party individuals know you're not going to change Washington unless you bring an outsider like myself in, who's not wedded to the old way of doing business—the Wall Street, Washington cabal that's been calling the shots and created this huge debt and the problems of government that's too big" (Helderman and Tumulty 2012).

In an effort to unite social conservatives, religious leaders and influential conservative political strategists met in Texas a week before the South Carolina primary to talk about who to support (Eckholm 2012). Attending the meeting were, among others, James Dobson, founder of Focus on the Family, and Donald Wildmon, the retired president of the American Family Association. The meeting focused on the pros and cons of Gingrich, Perry, and Santorum as the potential nominee (Eckholm 2012). The group sought an alternative to Romney, not trusting his shifting policy positions on gay marriage and abortion (Eckholm 2012). Participants in the Texas meeting also worried about what happened in the 2008 South Carolina primary, when white evangelical Christians did not rally behind Baptist minister and Iowa caucus winner Mike Huckabee (Eckholm 2012). Given concerns about Gingrich's electoral viability and marital history, the religious leaders voted to support Santorum (Eckholm and Zeleny 2012). Coming out of the weekend meeting, Tony Perkins, president of the Family Research Council, made the case for why South Carolina was the right state for social conservatives to take a stand on: "South Carolina is probably a state that is more reflective of the social conservative movement. It has a higher than average percentage of evangelical social conservative voters. . . . This is a good time to see movement toward a particular candidate as a consensus candidate for social conservatives" (Beam 2012d).

In addition to courting Christian conservatives, the 2012 contenders worked to gain support from South Carolina's military veterans. The state had more than four hundred thousand veterans and eight military bases at the time (Beam 2012f), but only two of the 2012 GOP candidates, Rick Perry and Ron Paul, served in the military (Beam 2012f). James Livingston, a retired major general, Medal of Honor recipient, and Mt. Pleasant resident, switched his support from Perry to Gingrich after Perry on account of his low poll numbers. According to Livingston, "We need a firewall out there that can stop this juggernaut called the Democratic Party from taking over our nation. The man that I think is the street fighter and the guy with the savvy and knowledge of Washington to take that on from the get-go . . . is Newt" (Beam 2012f). Romney, meanwhile, had support from Medal of Honor recipients Sergeant John Baker and Captain James Mc-Ginty (Beam 2012f).

Endorsements from South Carolina's leading politicos were split in 2012 between Romney and Gingrich. The state's two U.S. senators, Jim DeMint and Lindsey Graham, did not endorse anyone prior to the South Carolina GOP primary (Kropf 2012). Newly elected governor Nikki Haley endorsed Romney on *Fox & Friends* in December 2011 (Parker and Shear 2011), asserting that "now more than ever, we need someone who has the leadership to deal with a broken Washington" (Parker and Shear 2011). Haley also defended Romney when he was criticized for not releasing his tax returns: "The people of South Carolina are not talking about tax returns. They're talking about jobs, spending, and the economy, and in all honesty, I've heard more people wondering why you guys aren't asking about ethics reports and ethics problems with the Gingrich campaign" (Parker 2012). On January 17, Sarah Palin told Fox News political commentator Sean Hannity that she would vote for Gingrich in South Carolina if she could (Helderman and Tumulty 2012). Gingrich also received an endorsement from the powerful speaker of the South Carolina House of Representatives, Bobby Harrell (Clark 2014).

The 2012 contest included two high-profile debates in the final week of the campaign. The first debate was held in Myrtle Beach on January 16 and sponsored by the *Wall Street Journal* and the Fox News Channel, and featured Gingrich, Paul, Perry, Romney, and Santorum. Throughout the evening, Romney was hammered by his opponent for the work he did with Bain Capital and on the topic of his tax returns (Tumulty and Rucker 2012). In one of the debate's key moments, Gingrich took on President Obama and his policies around job training and food stamps. According to Gingrich, "Unconditional efforts by the best food-stamp president in American history to maximize dependency is terrible for the future of our country" (Tumulty and Rucker 2012). Gingrich also scored political points in his response to a question from Fox News contributor Juan Williams. Williams asked whether Gingrich's suggestion that poor school children could work as janitors to earn money and develop a work ethic was racially insensitive (Balz 2013). During the back-and-forth, Gingrich launched into a critique of the Obama administration and proclaimed that "every American of every background has been endowed by their creator with the right to pursue a happiness. . . . And if that makes liberals unhappy, I'm going to continue to find ways to help poor people learn how to get a job, learn how to get a better job, and learn someday to own the job" (Balz 2013, 189). Dan Balz (2013, 189) reported that "the audience's reaction to the exchange captured the pent-up anger of the party's base" and noted that "conservatives wanted a nominee who would go after the president and the liberal elites, and in Gingrich they saw someone doing it." Most postdebate prognosticators declared Gingrich the winner of the debate (G. Smith 2012c), and Gingrich received substantial media attention over the subsequent days.

As the election approached, Gingrich warned GOP voters that they were facing a repeat of 2008. He told the Faith and Freedom Coalition that "unless a conservative wins on Saturday, we're going to end up with a moderate nominee who in my judgment will have a very, very hard time beating Barack Obama" (Tumulty and Rucker 2012). In the contest's waning days, the pressure continued to build on Romney. He was forced to provide more details about his tax returns, describing the amount of money he made from speeches as "not very much," though the amount in 2011 was $374,000 (Rucker and Balz 2012, A5). This episode provided another example of how the multimillionaire Romney appeared out of touch with mainstream South Carolina voters. This sentiment among South Carolinians was exacerbated when Romney left the state on January 17 for a fund-raiser in New York (Zeleny and Parker 2012). However, there were some political experts who questioned the strategy behind the negative attacks against Romney's business record. Polls showed that the attacks on Romney's private sector work experience were actually hurting Gingrich with South Carolina Republican voters (Balz 2013). As Clemson political scientist David Woodard said, "When I first saw the [Bain] strategy I thought, 'This is the stupidest thing I've ever seen.' They're giving him more momentum. We've got BMW here, Fujifilm, Bosch and Michelin because we have a free-trade philosophy and it's engrained in our culture here. Beating up on free markets and capitalism—that's not going to work here" (G. Smith 2012a, 1).

The second debate between Gingrich, Paul, Romney, and Santorum took place just two days before the primary, on January 19. Perhaps the most memorable highlight from the debate was when just a few minutes in, CNN's John King asked Gingrich about recently released allegations he had asked his ex-wife for an open marriage. In a heated response, Gingrich slammed the media for asking this type of question at a presidential debate and protecting Obama. Gingrich said, "I think the destructive, vicious, negative nature of much of the news media makes it harder to govern this country, harder to attract decent people to run for public office and I am appalled that you would begin a presidential debate on a topic like that" (Byers 2012). The audience erupted approvingly and the exchange dominated the postdebate media coverage, giving Gingrich a key advantage over Romney. According to Clark (2014, 29), "For South Carolinians seeking a nominee that would wage an aggressive general election campaign against Obama, Gingrich showed that he would not be pushed around." Winthrop University political scientist Scott Huffmon pointed to Romney's decision to attack Gingrich as a sign that the race was tightening, "Going after Gingrich by name was, near the end, an acknowledgement that Gingrich might be threatening what Romney hoped was a coronation" (Beam 2012e, A1). As with the first debate, most observers declared Gingrich the victor.

There were two other noteworthy aspects of Gingrich's campaign. First, he acted as his own chief strategist following the "mass exodus" of his political consultants in June 2011 (Gabriel 2012). He did, however, get help from an upstart firm owned by two women, Leslie Gaines and Ruth Sherlock (G. Smith 2012d). According to Gina Smith, a political reporter at the *State,* Sherlock & Gaines Consulting Group was "the first woman-owned firm to play such a big role in winning a Republican presidential primary in South Carolina, a state often knocked for its paucity of women lawmakers and women in political roles" (G. Smith 2012d, A1). In addition, Gingrich was the candidate who most effectively represented GOP voters angry with the state of American politics, particularly frustrated male Republicans (Washington and Smith 2012). According to political consultant Shell Suber, "Gingrich is giving voice to all the voters frustrated with the direction of government" (Washington and Smith 2012, 1).

As the contest was heating up, veteran South Carolina political operative Larry Marchant anticipated that the campaigns would engage in dirty tricks: "History always repeats itself, and this state has the reputation of playing hard. I expect it to get bare knuckles here" (G. Smith 2012b, 1). And he was right. Unlike in 1988 or 2000, however, in 2012 the dirty tricks came in the form of fake emails. One email, designed to look like it came from CNN, claimed that Gingrich forced his ex-wife to have an abortion (Hamby 2012). A second email was designed to look like an apology from Gingrich's campaign. In the fake press release, Gingrich purportedly said, "I have said many times, including on the debate stage last night, that I am not a perfect human being and that I have made mistakes in my life. This was one of them. I have had to apologize to God and seek reconciliation" (Montopoli and Huisenga 2012). South Carolina's State Law Enforcement Division launched an investigation ("Fake CNN Email Alert" 2012), but the perpetrator was never identified.

In a stunning turn of events during the final days of the campaign, Perry dropped out of the race and endorsed Gingrich (Helderman and Balz 2012).

Gingrich told a rally in Orangeburg on January 20 that "the only effective conservative vote to stop the Massachusetts moderate is a vote for me" (Helderman and Balz 2012). Romney responded by trying to lower expectations: "I said from the beginning South Carolina is an uphill battle for a guy from Massachusetts" (Helderman and Balz 2012). South Carolina's two senators handicapped the race two days before the primary. Graham said, "The wind's at Newt's back," while DeMint noted that South Carolina is "clearly a two-man race" between Gingrich and Romney (Helderman and Balz 2012).

In one of the campaign's lighter moments, Charleston native and Comedy Central host Stephen Colbert flirted with getting on the ballot in his home state. Having previously formed a super PAC under the name Making a Better Tomorrow, Tomorrow, Colbert announced that he was forming an exploratory committee to become "president of the United States of South Carolina" on January 12 (Beam 2012c). Though he was not ultimately on the South Carolina ballot, Colbert encouraged his supporters to vote for Herman Cain instead, a candidate who had previously suspended his campaign. Colbert appeared with Herman Cain for a "Rock Me like a Herman Cain-olina Primary Rally" at the College of Charleston (see figure 5.1) the night before the election to raise awareness about the role of money in the U.S. political system ("Late Night" 2012).

FIGURE 5.1. Stephen Colbert Campaigning during the 2012 GOP Primary
Source: College of Charleston

When the polls closed on Saturday, January 21, Gingrich had defeated the Republican establishment's leading candidate to win the South Carolina primary. Gingrich received 40.4 percent of the vote, followed by Romney (27.9 percent), Santorum (17 percent), and Paul (13 percent).[5] According to exit polls, Gingrich had a strong showing among born-again/evangelical Christians, beating Romney 44 percent to 22 percent among this group.[6] Gingrich also won considerable support from voters who said abortion should be illegal, besting Romney 45 percent to 21 percent on this question.[7]

One of the notable features of the 2012 GOP primary was the fact that, for the first time in history, South Carolina's Republican voters did not select a candidate who won in either Iowa or New Hampshire. Even more notable, 2012 represents the one case in the history of the South Carolina GOP primary that the state did not back the eventual nominee. Romney secured the nomination by winning the Texas primary on May 29 (Gibson 2012). The day after the South Carolina primary, the state's political observers were already questioning whether the state had ceded the "we-pick-presidents" role (Beam 2012b). According to Andy Beam, a political reporter at the *State*, "Gingrich's victory transformed South Carolina from its traditional role of kingmaker of the Republican establishment candidate—this year, Romney—to disrupter—resurrecting the candidacy of Gingrich, who had finished fourth in Iowa and fifth in New Hampshire, and restarting the Republican primary process" (Beam 2012b).

Unlike previous cycles, the 2012 South Carolina GOP results were not a very good barometer for the upcoming southern states, either. Romney won the February 1 Florida primary with 46.4 percent. In the March 6 Super Tuesday contests, Gingrich won his home state of Georgia (47.2 percent), Santorum won Tennessee (37.1 percent), and Romney won Virginia (59.5 percent). One important dynamic in 2012 that may partially explain these results is the length of time between the South Carolina primary on January 21 and Super Tuesday on March 6. During the six weeks between these two contests, a number of states held primaries and caucuses, giving Romney and Santorum a chance to build momentum. In addition to winning in Florida, Romney won in Michigan, Nevada, and Washington, while Santorum won in Colorado and Minnesota.[8]

Although Gingrich's victory surprised many observers, our analysis in the prior chapter identifies four key reasons Gingrich won. First, Gingrich likely benefited from greater name recognition and familiarity with South Carolina politics given that his home state is Georgia. According to our model, neighboring state candidates enjoy a sizable 14 percent advantage in South Carolina primaries. Second, Gingrich had the added benefit of being a southerner. Like George H. W. Bush in 1988, and George W. Bush in 2000, candidates from the South perform better than candidates from other regions, according to our analysis. A third reason Gingrich performed well in South Carolina was his share of endorsements. Although Haley's endorsement of Romney was the most notable, Gingrich had a number of key endorsements as well. Fourth, Gingrich received a substantial amount of media attention, much of it favorable postdebate coverage. Although Romney garnered the most media coverage given his front-runner status, Gingrich came in a very close second, according to our data. As noted in the last chapter, media coverage and endorsements are key predictors of a candidate's performance in South Carolina's primary.

A host of additional factors not included in last chapter's analysis explain Gingrich's victory over Romney in 2012 as well. First, Gingrich was likely a better fit for South Carolina's Republican electorate than Mitt Romney. On the one hand, the state's GOP voters had serious questions about Romney's conservatism (Balz 2013). On the other hand, there is not a lot of racial diversity among South Carolina GOP voters, and this lack of diversity favored Gingrich (Clark 2014). Indeed, Romney performed much better in Florida, a southern state with a more racially diverse GOP electorate. Second, Gingrich ran a better campaign. Romney made mistakes in the weeks leading up to the South Carolina primary, particularly the way he handled the release of his tax returns. Gingrich, on the other hand, benefited from the new campaign finance rules and the financial support from Los Vegas billionaire Sheldon Adelson, who helped fund Gingrich's Winning Our Future super PAC (Grimaldi 2012). Gingrich also benefited from a strong and fiery debate performances, both within one week of the election. Reporting for the *Washington Post,* Philip Rucker and David Fahrenthold (2012) wrote that Gingrich won "a stunning come-from-behind victory . . . using hard-edged debate performances to vault over former Massachusetts governor Mitt Romney." Two-thirds of primary voters, they reported, noted the debate as critical to their decision.[9]

All in all, the 2012 election once again illustrated the benefits of being a southern candidate in the South Carolina primary, and the positives of being a southern candidate were compounded for Gingrich since he was also from a neighboring state. Although it is difficult to pin the outcome on any set of factors, these two built-in advantages for Gingrich likely proved decisive. Endorsements and media attention were key factors as well. Finally, the 2012 contest further highlighted the difficulties evangelical candidates face in the South Carolina primary. Though Christian conservatives play an important role in selecting GOP nominees, there is not a noticeable benefit for evangelical candidates.

"The Donald" Dominates the Headlines

For our final case, we selected the 2016 GOP primary. We picked this case for several reasons. First, it best illustrates the importance of media attention to winning the South Carolina primary. Despite being new to politics, Donald Trump dominated the airwaves, to put it mildly. Second, the 2016 GOP primary is perhaps the best example of the conventional wisdom among journalists and other observers failing. Not only does this contest provide yet another example of evangelical candidates underperforming despite the importance of evangelical voters in the state but it also illustrates our finding that spending the most money or having the most political experience is not predictive of who will win in the South Carolina primary. Trump was, after all, a political outsider who was outspent by several of his rivals in the Palmetto State. Many observers believed these characteristics would doom his candidacy. And third, we selected 2016 because it is the most recent primary.

In 2016, a large field of Republicans competed for the presidential nomination and the chance to reverse Obama's policies. Over a dozen candidates sought the GOP nomination. The main contenders were former Florida governor Jeb Bush, neurosurgeon Ben Carson, Texas senator Ted Cruz, Ohio governor John Kasich, Florida senator Marco Rubio, and billionaire businessman and reality television star Donald Trump. Other notable candidates included New Jersey governor Chris Christie, Kentucky senator Rand Paul, former Arkansas governor Mike Huckabee, and former Hewlett-Packard CEO Carly Fiorina.

On February 1, Ted Cruz won the Iowa caucuses with 27.6 percent of the vote, followed by Trump (24.3 percent), and Rubio (23.1 percent). The pattern of a close connection between the results in Iowa and South Carolina was borne out again, as the Palmetto State had the same top three, albeit in a different order. After a disappointing showing in Iowa, Ben Carson announced that he would focus on South Carolina instead of New Hampshire, saying "New Hampshire tends to be a little more liberal state, and I am not really going to resonate with liberals very well, which is okay" (Shain 2016b, 3). Trump did very well in New Hampshire, winning the primary with 35.2 percent. Unlike in Iowa, Kasich came in second (15.7 percent), followed by Cruz (11.6 percent), Bush (11 percent), and Rubio (10.5 percent).[10] Trump hoped to capitalize on his New Hampshire momentum in the February 20 South Carolina primary, while his rivals viewed the South Carolina primary as a chance to emerge as the main alternative to Trump.

Despite his strong showing in New Hampshire, there were reasons to doubt Trump's viability in a state like South Carolina. First, there were questions about how the thrice-married and brash New York businessman would relate to the state's GOP voters, particularly conservative Christians. At the same time, some wondered whether Trump's tepid support for military spending and his Vietnam draft deferments would hurt in him the promilitary state of South Carolina (Gabriel 2016). Second, there were certainly other 2016 candidates that had the potential to do very well in the Palmetto State. Despite his poor performances in Iowa and New Hampshire, Jeb Bush was, in many ways, the perfect candidate to win the South Carolina primary. South Carolina had been a firewall for his father in 1988 and 1992 and his older brother in 2000. Moreover, according to our model, southern candidates like Bush have an advantage in the Palmetto State. Of course Bush's Texas colleague, Senator Ted Cruz, enjoyed the same regional advantage, as well as the advantage of having won the Iowa caucus. Finally, South Carolina also set up very nicely for Marco Rubio. Rubio hailed from a southern state and had several key state endorsements, two predictors of success that we identified in our model. Notably, most observers expected Rubio to finish in third or fourth in South Carolina, whereas our analysis in the last chapter suggests he should have performed better than that.

Both nationally and in South Carolina, Republicans were debating about which type of nominee could win back the White House. Political reporters Alex Burns and Jonathan Martin argued in a piece in the *New York Times* that "the Republican Party in South Carolina is a lot like the party writ large. It is torn between activists enraged by President Obama and eager for the bald confrontation promised by Mr. Trump and Mr. Cruz, and party leaders hungry to take back the White House and considering candidates such as Mr. Rubio and Jeb Bush" (Burns and Martin 2016). However, support for Gingrich foreshadowed a shift in the South Carolina GOP. Burns and Martin posited that "Mr. Gingrich's win here reflected the state's drift in recent years away from conventional Republican candidates and toward a more populist, and at times, purer brand of conservatism" (Burns and Martin 2016).

As was the case in 2012, Christian conservatives were split among several candidates. "In South Carolina, evangelicals are a key part of any winning coalition," Winthrop University political scientist Scott Huffmon notes, "but they are not a singular constituency that can be grabbed by any one candidate" (Funk 2016, 3). Nevertheless, the emergence of Donald Trump as a leading contender for the Republican Party's nomination prompted national Christian conservatives "to make things simpler by forging a consensus behind a single favorite to guide local activists, thereby heading off Trump, then surging in the polls" (O. Smith and Guth 2018, 168). Two candidates emerged from these discussions, Ted Cruz and Marco Rubio, and both made strong appeals to South Carolina's Christian conservatives. Cruz organized a "pastors roundtable" and spoke to religious audiences across the state, while Rubio courted Christian conservatives by beginning rallies with a prayer, playing Christian rock at his events, and using "evangelical language" in his speeches (O. Smith and Guth 2018, 169). Though Trump skipped the February 12 Palmetto Family Council's Faith and Family Forum at Bob Jones University, he did improve his standing with the state's Christian conservatives by giving the convocation address at Liberty University on January 18 (O. Smith and Guth 2018). Trump also had surrogates, such as Pastor Mark Burns, an African American minister form the Upstate region, vouching for his conservative credentials (Shain 2016g, 1).

As he did throughout the nomination season, Trump held large campaign rallies across South Carolina. According to our data from the last chapter, Trump captured the lion's share of media attention in 2016, and it is difficult to overstate the value of Trump's media advantage. During a January 7 rally at the Winthrop Coliseum in Rock Hill, Trump picked on one of his favorite targets, Jeb Bush, telling the crowd, "But Jeb spent $68 million on his campaign and he's down here, like really low, I spent nothing and I'm number one" (Jackson 2016c, 1). On February 5, he spoke to thousands at the Florence Civic Center, hitting on many of his common campaign themes (Lloyd 2016). He talked about the middle class, telling the crowd, "We're going to take care of the middle class. The middle class is almost like the forgotten class. They take care of people at the low end and the high end, and they've forgotten the people in the middle" (Roldan 2016c, 1). He also focused on trade, saying "I like China but they kill us because their leaders are smarter than our leaders. We have a bunch of hacks trying to make deals" (Lloyd 2016, 3). In addition, Trump attacked the Obama administration: "We are led by people that are stupid. We are led by people that are incompetent" (Lloyd 2016, 3). At a February 11 rally in Clemson, Pastor Mark Burns gave a "fiery" invocation, thanking God that Trump "has the boldness to say what others will not say" (Coyne 2016, 3). Speaking to supporters in Sumter on February 18, Trump focused on economic issues, saying, "We're going to be rich again, we're going to

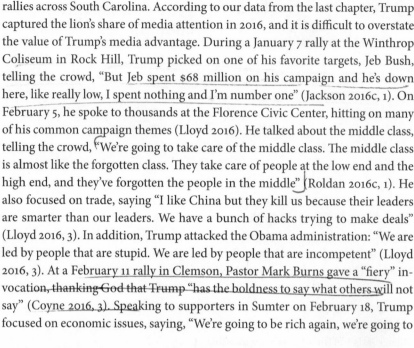

FIGURE 5.2. Donald Trump Campaign Postcard from 2016
Source: Zuma Press, Inc./Alamy Stock

be strong again, we're going to be respected again" (Flach 2016, 6). He built on themes of American exceptionalism used by Ronald Reagan in the initial 1980 South Carolina primary. The Trump campaign even sent out campaign material connecting Trump and Reagan (see fig. 5.1).

Endorsements from the state's top political leaders were split in 2016. In the early iterations of the South Carolina primary, support from kingmakers like Lee Atwater and Carroll Campbell could propel a candidate to victory. By 2016, a new generation of South Carolina leaders had emerged. Perhaps the two most popular Republicans of this new generation were Governor Nikki Haley and Senator Tim Scott, who both backed Rubio. Scott endorsed Rubio in early February (Kane 2016), and Haley endorsed the Florida senator three days before the primary (Haberman 2016a). Congressman Trey Gowdy, another rising star in South Carolina politics, also supported Rubio (Shain 2016e). Longtime GOP insider Katon Dawson noted that Rubio had the support of "three superstars who are trusted" (Self 2016c, 1). Lindsey Graham, who dropped out of the presidential race on December 21 (Self 2015), endorsed Jeb Bush (Isenstadt 2016). According to Graham, Bush was "ready to be a commander-in-chief on Day One" (Isenstadt 2016). And in response to Trump's plan to ban Muslims from entering the United States, Graham noted, "Don't run for president if you are going to double-down on crazy" (Kropf 2016d, 10). Not to be outdone, Cruz had endorsements from former governor and current U.S. representatives Mark Sanford as well as U.S. representative Jeff Duncan (Shain 2016e). In the endorsement race, lieutenant governor and former South Carolina GOP chair Henry McMaster was the only statewide elected official to formally back Trump (Gabriel 2016). At the time, McMaster was one of the highest-ranking elected officials to back Trump's candidacy across the nation. Trump also received endorsements from South Carolina House members Jim Merrill and Mike Ryhal as well as the state's former lieutenant governor and CNN commentator Andre Bauer (Graham and Buchanan 2018).

Of all the candidates, Cruz made the most direct appeals to voters' southern identity. When the Texan spoke to a Republican women's club event in Greenville, he said, "I'm told people in South Carolina kind of like their guns. I have to say, as a Texan, I understand. Remember the Alamo" (Martin and Burns 2016). He also attended an event at College of Charleston hosted by Sean Hannity at which Mark Sanford and "Duck Dynasty" patriarch Phil Robertson made appearances. Admittedly, the 2016 outcome belies our finding that southern candidates are advantaged in the South Carolina primary. In retrospect, however, 2016 was unique in that it had the largest field of southern candidates of any GOP contest in our analysis.[11] In addition to Cruz, Jeb Bush (Texas) and Marco Rubio (Florida) appeared on the ballot, making half the candidates southerners. Just as the benefit of being an evangelical candidate, was often split among voters the benefit of being from the South got split in 2016, as Rubio, Cruz, and Bush finished second, third, and fourth, respectively.

As it has in past contests, the Republican primary got heated at times in 2016, the usual bare-knuckle campaign tactics and dirty tricks making an appearance. After Cruz ran a television ad pointing out Trump's shifting position on abortion, Trump sent Cruz a cease-and-desist letter. Rubio claimed that Cruz had lied about his record and accused Cruz of "saying anything to get elected" (Recio 2016, 4). Rubio also predicted that voters would reject Cruz's "campaign of personal insult, deceptions, push polls and ads so misleading they can't be aired" (Recio 2016, 4). In perhaps the biggest dirty trick of the campaign, someone created a fake Facebook post indicating that Representative Gowdy was changing his support from Rubio to Cruz. Rubio supporters placed the blame squarely on team Cruz (Recio 2016). In addition, a pro-Cruz robocall began with Trump's suggestion to "put [the Confederate flag] in a museum, let it go," which was followed by an announcer saying "that's Donald Trump supporting Nikki Haley removing the battle flag from the Confederate memorial in Columbia" (Kropf 2016g, 1). The announcer also noted that "people like Donald Trump are always butting their noses into other people's business" and that "Trump talks about our flag like it's a social disease" (Kropf 2016g, 1).

As was the case in 2012, there were two South Carolina GOP debates in 2016. The first debate took place in North Charleston on January 14 and featured an undercard (Fiorina, Huckabee, and Santorum) and the main event (Bush, Carson, Christie, Cruz, Kasich, Rubio, and Trump). Rand Paul was also invited to participate in the undercard but boycotted the debate, telling the press, "We will not participate in anything that's not first-tier" (Kropf 2016f, 4). The main debate was dominated by exchanges between Cruz and Trump, with Trump raising questions about whether Cruz was eligible to be president since he was born in Canada to a U.S. mother (Shain 2016d). "You have a big lawsuit over your head," Trump said. "Why are you running?" (Shain 2016d, 1). Trump also doubled down on his pledge to ban Muslims, something he announced while speaking at a campaign rally aboard the USS Yorktown on December 7, 2015. When asked about his controversial comments at the North Charleston debate Trump said, "We have to stop with the political correctness" (Shain 2016d, 1). There was also a debate in Greenville on February 13, one week before the Republican primary. In a direct assault on Jeb Bush, Trump accused his brother's administration of lying about weapons of mass destruction and castigated George W. Bush for letting the World Trade Center's twin towers come down while he was president (Haberman 2016b). According to the *New York Times* political reporter Maggie Haberman (2016b), Trump "doused the Republican Party with the verbal equivalent of napalm." Jeb Bush shot back, saying, "While Donald Trump was building a reality TV show, my brother was building a security apparatus to keep us safe. I'm proud of what he did" (Roldan 2016b, 1). Following the debate, Graham came to Jeb Bush's defense, saying "The market for those who like Putin and believe W. is a liar, is pretty small in South Carolina" (Roldan 2016a). Notably, the debate took place a few days after the death of Supreme Court Justice Antonin Scalia. Despite contentious moments on other issues, the candidates all agreed that the newly elected president should select Scalia's replacement (Shain 2016a).

In the end, Trump won South Carolina in 2016 by an impressive ten-point margin, securing 32.4 percent of vote. Rubio and Cruz were neck and neck, with Rubio winning 22.4 percent and Cruz 22.2 percent. This was the same top three as Iowa. Bush finished a disappointing fourth with just 7.8 percent. Kasich came in fifth (7.6 percent) and Carson sixth (7.2 percent).[12] Unlike candidates of the past, Trump had been able to forge a unique connection with South Carolina voters. "When he spoke to thousands of supporters at convention halls and civic centers across South Carolina," political reporter Andy Shain observed, "Trump promised to reconnect voters to a government that they felt had left them behind. He pledged to protect them from undocumented immigrants, and stop China and Iran from taking advantage of the United States. He also insisted his business expertise would improve the economy" (2016f, 1). And they believed him. Trump did particularly well in rural South Carolina and in the high growth counties of Beaufort, Greenville, and Horry (Graham and Buchanan 2018). There are not, however, just one or two simple explanations for Trump's success. In fact, the only factor that mattered in a post-election analysis of support for Trump among likely voters was Republican self-identification (Huffmon, Knotts, and McKee 2017).

In an effort to better understand Trump's support among Christian conservatives in South Carolina, Oran Smith and James Guth (2018) analyzed data from the Cooperative Congressional Election Study. Trump received more support from mainline Protestants than he did from evangelicals (54 to 37 percent), but perhaps most interestingly, Trump did better among voters with less "religious commitment" (O. Smith and Guth 2018). According to Smith and Guth (2018, 172), "Among evangelicals, the major dividing line was indeed the extent of a voter's religious commitment. Trump's strongest showing was among those scoring lowest on the importance of religion, church attendance, or frequency of prayer." Trump's skepticism about climate change may have also helped him, since it "fed into a persistent stream of evangelical concerns about 'environmental idolatry'" (172). Finally, some of South Carolina's white evangelicals used biblical passages to justify support for Trump, suggesting that "God had used secular, pagan, or evil rulers to accomplish His purposes" (173).

Despite veering off track in 2012, South Carolina GOP voters once again selected the party's eventual nominee and served as a barometer for upcoming southern states. On Super Tuesday, Trump won five of six contests in the South, only losing in Cruz's home state of Texas.[13] The 2016 GOP contest also represented another instance of South Carolina Republicans bucking the establishment. This antiestablishment sentiment had bubbled up in the 2010 election of Governor Nikki Haley and had also manifested itself in 2012 with Gingrich's presidential primary victory. Trump was able to capitalize on the same anger in 2016, which helped him emerge as the winner in South Carolina, secure the eventual Republican nomination, and become the nation's forty-fifth president.

In summary, one of Trump's keys to victory in the South Carolina primary was his domination in preelection media coverage, which is a key predictor of success in our model. On the flip side, lack of political experience and spending less money than one's rivals are not significant predictors of success in South Carolina, according to our analysis, and so it is not surprisng that despite many observers' claims that these were Trump's weaknesses, they did not have a significant impact on his standing. On this point, it is likewise perhaps no surprise that one of Trump's key rivals, Jeb Bush, performed so poorly: his massive spending advantage and lengthy political resume were not as advantageous as most believed. Finally, although Trump did not have the benefit of being a southerner nor the advantage in the endorsement race, he was helped in 2016 by the fact that these two key characteristics were split among multiple candidates.

Conclusion

Our four Republican cases reiterate many of the key arguments and findings from earlier in this book, yet they also challenge some of our claims and provide additional context for understanding what it takes to win in South Carolina. First, these cases exemplify many of our claims in chapter 1 about the importance of South Carolina's first-in-the-South primary. In every instance, Iowa and New Hampshire were won by different candidates, and in every case but 2012, South Carolina provided a critical tie-breaking vote in favor of the eventual nominee. Likewise, in each contest except for 2012, the winner of South Carolina went on to quickly amass a significant delegate advantage in the subsequent states, largely on the basis of early primaries in other southern states. Once again, being first matters, but being first in the South is uniquely important.

Second, our cases highlight the importance of two candidate resources: endorsements and media coverage. George H. W. Bush and his son George W. Bush received the largest share of statewide endorsements in their successful runs for the GOP nomination in 1988 and 2000, respectively. Both had the backing of Governor Carroll Campbell, and the younger Bush received the endorsement of Senator Strom Thurmond. Of course, there are certainly examples of candidates who secured prominent endorsements and lost the South Carolina primary. It is important to point out, however, that many of these candidates still outperformed expectations. For example, we think Haley's endorsement played a role in Rubio's second-place finish in 2016, worth roughly 9 percent of the vote according to our model, enough to have propelled Rubio past Ted Cruz. On media attention, there are a number of notable examples that mirror our findings. Donald Trump's victory in the 2016 contest is perhaps the quintessential example of the value of media attention. Trump dominated national and local media coverage in the week prior to the South Carolina primary, according to our data. Another example is Newt Gingrich's surprise victory in 2012. After lackluster results in both Iowa and New Hampshire, finishing fourth and fifth, respectively, Gingrich received a boost in media attention after strong performances in two South Carolina debates. According to our data, Gingrich received the greatest volume of media coverage in the state in the two weeks before the primary and the second most national media coverage.

We also found that money—a key candidate resource—did not always translate into victory in South Carolina. Although perhaps surprising, there are many examples of this phenomenon. While George W. Bush had a greater share of campaign contributions relative to his Republican opponents in 2000, his brother, Jeb, lost South Carolina by a wide margin in 2016 despite an equally sizable money advantage over his main competitors. And, in 2012, Mitt Romney secured the largest money advantage on the GOP side, yet he was upset by Gingrich that year, whose campaign receipts were well below average. A deeper look at the 2012 primary reveals a limitation with our analysis in the last chapter: our dataset does not take into consideration outside spending. After all, Gingrich was aided in the 2012 contests by $20 million in super PAC spending linked to the family of casino mogul Sheldon Adelson (Grimaldi 2012).

A third and final point that our cases illustrate is the built-in advantages of two candidate characteristics, namely, being from the South and being from a neighboring state. Of the four cases we selected, three winning candidates were from the South: George H. W. Bush (1988), George W. Bush (2000), and Newt Gingrich (2012). If we broaden our focus to include all nonincumbents since 1980, including Democrats, a whopping six of fourteen winners—just over 40 percent—were from the South. The 2012 case helps illustrate that candidates from a neighboring state have an additional advantage, this being the one instance in which South Carolina failed to select the eventual Republican nominee. If there is one surprising conclusion in our analysis, it is the fact that evangelical candidates do not have a built-in advantage in South Carolina, a point supported by the four cases outlined here.

★ 6 ★
LESSONS FROM KEY DEMOCRATIC CONTESTS

What does it take to win the South Carolina Democratic primary? As we demonstrated in our examination of each state's primary electorate, aspiring Democratic nominees navigate a much different electoral environment in South Carolina than they do in other early states. Most importantly, the South Carolina Democratic primary is the first contest where candidates face a majority black electorate, a key Democratic voting bloc. In this chapter, we expand on our findings thus far in the book, focusing in depth on four of the most historically significant Democratic presidential primaries in South Carolina. As in the last chapter, these primaries were selected because they illustrate many of the key predictors of electoral success we identify in chapter 4 and help us gain a more in-depth understanding of the political dynamics facing Democratic candidates in South Carolina. And like in the previous chapter, we also selected a case where South Carolina voters did not select the party's eventual nominee.

We begin this chapter with the 1992 Democratic primary, a contest where Arkansas governor Bill Clinton won a convincing victory in the Palmetto State over a fairly weak field of candidates. Then we turn our attention to the 2004 primary, a case when another southerner, Senator John Edwards from neighboring North Carolina, defeated party favorite John Kerry. For our third case, we investigate the 2008 primary battle between Edwards, Illinois senator Barack Obama, and New York senator and former First Lady Hillary Clinton. The 2008 primary set records for voter participation in South Carolina and provided a convincing victory to Obama, the party's eventual nominee. We conclude with an examination of the 2016 contest between Hillary Clinton and Vermont senator Bernie Sanders. In this contest, Clinton gained support from the vast majority of African American voters and secured nearly all of the state's key endorsements.

Triumph of a Southern Governor

The 1992 Democratic presidential primary highlights many of the key predictors of what it takes to win in South Carolina. Perhaps most importantly, it shows the appeal of a southern candidate in South Carolina and the importance of both endorsements and media attention. Further, the 1992 cycle is interesting because there was no African American candidate on the ballot. In the two previous Democratic contests in South Carolina, Jesse Jackson ran competitive campaigns, receiving a plurality in the 1984 caucuses and winning the 1988 caucuses. Interestingly, there was a very highly qualified black presidential candidate early in the 1992 election cycle. Virginia governor Douglas Wilder, the first African American to be elected governor, declared his candidacy for president during the late summer of 1991, but citing budget problems in Virginia, he withdrew from the race about a month before the Iowa caucuses and two months before the South Carolina primary (Ayers 1992). Wilder was expected to do very well in the Palmetto State (Ayers 1992), and as we have noted, our analysis in chapter 4 indicates the sizable advantage for African American candidates.

In addition to being the state's first Democratic presidential primary, the 1992 nomination contest was the first time state Democrats secured an early slot on the election calendar and the first time that results from South Carolina played a part in who would become the eventual nominee. It was also an attempt by state Democrats to capture some of the spotlight Republicans had received by holding early primaries in 1980 and 1988. South Carolina Democrats, we recall, had hoped to secure first-in-theSouth status in 1992 but were leapfrogged by Georgia's Democratic leadership. Nevertheless, the March 7 contest in South Carolina was an opportunity for the state's Democrats to hold its first ever presidential primary, engage voters on issues important to the party, and influence national Democratic politics.

As is often the case, the election results were mixed coming out of Iowa and New Hampshire. Native son and senator Tom Harkin won the Iowa caucuses in 1992 with a whopping 77.2 percent of the vote. Coming in second was Massachusetts senator Paul Tsongas (4.3 percent), followed by Arkansas governor Bill Clinton (2.5 percent) and Nebraska senator Bob Kerrey (2.4 percent).[1] In New Hampshire, Tsongas won with 33.2 percent, Clinton was second (24.7 percent), Kerrey was third (11.1 percent), and Harkin came in fourth (10.2 percent) (Cook 2000). Although Tsongas emerged victorious, the result was a remarkably strong showing for Clinton after he had suffered a series of setbacks including reports of an affair with Gennifer Flowers and efforts to avoid the Vietnam draft (Bullock 1994). Many political analysts, including Emory University's Merle Black, also were of the opinion that the 1992 Democratic field of candidates was a weak one (Bandy 1992a).

For South Carolina Democrats and southern Democrats more broadly, the 1992 contest represented a prime opportunity to influence who would become the party's standard-bearer. After the failure of Walter Mondale in 1984 and Michael Dukakis in 1988 to earn the presidency, many thought the path back to the White House was to nominate a moderate candidate who could compete in the South. Many believed this strategy required a candidate who could win support from African Americans but also appeal to conservative, blue-collar whites (Applebome 1992). There was also a belief that such a candidate would be more competitive in the general election. In 1992, Clinton was the best hope for southern Democrats—a chance to attract moderates and independents in November.

Clinton's message on the campaign trail was tailor made for white southern moderates. Writing for the *New York Times,* Gwen Ifill (1992a) noted that "in each appearance, he has offered an assessment of the state of the American economy that borrows as much from Republicans like Jack Kemp as it does from liberals like Jesse Jackson" and called Clinton "self-consciously centrist," asserting that Clinton advocated "a marriage of traditional Democratic social concerns with economic policies borrowed from Republicans." While campaigning at Georgetown University, two months before the South Carolina primary, Clinton responded to a question about support for the poor. Clinton said, "There is no hostility to the poor in my plan," but he also noted that "if you're going to help the poor with tax money, somebody's got to earn the money to pay the taxes. The best way to help the poor is to expand the middle class" (Ifill 1992a). In addition, Clinton was a strong supporter of the death penalty, described by Georgia governor Zell Miller as a "tough-on-crime governor who not only supports the death penalty but has carried it out" (Cannon 1992, 11C).

As the first southern primary in 1992, Georgia had the potential to elevate the Clinton candidacy and serve as a gateway to the South Carolina primary and the remainder of the South. In Georgia, Clinton secured endorsements from several of the state's leading politicians including Governor Miller, House Speaker Tom Murphy, Representative John Lewis, and Atlanta mayor Andrew Young (Bullock 1994). Though the South was likely to be hospitable turf for Clinton, there were some concerns about his regional appeal. As political scientist Charles Bullock (1994, 11) noted, "There was speculation that southerners might be less willing to forgive a man accused of cheating on his wife and dodging the draft than were New Hampshire voters." Despite these concerns, Clinton secured a resounding victory over Paul Tsongas in the Georgia primary, 57.1 percent to 24.0 percent (Cook 2000). Clinton won by a five to one margin among black voters and was victorious in 158 of 159 Georgia counties (Bullock 1994).

In South Carolina, Clinton secured several key endorsements, garnered substantial media coverage, and worked to win support from the state's African American voters. In 1992, former governor Dick Riley was the chairman of Clinton's South Carolina committee, and the state's former Democratic party chair, Frank Holleman, was Clinton's South Carolina campaign director (Ifill 1992b). Clinton's Democratic opponents received far fewer key statewide endorsements. Clinton also had a sizable advantage in media attention in the week prior to the primary, another key factor in our analysis. Clinton also worked to win the support of the state's African American voters. In a speech at Atlanta's Morehouse College, Clinton addressed race relations in the South, saying, "Every time we have permitted ourselves to be divided by race in this region, we have been kept dumb and poor" (Ifill 1992b). South Carolina state senator McKinley Washington from Charleston, who served as co-chair of Clinton's South Carolina campaign, said, "He's emotional; he's charismatic; and he gets his message across to black people." (Miller 1992a). South Carolina State University political scientist Ricky Hill was less convinced, arguing instead that black voters were getting "overlooked" in favor of Reagan Democrats (Miller 1992a, 1A).

Clinton campaigned as a moderate "New South" governor, mixing progressive themes with policies more typically touted by Republican candidates. On a campaign swing in South Carolina the day after winning the Georgia primary, Clinton told a crowd "I live in a state, not unlike yours, where we struggle to get and keep good jobs and to educate our children. I have worked as hard as I can as governor with the practical problems of real people" (Brook and Greene 1992, 15A). He also addressed the character issues raised by his opponents head on. Speaking to reporters in Florence, he said "I don't think most Americans want anyone who pretends to be perfect. I think what you want is someone who's struggled and improved. I think here in our part of the country we appreciate and respect people who are honest enough to tell us they've had problems and dealt with them" (Brook and Greene 1992, 15A). Clinton even sounded like a general election candidate, at times touting Democrats' ability to win back the South. At one rally he urged South Carolinians to send a message: "I want you to say we may be Southerners and we may be regional, but we ain't crazy. We don't want four more years of this" (Scoppe, Greene, and Miller 1992, 8A).

Clinton's two biggest rivals in South Carolina were Tom Harkin and Paul Tsongas. Harkin put considerable effort into the primary, working to gain support from the state's politically important African American voters. For Harkin, South Carolina was a last stand of sorts, after winning his home state of Iowa but finishing worse than expected in New Hampshire and Maine (Bandy 1992c). During the week before the South Carolina primary, Harkin targeted African Americans and organized labor, telling voters that "My agenda is the National Rainbow Coalition agenda" (Bandy 1992c, 4C). Harkin even campaigned with

Jesse Jackson, though Jackson did not formally endorse a candidate during the 1992 South Carolina primary (Bandy 1992c). Tsongas, however, was the biggest threat to a Clinton victory in the Palmetto State. Though Tsongas finished second to Clinton in Georgia, he defeated Clinton in Maryland and hoped to ride the momentum from this win into South Carolina. Tsongas was able to secure support from some of the state's prominent business leaders, including Samuel Tenenbaum and Hootie Johnson (Miller 1992b). Tsongas preached a message of unity, often holding a canoe oar and saying, "We're all in the same boat" (Miller 1992b, 10A). Yet as the primary approached, Tsongas began to downplay expectations. He said his goal in the South was "to show the flag and get my message out," noting that "obviously, Bill Clinton has the advantage in the South. . . . I just have to be competitive here" (Bandy 1992d, 15A).

As was the case across the South, the South Carolina electorate was in the midst of significant electoral change during the 1990s. Many white Democrats began to support Republican candidates, first for president and then for governor and other offices (Kuzenski 2003). Blacks voted predominantly Democratic, and newcomers to the region, often from the Northeast and Midwest, brought more moderate views to the state (Applebome 1992). Republicans and Democrats competed for these newcomers, but since they came from regions of the country that leaned Democratic, many cast ballots for Democratic candidates.

As primary day approached in South Carolina, polls showed support for Clinton was strong. According to a *Post and Courier*/WCBD-TV poll about a week before voting, Clinton had 33 percent, Tsongas 14 percent, Kerrey 9 percent, Harkin 6 percent, and former California governor Jerry Brown 3 percent (Bandy 1992a). A few days before the South Carolina primary and subsequent Super Tuesday states, the campaign took a negative turn. The *New York Times* printed a photograph of Clinton and the powerful Georgia senator Sam Nunn standing before a group of mostly black inmates at a Georgia correctional facility (Efron and Richter 1992). Jerry Brown criticized Clinton for participating in the photo op, saying Clinton and Nunn look "like colonial masters," while Tom Harkin said the picture demonstrated "insensitivity" (Efron and Richter 1992, 24). Clinton rebutted the criticism, noting that facility had a rehabilitation mission to help convicted young people to "get their lives back together" (Efron and Richter 1992, 24). In an Atwater type move, Harkin's team passed out eighty thousand copies of a flyer that had the Clinton/Nunn correctional facility picture alongside a picture of Harkin and Jesse Jackson (Efron and Richter 1992). This was an effort to send a clear signal that Harkin was the candidate more attuned to the interests of African Americans.

The bare-knuckle tactics did not work, however, and Clinton won the South Carolina Democratic primary with 62.9 percent of vote. Tsongas was a distant second (8.3 percent) and Harkin finished third (6.6 percent).[2] As expected,

Clinton did very well with the state's African American voters. Exit polls indicated that Clinton got 75 percent of the black vote compared to 3 percent for Tsongas and 15 percent for Harkin (Edsall 1992). Harkin dropped out of the race two days after the South Carolina primary. Since this was the first early primary for South Carolina Democrats, it was also an opportunity to see whether the results on the Democratic side were a good bellwether for the Super Tuesday states. Five southern states held contests on March 10, just three days after South Carolina's primary. Clinton won in all five states: Mississippi (73.1 percent), Louisiana (69.5 percent), Tennessee (67.3 percent), Texas (65.6 percent), and Florida (50.8 percent) (Cook 2000).

In summary, the 1992 contest demonstrated the built-in advantages for southern candidates. Clinton connected with the state's Democratic voters, both whites and blacks, advocating moderate policy positions, economic growth, and racial healing. The primary also highlighted the importance of state endorsements for presidential contenders in South Carolina. Clinton secured far more key endorsements than his two closest rivals. Given Clinton's ability to connect with voters and secure key endorsements, it is no surprise he dominated his Democratic competitors in media attention as well. The 1992 Democratic primary was also a triumph for the South Carolina Democratic Party. Political participation was up from previous cycles, and some have suggested that the excitement from the 1992 South Carolina primary played a role in the increased participation of black South Carolinians in the 1992 general election (Kuzenski 2003). Though not first in the South, the primary also helped propel a moderate southern governor toward the Democratic nomination and eventually the presidency. Given that Democrats had lost the presidency in five of the last six contests, this was welcome news for the state's Democrats.

Democrats Miss the Mark

For our second case, we investigate the 2004 Democratic contest. We selected this case for several key reasons. First, the state's Democratic voters did not back the party's eventual nominee in 2004, making this deviant case worthy of investigation. Though Democrats have a less reliable track record than Republicans, Democrats have selected the nominee in three of four contested primaries since 1992, so it is important to better understand why South Carolina voters got it wrong in 2004. Second, 2004 yet again illustrates the advantages enjoyed by southern candidates in the South Carolina primary. Third, this election also demonstrates the added benefit of being from a neighboring state. In addition to representing North Carolina in the Senate, the 2004 winner, John Edwards, had the added bonus of being born in South Carolina. Fourth, the 2004 Democratic primary is worthy of investigation because South Carolina voters did not give the lone African American candidate, the Reverend Al Sharpton, the electoral victory. Our model highlights the advantages black candidates have in South Carolina's Democratic primaries, and Sharpton's lack of success in 2004 is important to investigate. And, finally, the 2004 primary is interesting because Edwards won despite having fewer major state endorsements than Massachusetts senator John Kerry.

South Carolina Democrats had the spotlight to themselves in 2004, since President George W. Bush was running for a second term and did not receive a serious primary challenge. Bush was a popular wartime president, focused on fighting terrorism and helping the country recover after the September 11 attacks. The Democratic contest that year featured a crowded and experienced field of contenders for the party's nomination. In addition to Edwards, Kerry, and Sharpton, the candidates included former general Wesley Clark, Vermont governor Howard Dean, Missouri congressman Richard Gephardt, Florida senator Bob Graham, Ohio congressman Dennis Kucinich, Connecticut senator Joe Lieberman, and former Illinois senator Carol Mosley-Braun (Cook 2007). In anticipation of the South Carolina primary, the state hosted the first Democratic debate of the 2004 campaign season. Each candidate (minus Wesley Clark) participated in a May 3, 2003, debate in Columbia. The debate featured heated exchanges between Dean and Kerry, particularly about the Iraq War. At one point, Kerry warned Dean that he did "not need any lectures in courage" from him (Sheinin 2003, A1). Playing the role of peacemaker, Sharpton intervened: "Republicans are watching. . . . We should not have the bottom-line tonight be that George Bush won because we were taking cheap shots at one another" (Nagourney 2003, N30).

Although it does not happen very often, the same candidate won both the Iowa Caucus and the New Hampshire Primary in 2004. Kerry won Iowa with 38 percent of vote, followed by Edwards (32 percent), Dean (18 percent), and Gephardt (11 percent) (Cook 2007). Clark and Lieberman did not prioritize campaigning in Iowa, instead focusing on both New Hampshire and South Carolina (Sheinin 2004e). In New Hampshire, Kerry won again, securing 38.4 percent of the vote (Cook 2007). Dean was second (26.3 percent), Clark third (12.4 percent), and Edwards fourth (12.1 percent) (Cook 2007). Unlike in most contested nomination contests since the state became first in the South, the Palmetto State would not play a tie-breaking role. Yet as we argue in chapter 1, South Carolina provides a different test than New Hampshire and Iowa.

While this was the Democrat's initial first-in-the-South primary, South Carolina was not the only state in the spotlight on February 3. Six other states held contests the same day: Arizona, Oklahoma, New Mexico, Missouri, North Dakota, and Delaware (FrontloadingHQ 2009b). Winthrop University political scientist Scott Huffmon said, "We're now part of a more broadly-based target. We've lost a little bit of our luster. Attention is more divided" (Bandy 2004, A13). Similarly, Furman University political scientist Danielle Vinson noted that "if this had been a showdown state, all seven candidates would have felt compelled to compete here" (Bandy 2004, A13).

Edwards and Kerry were the favorites to win the 2004 South Carolina primary, according to most observers. Edwards played up his southern roots during the campaign, labeled the Bringing It Home tour, and secured the backing of Hootie and the Blowfish, a popular rock band from South Carolina (Archibold 2004). Ferrel Guillory, director of the Program on Southern Politics, Media, and Public Life at the University of North Carolina talked about Edwards's message of economic revitalization in South: "Think of the significance of that in a region that is the poorest region in the country and has large rural regions of persistent poverty" (Drake 2004b, A1). Kerry had a number of advantages as well. He was the national frontrunner, had support from much of the Democratic establishment, and had done what others were unable to do, win in both Iowa and New Hampshire. However, there were questions about whether a New Englander could win in a place like South Carolina. Scott Huffmon talked about the uphill battle and "regional biases" facing the Massachusetts senator: "Kerry suffers from that wealthy Northeastern Boston Brahmin image" (Sheinin 2004d, A1).

Two other candidates also had the potential to do well in South Carolina despite receiving less media attention. Al Sharpton hoped to follow in the footsteps of Jesse Jackson's strong showings in South Carolina Democratic caucuses. Though he could not afford television advertising, Sharpton spent considerable time campaigning in black churches across the Palmetto State (Moreland and Steed 2005b). General Wesley Clark also prioritized the South Carolina primary, hoping "his stellar military credentials, his campaign themes of leadership and patriotism, and his southern roots would be irresistible to South Carolina primary voters by combining Kerry's military background and Edwards' southern origins" (Moreland and Steed 2005b, 111).

The amount of time the major Democratic contenders spent in the Palmetto State varied widely because of the other nomination contests occurring on the same day. Sharpton campaigned the most in South Carolina, followed by Edwards, who made twenty-seven trips to the state (Moreland and Steed 2005b). Leading up to the primary, Kerry went four months without campaigning in South Carolina and did not run any television ads until a week before the election (Sheinin 2004e). Citadel political scientists Laurence Moreland and Robert Steed (2005b, 111) described Kerry's South Carolina campaign as "somewhat of enigma." Back in September 2003, Kerry announced his presidential bid aboard the USS Yorktown in Charleston, but he only campaigned for three days in the state (Moreland and Steed 2005b). As primary day approached, College of Charleston political scientist William Moore remarked that "it's all falling apart.

It's kind of like the race here is being left by default to John Edwards, so a victory here won't look like much" (Seelye 2004).

In terms of endorsements, the state's Democratic leaders were split. Senator Fritz Hollings endorsed Kerry, while Representative James Clyburn backed Gephardt (Seelye 2004). John Edwards had fewer high-profile endorsements, but he did have the backing of influential state senators Robert Ford and Maggie Glover (Bauerlein 2004). Though he did not secure any notable endorsements from South Carolina's leading politicians and pundits, Al Sharpton had the support of music mogul Russell Simmons and famed O. J. Simpson attorney Johnnie Cochran (Seelye 2004).

A key event of the 2004 race was Dick Gephardt's dropping out following his disappointing fourth place finish in the Iowa caucuses ("Gephardt to Drop Out of Race" 2004). Gephardt's departure put the Missouri primary into play, a contest that was scheduled the same day as South Carolina's Democratic primary. Though Missouri did not threaten South Carolina's first-in-the-South status, as most observers do not consider Missouri a southern state, the newly competitive primary led candidates to alter travel schedules and likely meant that they would spend less time in South Carolina. Gephardt's exit from the race also caused the remaining candidates to scramble for the support of the politicians who had endorsed Gephardt. The biggest prize was Clyburn, the state's top ranking African American elected official (Sheinin 2004c, A6), who eventually shifted his support to Kerry (Moreland and Steed 2005b).

Although he had not prioritized South Carolina in several months,.Kerry made a last-minute push during the final week of campaigning. Perhaps Kerry's biggest weakness in South Carolina was his lack of organization. Clark, Edwards, and Dean all had more volunteers and paid staff than Kerry (Markoe 2004) despite the fact that Kerry's campaign was very well funded according to Federal Election Commission campaign receipts. In fact, Kerry had the most campaign receipts of any candidate with the exception of Howard Dean. Kerry also made a late advertising push in South Carolina, spending $300,000 in the final week of the race (Associated Press 2004). This was much less than the $2.3 million Clark spent in the state or the $1.7 spent by Edwards, however (Associated Press 2004).

It is also worth highlighting the specific struggles of Wesley Clark during the 2004 South Carolina Democratic primary. His campaign had committed considerable time and money to South Carolina, but just before Election Day, he faced a host of problems. The Clark campaign booked the rock band Blues Traveler to perform in Columbia, but icy conditions forced the event to be canceled (Drake 2004a). And, when Clark tried to leave Charleston for a campaign swing through Oklahoma, New Mexico, and Arizona, his plane was grounded because of mechanical trouble (Drake 2004a). He and other candidates must also have realized that Edwards had won the battle of who was most perceived as the "southern candidate" and therefore was most likely the candidate who would get the bump in the primary from that advantage. Clark was born in Chicago but grew up in Arkansas. According to political reporter John Drake, "Clark's national spokesman, Bill Buck, on Tuesday stressed the natural advantage John Edwards has here as a South Carolina native and a Senator from North Carolina" (Drake 2004a, A7). Just two days before the primary, Clark's communication director, Matt Bennet said, "We're realistic about South Carolina. But we are doing our damnedest" (Nagourney and Rutenberg 2004, A21).

South Carolina's second Democratic debate was held at the Peace Center in Greenville, just five days before the election and included seven candidates: Wesley Clark, Howard Dean, John Edwards, John Kerry, Dennis Kucinich, Joe Lieberman, and Al Sharpton. The debate was generally civil with the bulk of the criticism directed at President Bush. Dean lashed out at the frontrunner, John Kerry, noting that he had not produced many results during his time in the U.S. Senate. Kerry, who at an earlier forum had said Democrats could win without the South, reassured South Carolina Democrats that "I've always said I will compete in the South" (Seelye and Halbfinger 2004). As he had throughout his time campaigning in South Carolina, Edwards reminded voters of his ties to the region. Responding to a question about economic challenges Edwards said, "This is personal to me. I've seen mills close, I've seen what it does to communities, I've seen what it does to families" (Seelye and Halbfinger 2004). Sharpton brought the issue of race into the conversation, responding to Edwards's constant references to his being the son of mill workers: "I've been inspired in this campaign, hearing John Edwards talk about how he's a son of a mill worker. Well, I'm the son of a man who couldn't be a mill worker because of the color of his skin. But his son can be the president of the United States" (Sheinin 2004a, A1).

In the end, Edwards won the 2004 South Carolina primary with 45.2 percent of the vote. Kerry finished second (29.8 percent), and Sharpton was third (9.7 percent) (Cook 2007). Clark (7.2 percent), Howard Dean (4.8 percent), and Joe Lieberman (2.4 percent) were further back (Cook 2007). Edwards had a strong showing in the state's Midlands region, an area of South Carolina with higher unemployment and a fading industrial sector where his populist appeal likely played well (Moreland and Steed 2005b). Kerry may have beaten expectations in part because of late endorsements from Senator Hollings and Representative Clyburn (Moreland and Steed 2005b). In the day's other contests, Clark won in Oklahoma and Kerry won in the remaining five states (Sheinin 2004b).

Looking back at the results, we can see that Edwards did particularly well with white Democrats. According to exit polls, whites made up 51 percent of primary voters in 2004, and Edwards beat Kerry 52 percent to 27 percent among this group.[3] Edwards also won a plurality of the state's black vote, but the margin was only 37 percent to 34 percent.[4] Laurence Moreland and Robert Steed (2005a,

4) explained Edwards's South Carolina victory by noting that "he was born in the state, represented a neighboring state in the U.S. Senate, and gave that state a very high priority in terms of time and money." University of Virginia political scientist Larry Sabato echoed these points but downplayed Edwards's victory, saying that he won "the state he was born in, which is next to the state he serves as U.S. senator, which has the same name—Carolina. He's got a long way to go" (Sheinin 2004a). Some have suggested, however, that Edwards's strong showing in South Carolina may have played a role in Kerry's decision to select him as a running mate—it was seen as an effort to make the ticket more competitive in the South (Moreland and Steed 2005b, Steed and Moreland 2007).

Another reason 2004 represents an interesting case is Sharpton's mediocre performance in South Carolina. We think a few factors explain this result. First, Sharpton was not able to raise much money and was not able to advertise on television (Slackman 2004). Once again, media attention is a strong predictor of success, according to our analysis. Second, he did not secure the endorsement of any notable South Carolina elected officials. And as we have demonstrated, endorsements from elected officials have an impact on how well candidates perform in the Palmetto State. Finally, Sharpton may have been hurt by Jackson's 1984 and 1988 campaign. As David Bositis, an analyst with the Joint Center for Political and Economic Studies, told the *New York Times,* "The black vote is looking for a winner and they are not looking to make a statement about race. John Kerry is one of the whitest guys, you know what I mean. The fact that he is getting twice as much as Sharpton is getting, that sends a message" (Slackman 2004). Although Sharpton certainly unperformed, there is an important caveat: he did better in South Carolina than any other state. In this respect, Sharpton's performance does not undermine our conclusion that African American candidates enjoy a sizable advantage in South Carolina Democratic primaries.

Another interesting feature of the 2004 contest is that it was the first time the South Carolina primary results were not a barometer of the upcoming southern contests. Although Edwards won the Palmetto State in 2004, he lost to Kerry a week later in Tennessee and Texas. Kerry received 41.0 percent of the vote in Tennessee, compared to just 26.5 percent for Edwards (Cook 2007). In Virginia, Kerry won 51.5 percent, while Edwards received just 26.6 percent (Cook 2007). A few weeks later, on March 2, Georgia held a primary, and Kerry was again the winner, 46.8 percent to Edwards's 41.4 percent (Cook 2007). Edwards dropped out the race the next day (Simon and Coile 2004).

In summary, John Edwards's success in the 2004 South Carolina primary is best explained by his appeal as both a southerner and a resident of a neighboring state. Both yield sizable advantages in the South Carolina primary according to our analysis. In addition, his closet rival, John Kerry, spent very little time campaigning in South Carolina and had a small campaign staff in the state. The 2004 contest also illustrates that campaign spending has little effect on South Carolina outcomes as Edwards was at a substantial fundraising disadvantage to both Kerry and Howard Dean. Ultimately, as a wealthy New Englander, Kerry likely had a hard time connecting with South Carolina Democratic primary voters. Finally, Al Sharpton, the only African American in the race, was not able to mount a serious challenge and was likely penalized because many black voters did not think he had a good chance of winning the nomination. Although Sharpton likely benefited from the state's high percentage of African American voters in Democratic contests, he trailed his primary opponents in virtually every other key factor in our analysis.

The Power of Race in Democratic Contests

For our third case, we selected the 2008 Democratic primary, perhaps the most important presidential nomination contest in South Carolina history. In this contest, the state's voters backed African American candidate Barack Obama over his more experienced and more well-known challengers, Hillary Clinton and John Edwards. This race illustrates the advantages African American candidates have in the South Carolina Democratic primary and serves as another example of South Carolina voters backing the eventual nominee. Also of note is the fact that there was a shift between the 2004 and 2008 contests from a majority white to a majority black Democratic primary electorate. The 2008 contest also confirms the importance of state endorsements, as Obama was able to secure more high-profile endorsements than either Edwards or Clinton. A final reason we picked this case is that it was an instance where a southern candidate, Edwards, did not win in South Carolina, contrary to what our model predicts—regional appeal was not enough to help Edwards win in 2008.

By the time of the Iowa caucuses, the 2008 Democratic contest in South Carolina was a three-person race. In Iowa, Obama shocked the political establishment winning the caucuses with 34.9 percent of the vote. Edwards was second in Iowa (31.2 percent), while Clinton came in a surprising third (30.4 percent). Clinton bounced back five days later, winning New Hampshire with 39.1 percent of the vote. Obama came in second in New Hampshire (36.5 percent), while Edwards was further back (16.9 percent). Clinton won the Nevada caucuses, another early primary state, with 50.8 percent of the vote to Obama's 45.1 percent. Edwards won a paltry 3.7 percent in Nevada.[5]

True to form, South Carolina was a showdown between the winners in Iowa and New Hampshire. But the first-in-the-South primary was also an opportunity for Edwards, a native son and winner of the South Carolina primary four years earlier, to resurrect his campaign. According to most political observers, doing well in South Carolina was vital for Edwards, and as he did in 2004, Edwards made appeals to his southern heritage (Balz 2008): In response to the question of what made him think he could win the South Carolina primary, one source reported that Edwards, "stretching out his Southern drawl," replied that there was "one simple answer: I talk like this'" (Bosman 2008). South Carolina also presented an opportunity for Obama, who was expected to do well with African American voters (Balz 2008). The 2008 contest was thus a test between two of the strongest factors that predict who wins Democratic contests in the state: geography and race. Given the perceived advantages for Edwards and Obama with respect to these two factors, there was some discussion that Clinton would not compete in the Palmetto State, but she ultimately decided to participate (Balz 2008).

It is hard to overestimate the importance of Obama's victory in Iowa. In a country with a long and troubling history of racial discrimination, it was a major accomplishment for a black candidate to win in an overwhelmingly white state. Obama's victory in Iowa also made him more competitive in the South. According to political scientist Blease Graham (2009, 102), Obama's Iowa victory "broke a psychological barrier and gave a clear signal it was acceptable for a Democrat, even a white Democrat in the South, to vote for a black man." Although our analysis reveals a strong connection between Iowa and South Carolina in Republican contests only, certainly the symbolic nature of Obama's Iowa victory mattered in ways that are hard to quantify.

Obama secured the most high-profile endorsements in South Carolina. He received the backing of Jim Hodges, the last Democrat to be elected governor in the Palmetto State. Hodges described Obama as a "once-in-a-lifetime political figure," saying, "He's the real deal" (Washington 2008c, B3). Obama also got endorsements from Dick Harpootlian, former chair of the South Carolina Democratic Party, Inez Tenenbaum, former state superintendent of education, and popular state representative Bakari Sellers (Washington 2008d). Hillary Clinton was endorsed by former Democratic governor Dick Riley (Washington 2008c). James Clyburn, perhaps the most coveted Democratic endorsement in South Carolina, remained neutral during the 2008 contest.

A bone of contention during the South Carolina Democratic primary was who would make the best general election candidate. State senator Robert Ford, a Clinton supporter, said that Democrats would suffer huge losses if Obama became the nominee (O'Connor 2008b). Edwards cited polls indicating that he would fare best in November and pledged to campaign in the South (O'Connor 2008b). Obama talked about creating a new Democratic collation with religious voters, independents, and Republicans (O'Connor 2008b). Clinton emphasized her experience and ability to withstand attacks from Republicans, "If it is, indeed, the classic Republican campaign, I've been there. I've done that. They've been after me for 16 years, and much to their dismay, I am still here" (O'Connor 2008b, A4).

As was the case in the 1990s, the South Carolina electorate continued to realign politically in the years prior to the 2008 contest. By 2008, most white voters backed GOP candidates and Republicans held nearly all statewide offices and majorities in the general assembly. Perhaps most notably, the Democratic primary electorate shifted from a majority white makeup to a majority black makeup between 2004 and 2008 (Huffmon, Knotts, and McKee 2017). It also shifted slightly to the left of the ideological spectrum, with the percentage of Democrats identifying as liberal increasing from 39 percent to 44 percent (Huffmon, Knotts, and McKee 2017). Moreover, support for the 2008 Democratic candidates tended to split along racial and generational lines (Washington and Smith 2008). African Americans leaned toward Obama, while whites gave Clinton the edge (Washington and Smith 2008). Younger voters tended to support Obama, while older voters backed Clinton (Washington and Smith 2008).

One week before the primary, the three contenders debated at the Palace Theater in Myrtle Beach. The gloves came off in the debate, with Clinton accusing Obama of taking campaign donations from a "slumlord" in inner-city Chicago (Healy and Zeleny 2008). Obama countered, lamenting that he was having to run against Bill *and* Hillary Clinton (Healy and Zeleny 2008). Obama also criticized Hillary Clinton's corporate ties, saying that "While I was working on those streets, watching those folks see their jobs shift overseas, you were a corporate lawyer sitting on the board of Wal-Mart" (C-SPAN 2008). Edwards was often caught between the bickering and, at one point asked rhetorically, "Are there three people in the debate, not two?" (O'Connor 2008a, A1). On a lighter note, Obama was asked if Bill Clinton was the first black president. He said he would have to "investigate more of Bill's dancing abilities" to determine "whether he was, in fact, a brother" (Healy and Zeleny 2008).

The campaign strategies of Obama and Clinton were notably different. Obama employed a sophisticated voter mobilization effort in South Carolina, spending money early on in the state and targeting younger voters (Graham, Moreland, and Steed 2010). Obama was a frequent visitor to the state's colleges and universities, including the College of Charleston (see figure 6.1). Conversely, Clinton ran a more traditional campaign, employing party leaders as consultants (Graham, Moreland, and Steed 2010). According to Blease Graham (2009, 102), "The Clinton campaign was run poorly, spending seven million dollars in the state. In an early effort to head off opposition, Senator Clinton engaged consultants among ranking and established state leaders to win the state's Democratic power structure." In addition, President Bill Clinton criss-crossed South Carolina campaigning for his wife, while Hillary Clinton campaigned in other states (Healy and Zeleny 2008). While traveling through South Carolina, Bill

FIGURE 6.1. Barack Obama Campaigning at the College of Charleston in 2008
Source: College of Charleston

Clinton had some harsh words for Obama, criticizing his voting record and positions related to the Iraq War (Healy 2008). This rhetoric caused a rift between the Clintons and many in the state's African American community. Graham reported that Clinton "missed Obama's broader professional appeal compared to the usual narrower representational interest in African American interests by black candidates" (2009, 102). Another controversy stemmed from comments by Robert Johnson, a Clinton backer and founder of Black Entertainment Television. Johnson told an audience at Columbia College that the Clintons were "deeply and emotionally involved in black issues when Barack Obama was doing something in the neighborhood that I won't say he was doing, [but] he said in his book" (Washington 2008b, A1). These remarks were understood to reference Obama's "youthful drug use," but Johnson later said his comments referred to Obama's time as a community organizer (Washington 2008b, A1).

Obama ended up scoring a resounding victory in the South Carolina Democratic primary, besting Clinton by a whopping 55.4 percent to 26.5 percent. Edwards was further behind, with 17.6 percent, a disappointing performance in a state he had won four years earlier.[6] In addition, a record number of voters, 532,151, participated in the primary, with more Democrats voting in 2008 than in any other Democratic presidential primary in state history. The day after the primary, Clyburn praised the effort: "Young people who had been sitting on the sidelines for years are now engaged in the process. African-Americans are really demonstrating a willingness and excitement to be involved in the process. Women are engaged. All of that is what we are looking at" (Washington 2008a, A1). In fact, there were even more people participating in the Democratic primary than in the state's 2008 Republican primary. It is important to note, however, that GOP voters faced cold and icy conditions during their 2008 contest, and some have suggested that the weather affected Republican turnout (Behre 2008).

According to exit polls, Obama won 78 percent of the black vote, compared to 19 percent for Clinton.[7] Obama also did very well with younger voters, winning 67 percent support in the eighteen to twenty-nine category and 62 percent in the thirty to forty-four category.[8] There was not a noticeable gender gap in the 2008 Democratic primary, however. Obama was the choice for 54 percent of male voters and 54 percent of female voters.[9] According to political scientists Blease Graham, Laurence Moreland, and Robert Steed (2010, 41), "Obama's increasingly professional image ran beyond the usually limited appeal to African American voters by an African American candidate . . . Now Obama could count on support not only from younger voters, but from many white moderates and reformers as well as from his African American base." In his victory speech at a Columbia convention center, Obama echoed familiar campaign themes. He spoke about healing the racial divide and moving toward a postracial society, "I did not travel around this state over the last year and see a white South Carolina and a black South Carolina. I saw South Carolina" (Zeleny and Connelly 2008).

Unfortunately for Democrats, the bitter rivalry between Obama and Clinton continued well beyond the South Carolina primary. After the votes were counted in the Palmetto State, Bill Clinton compared the Obama victory in South Carolina to Jesse Jackson's strong showing in the state: "Jesse Jackson won South Carolina in '84 and '88. Jackson ran a good campaign. And Obama ran a good campaign here. He's run a good campaign everywhere" (Kristol 2008). The comparison did not sit well with Obama supporters. According to Andy Sullivan (2008), a columnist for Reuters, "Many blacks were angered when he compared Barack Obama to Jesse Jackson, seeing it as an attempt to marginalize a black candidate who has drawn white support." Bill Clinton also made a late-night phone call to his old friend and political ally Representative James Clyburn to say that "if you bastards want a fight, you damn well will get one" (Clyburn 2014, 3).

As was the case in 2004, the 2008 South Carolina Democratic primary results were not a very good indicator of what would happen in the other southern states. Florida's primary occurred just three days after the South Carolina Democratic primary on January 29. Clinton won in Florida with 49.8 percent compared to Obama's 32.9 percent. Four southern states held contests on February 5: Alabama, Arkansas, Georgia, and Tennessee. Obama won Georgia (66.4 percent) and Alabama (56 percent), while Clinton won majorities in Arkansas (70.1 percent), and Tennessee (53.8 percent).[10] Although the general pattern for both parties is that victory in South Carolina correlates with success in subsequent southern states, the 2004 and 2008 Democratic results suggest the relationship is perhaps weaker for Democratic contests.

In summary, the case of the 2008 presidential primary illustrates the unmistakable advantages of being an African American candidate in the South Carolina Democratic primary, and 2008 indicates that a pivotal shift had taken place from a majority white to a majority black Democratic primary electorate in the state. Yet Obama's victory in 2008 was not due to race, alone. Ultimately the 2008 contest also highlights the power of securing state endorsements and, in particular, the importance of having the backing of the state's political establishment. Lastly, even though the results in South Carolina were not a barometer of what would happen in other southern states, the 2008 contest was important because of the record turnout and the boost it gave to Obama, the eventual Democratic nominee.

The Endorsement Advantage

Our final Democratic case is the 2016 primary between Hillary Clinton and Bernie Sanders. We selected this primary because it illustrates the importance of endorsements, media attention, and the crucial role African American voters continue to play in selecting winners and losers in South Carolina Democratic presidential contests. Additionally, the race has historical significance, since 2016 was the first time a woman won a presidential primary in the Palmetto State.

For Hillary Clinton, the 2016 election was a chance for redemption. She lost the South Carolina primary and the Democratic nomination to Barack Obama in 2008. After the loss, she served as U.S. Secretary of State under President Obama and worked to secure the backing of the Democratic Party's establishment for her candidacy in 2016. Though Clinton was always the favorite to secure the nomination in 2016, she received a vigorous, and somewhat unexpected, nomination challenge from Sanders, the independent senator from Vermont. Martin O'Malley, former governor of Maryland, was also a candidate for the Democratic nomination, though he was much less competitive and dropped out after a poor showing in Iowa (Preston, Zeleny, Krieg, and Bradner 2016). Clinton and Sanders fought to what amounted to a draw in the Iowa caucuses. Clinton received 350 more votes than Sanders, winning 49.8 percent to Sanders's 49.6 percent. Eight days later, in the New Hampshire primary, Sanders scored an impressive victory, receiving 60.2 percent to Clinton's 37.7 percent.[11] Once again, Iowa and New Hampshire selected different candidates, placing South Carolina in the critical role of tiebreaker.

As the establishment pick, Clinton received nearly all the state's key endorsements. She was supported by former South Carolina governors Dick Riley and Jim Hodges, as well as by former South Carolina secretary of education Inez Tenenbaurm ("Winners & Losers" 2016). Columbia mayor Steve Benjamin, one of the state's leading African American politicians, backed Clinton as did former Charleston mayor Joe Riley ("Winners & Losers" 2016). Clinton also had the support from more than thirty state legislators and eighty local officials ("Winners & Losers" 2016). Clinton even secured the support of influential Representative James Clyburn, who endorsed her at Allen University on February 19, eight days before the South Carolina primary (Burns and Healy 2016). Sanders was not completely shut out of state endorsements, however. He received the endorsement of twenty-eight-year-old state representative Justin Bamberg (Prabhu 2016b). Bamberg had become well known as the attorney who represented the family of Walter Scott, the man who was shot and killed by a North Charleston police officer (Prabhu 2016b). Sanders was also endorsed by the former chair of the South Carolina Democratic Party, Dick Harppotlian (Kropf 2016e).

In addition to her sizable advantage in endorsements, Clinton garnered substantially more media attention in preelection media coverage than Sanders, according to the data used in chapter 4's analysis. In fact, the media attention gap between Clinton and Sanders is the largest between the top two candidates in our dataset. Clinton received nearly 50 percent more local media coverage than Sanders in the two weeks before the South Carolina primary and roughly 33 percent more national coverage in the final weeks. As a point of comparison, in the 2016 Republican contest Donald Trump garnered 9.5 percent more local coverage than his nearest competitor, Ted Cruz, and 19 percent more national coverage. One explanation for Clinton's media dominance—especially in local outlets—was her greater presence in South Carolina.

One of the key events of the 2016 campaign was the South Carolina Democratic Party's first-in-the-South dinner at the Marriott Hotel in downtown Charleston (Kropf 2016c). The event was attended by House minority leader Nancy Pelosi and a number of members of the Congressional Black Caucus (Kropf 2016c). During the event, Sanders shared stories about participating in the 1963 March on Washington (Chozick 2016) and also asserted that the national Democratic Party needed to pay more attention to the South (Kropf 2016c). According to Sanders, "We cannot simply be a party of East Coast, the

West Coast and the Midwest" (Kropf 2016c). Clinton praised Obama and talked about continuing his legacy (Chozick 2016). She also talked about the tragic shooting at Emanuel AME church, her belief that gun manufacturers should not have "limited liability," and her memories from the funeral of Reverend Clementa Pinckney (Kropf 2016c). After the dinner, the candidates attended Representative Clyburn's annual fish fry, also being held in downtown Charleston (Chozick 2016).

Not surprisingly, Clinton raised the most money in South Carolina. During the crucial final three months of 2015, Clinton outraised Sanders by a five to one margin (Shain 2016c). As was the case in many areas of the country, Sanders had smaller average contribution, just $70, compared to Clinton's average contribution of $338 (Shain 2016c). Clinton also had a strong ground game in South Carolina and carried out an effective get-out-the-vote effort (Self 2016a). Sanders had a noteworthy campaign organization in South Carolina as well, with 160 part-time staffers, making $15 an hour, in addition to 50 full-time aides (Self 2016d).

Clinton, O'Malley, and Sanders squared off at the Charleston's newly renovated Gilliard Auditorium on January 18 for a nationally televised debate. Sanders criticized Clinton's Wall Street connections and speaking fees, while Clinton talked about the injustices of the Flint, Michigan, water crisis and its impact on a poor black city (Healy and Chozick 2016). One of Clinton's key campaign strategies was to align herself closely with her one-time rival and former boss, President Barack Obama. According to Jamie Self, a political reporter at the *State*, Clinton "fully embraced Obama's legacy, pitching S.C. Democratic voters that she was the candidate best suited to protect the president's work and improve upon it" (Self 2016a). It was much more difficult for Sanders to align himself with Obama. As CNN commentator and former state legislator Bakari Sellers noted, "One of the most important takeaways is that Bernie Sanders is not Barack Obama. The Democratic Party in South Carolina is about building on the legacy of Barack Obama" (Dumain 2016, 1).

Clinton also drew on her extensive ties in the Palmetto State. During the 1970s, she worked in South Carolina for the Children's Defense Fund, and during the 1980s and 1990s she regularly traveled to Hilton Head for Renaissance Weekend, "a nonpartisan annual gathering in the Lowcountry of notables from diverging backgrounds and opinions on everything from civics, politics or academia, to the arts, science or business" (Self 2016a). Her extensive work in the state made her a particularly attractive candidate for African American voters. As Clyburn noted, "African-American voters are basically traditionalists; they're people who tend to stay with whom and what they know. Most African-American voters in this country, specifically South Carolina, just don't know Bernie Sanders" (Dumain 2016, 1). Much like fellow New Englander John Kerry in 2004, Sanders had a difficult time connecting with southern voters. At one point during the campaign, he appeared on the *The Late Show with Stephen Colbert*, where he received advice from the host about how to connect with South Carolina voters. According to Colbert, "To get the vote down there, you have to eat boiled peanuts" ("Colbert's Advice" 2016, 8). On the flip side, although Hillary Clinton was born in Chicago, and represented New York in the Senate, her time as First Lady of Arkansas gave her some southern credentials.

Both of the leading candidates recognized the importance of courting South Carolina's black voters. While Bill Clinton had always done well with African American voters, and was even dubbed the country's "first black president," South Carolina's black voters supported Obama overwhelmingly in 2008. And African Americans remembered Bill Clinton's campaign tactics during the 2008 nomination contest, which required fence-mending for the Clintons in the 2016 cycle. Nonetheless, Hillary Clinton was generally well liked by African Americans, in part because of her husband's policies as president and her commitment to continuing the Obama legacy. Clinton also campaigned with the "mothers of the movement," five mothers whose children were killed as a result of gun violence (Self 2016b) and had other high-profile surrogates including actress Angela Bassett and entertainer Vivian Fox (Douglas 2016). In addition, the Clinton campaign ran a commercial featuring Obama's former attorney general Eric Holder in which he tells viewers that Clinton has "fought her whole life for children, to protect civil rights, voting rights" (Kropf 2016b, 1). However, during the final week of the campaign, Black Lives Matter activists paid to attend a Clinton fund-raiser at a donor's house and in an "ambush-style interruption" criticized Clinton for her 1996 comments as first lady when she used the term "super-predators" in a speech about crime (Kropf 2016a, 1). According to one of the protestors, "We did this because we wanted to make sure that black people are paying attention to her record" (Kropf 2016a, 1).

Sanders also made direct appeals to the state's African American voters. During a campaign stop in Charleston, Sanders accused GOP frontrunner Donald Trump of leading an effort to delegitimize Obama by raising questions about his birthplace (Clark and Kumar 2016). Sanders also campaigned at the state's predominantly black colleges and universities, often appearing with Erica Garner, the daughter of Eric Garner, the man who died from a police chokehold in 2014 (Douglas 2016). Noted intellectual Cornel West also campaigned for Sanders in South Carolina (Douglas 2016).

For Clinton, winning the South Carolina primary was a family affair. Bill Clinton, the winner of the 1992 South Carolina primary, campaigned throughout the Palmetto State. During a rally at Allen University in Columbia, he rattled off the reasons his wife should be president, "So Hillary should be president, I think, because she's the best change-maker I've ever known. Because of her ideas for creating more jobs and raising incomes and including everybody. Including getting more women in the workforce. Equal pay, paid leave, child care—don't say that's a women's issue. It's a family issue" (Prabhu 2016a, 7). At rally at Francis Marion University, Bill Clinton talked about the state's decision to remove the Confederate flag from State House grounds. Clinton said, "South Carolina, after the horrible church shooting in Charleston, gave the country an incredible gift because we got to watch democracy come alive again" (Jackson 2016a, 7). Chelsea Clinton campaigned in the Palmetto State as well. During an event at the College of Charleston, she touted her mother's commitment to health care, referencing the 1993 health care reform effort and telling the crowd that "before it was called Obamacare, it was called Hillarycare" (Bowers 2016).

Although Hillary Clinton spent far more time in South Carolina, the Vermont Senator did make several campaign appearances in the Palmetto State. During one campaign swing, he told a crowd at Charleston's Memminger Auditorium that "in America, someone who works 40 hours a week should not live in poverty" (Jackson and Slade 2016, 1). Sanders also hit on a number of other familiar campaign themes such as the "corrupt campaign finance system," health care reform, and tuition-free college (Jackson and Slade 2016, 1). About a week later, during a campaign rally in Greenville, Sanders continued to make his case to South Carolina voters: "What the American people are demanding is a government which represents all of us, not just a handful of wealthy campaign contributors" (Jackson 2016b, 1). He also addressed concerns that South Carolina was already in the Clinton column: "This campaign is gaining momentum because we are listening to the American people and we are listening in a way other campaigns don't" (Jackson 2016b, 1). However, after a morning rally just four days before the South Carolina primary, Sanders left the state for events in Missouri and Oklahoma, a clear sign Sanders would likely lose (Roldan and Kropf 2016, 1). According to College of Charleston political scientist Kendra Stewart, "I think he's conceded the state" (Roldan and Kropf 2016, 1).

Clinton indeed scored a resounding victory in South Carolina. She received 73.5 percent of the vote, compared to 26.0 percent for Sanders.[12] According to exit polls, 86 percent of African Americans supported Clinton and made up 61 percent of the Democratic primary electorate that year.[13] In addition to blacks, self-identified Democrats, older voters, and more frequent church attendees were statistically more likely to support Clinton over Sanders (Huffmon, Knotts, and McKee 2017). Sanders outperformed his overall vote total among voters age seventeen to forty-four, winning 37 percent among this group.[14] Clinton did particularly well in the state's majority-black counties, while Sanders best showing was in urban counties and rural counties with higher percentages of white voters (Graham and Buchanan 2018).

It is important to point out the lower voter turnout among South Carolina Democrats in 2016 compared to 2008. Although the general trend since the first Democratic primary in 1992 was increasing voter participation, turnout in 2016 was just 12.5 percent of registered voters, down from 23 percent in the historic 2008 primary (Graham and Buchanan 2018). Finally, in 2016, South Carolina Democrats provided a perfect barometer of what to expect in the southern Super Tuesday event on March 1. Clinton won in Alabama (77.9 percent), Georgia (71.3 percent), Arkansas (66.1 percent), Tennessee (66.1 percent), Texas (65.2 percent), and Virginia (64.3 percent).[15]

Overall, the 2016 primary shows the power of both state endorsements and media attention in the South Carolina primary. Clinton had the backing of nearly all the state's leading Democrats, and her media attention advantage is the largest in our dataset. Indeed, a key strategy for Clinton was to closely align herself with Obama and convince South Carolina voters that she was the best candidate to continue his legacy. Despite her inherent advantages in South Carolina, Clinton spent time and money in the Palmetto State as well. Former governor Jim Hodges said, "I certainly think the mindset was: 'I'm not taking South Carolina for granted.' She wanted to communicate to voters, particularly African American voters, that she was going to work hard to win their support" (Self 2016a, 1).

Conclusion

Our four Democratic cases reinforce many of the key arguments in this book, challenge a few, and help better address one of our central questions: what does it take to win in South Carolina? Perhaps most importantly, these cases show the key role played by African American voters in South Carolina's Democratic presidential primaries. Black support played a vital role in each of the four cases we have profiled. Although the most obvious example is Barack Obama's victory over Hillary Clinton in 2008, support from African American voters also played a critical role in Clinton's victory over Bernie Sanders in 2016. In addition, our analysis in this chapter illustrates the importance of state endorsements and media attention in South Carolina. Hillary Clinton's 2016 campaign provides the clearest example of this, although Bill Clinton's 1992 campaign illustrates these two effects as well. Likewise, the chapter provides examples of southerners doing particularly well in the South Carolina primary. For Democrats, the southern advantage is best demonstrated in the campaigns of Bill Clinton in 1992 and John Edwards in 2004. Both Clinton and Edwards won the South Carolina primary, doing much better than they did in either Iowa or New Hampshire. And as we point out in the last chapter, it is notable that six of the fourteen candidates who won South Carolina between 1980 and 2016 on both sides of the aisle—just over 40 percent—were from the South.

Our cases also highlight factors that do *not* matter in the South Carolina primary. First, in some instances candidates who previously competed in the South Carolina primary did not seem to have an advantage over political newcomers. This finding is best demonstrated by John Edwards, who won the 2004 South Carolina Democratic primary with 45.2 percent of the vote yet finished third in 2008 with just 17.6 percent. At the same time, there were many newcomers who did very well in the South Carolina primary, most notably Bill Clinton in 1992 and Barack Obama in 2008. Second, our analysis suggests that candidates who outspend their opponents do not automatically win the South Carolina primary. Both John Kerry and Howard Dean had a significant fund-raising advantage in 2004 but could not overcome Edwards's geographic advantages, while Hillary Clinton had fund-raising advantages in both 2008 and 2016 and only won the latter contest.

Finally, the 2004 case allowed us to take a closer look at an instance where South Carolina's Democratic voters did not back the eventual nominee. As noted, since the state adopted a primary in 1992, South Carolina's Democratic voters have correctly selected the eventual nominee every cycle except 2004. In this contest, John Edwards received the most votes in South Carolina, even though he was defeated for the nomination by John Kerry. In addition to having the advantage of being a candidate from the South, Edwards also benefited from residing in a neighboring state. As our analysis demonstrated, there is a sizable benefit for candidates from neighboring states. Ultimately, this not only helps explains why Edwards won South Carolina, but why 2004 bucks the general pattern where candidates who do well in the South Carolina primary perform well in the subsequent southern contests.

★ 7 ★
THE CASE FOR THE
SOUTH CAROLINA
PRIMARY

When it comes to picking presidents, Iowa and New Hampshire receive the bulk of attention. And while these states play an important role in the current system, they are not particularly good barometers of who will win the nomination and nearly always back different candidates. In twelve of thirteen contested elections since 1980, Iowa and New Hampshire produced mixed results, the only exception being John Kerry's back-to-back victories in 2004. The historic 2016 nomination contest was just the latest example in which Iowa and New Hampshire produced a split decision: Clinton narrowly won Iowa before being routed by Bernie Sanders in New Hampshire, while Trump won New Hampshire after losing Iowa to Ted Cruz. As Elaine Kamarck (2016b) has aptly noted, Iowa and New Hampshire are where "winners lose, and losers win."

South Carolina's track record is different from Iowa's and New Hampshire's. South Carolinians have correctly selected the eventual nominee in six of seven Republican contests since 1980 and three of four Democratic contests since 1992. Not only did Donald Trump and Hillary Clinton emerge victorious in 2016, but they had sizable delegate leads after South Carolina: 74 percent and 58 percent, respectively. According to the delegate math, and most observers, the race was all but over after the South Carolina primary. If Iowa and New Hampshire are where "losers win," perhaps South Carolina is where "winners win."

Although we recognize the importance of both Iowa and New Hampshire, we have argued that South Carolina's vital role in the race for the White House deserves more attention. In discussing the importance of the first-in-the-South primary in chapter 1, we show that the volume of news coverage on South Carolina is far less than the coverage of Iowa and New Hampshire. Likewise, we noted that there are a number of excellent books on the Iowa caucus (Redlawsk, Tolbert, and Donovan 2011) and New Hampshire primary (Moore and Smith 2015), yet no book-length examination of the South Carolina primary.

We are certainly not the only ones to argue for the importance South Carolina in the presidential race. A number of politicians and political strategists have recognized the key role of the state's first-in-the-South primary. A common refrain is that in South Carolina "we pick presidents," a phrase popularized by Republican leaders after Reagan's victory in the first primary in 1980 ("First in the South" 2018). Steve Benjamin, the Democratic mayor of Columbia, South Carolina, said the "road to the White House starts in South Carolina" (Martin and Herndon 2019). South Carolina's former Republican governor David Beasley labels the state the "the gateway to the South" (Edsall 1996) while David Plouffe, Barack Obama's former campaign manager, calls South Carolina the "gateway to the nomination" (Martin and Herndon 2019). In addition to the "gateway" label, a range of superlatives are often used to describe the South Carolina primary including "tiebreaker," "make or break," and "firewall."

Yet the South Carolina primary has not always been the high-profile event that it has become. Chapter 1 documents the primary's growth over the past few decades, from the number of citizens participating to its increased media coverage. Chapter 2 then tells the story of how South Carolina achieved its coveted first-in-the-South status. On the Republican side, the scheduling of the first southern primary in 1980 represented an effort by entrepreneurial party leaders to secure in role in shaping national politics and wrestle control of state politics away from their Democratic rivals. South Carolina Democrats decided not to hold a primary for the very same reasons: it would not, in their estimation, benefit the party's electoral future. Ultimately, however, the success of the GOP primary, coupled with pressure from within the party, changed Democrats' minds. They held the first primary in 1992, and since 2004, the party has maintained the coveted first-in-the-South status.

Given its increased importance, and the state's reputation for picking winners, we believe the South Carolina primary has many positive qualities in the current nominating system. Drawing on findings from throughout the book, in this final chapter we argue that South Carolina should maintain its current position. In making the case for the South Carolina primary, we highlight the most frequently debated alternatives to the current system, discuss the positive qualities of the existing system (including Iowa and New Hampshire as the first two contests), the positive features unique to South Carolina, and the future of the South Carolina primary.

Alternative Nominating Systems

One of the most popular reform proposals is the idea that the United States should be divided into four or five regions and that each state in the region should hold their primary on the same day (Norrander 2010). Of course, this plan would be an expansion of the southern regional primaries, often called Super Tuesday, that have existed informally since 1988 (Norrander 1992). Advocates of regional primaries argue that candidates could concentrate on one part of the country, reducing travel time and advertising costs (Norrander 2010; S. Smith and Springer 2009). In addition, regional primaries could help focus campaigns on issues important to an entire region, not just a particular state (Norrander 2010).

Over the years, several regional primary plans have been proposed. The National Association of Secretaries of State endorsed a regional primary concept in 1999, and a version of this plan was introduced as the Regional Presidential Primary and Caucus Act of 2007 in the U. S. Congress (Kamarck 2016a). Some regional primary proposals even provide exceptions for Iowa and New Hampshire (Kamarck 2016a). However, none of these proposals have actually been approved by Congress, and there has not been a lot of recent movement toward a regional primary. Moreover, two of the main advocates of a regional primary, Michigan representative Sander Levin and, his brother, Michigan senator Carl Levin (Kamarck 2016a), have both retired from politics.

A number of other reform proposals seek to group states based on predetermined criteria. In the Delaware Plan, perhaps the most popular of the grouping options, states would be assigned to four pods according to their population (Kamarck 2016a; Norrander 2010). Advocates argue that this plan has the potential for more voters to influence the outcome, since states with the largest populations would vote last and likely extend the primary calendar (Norrander 2010). In one version of this plan, no southern states would be in the first pod, and South Carolina would be in the second group of states, along with Arkansas and Mississippi (Fair Vote 2009). The Delaware Plan was presented to the Republican National Committee Rules Committee in 2000, but opposition from big states, concerns over what Democrats would do, and opposition from George W. Bush ultimately derailed the proposal (Kamarck 2016c).

Finally, there have been calls for a national primary, a proposal whereby all states would hold nomination contests on a single day. In 1911, Alabama representative Richard Hobson introduced national primary legislation (Buell 2004), and President Woodrow Wilson endorsed the idea in a speech to Congress in 1913 (Norrander 2010). Proponents of a national primary emphasize its simplicity and fairness (Norrander 2010), as well as its ability to increase voter turnout and result in a more representative primary electorate (Altschuler 2008). Advocates also stress that a national primary would require candidates to run truly national campaigns (S. Smith and Springer 2009).

Positives of the Current System

Our book makes no normative claims about the "best" way to select a party's nominee for president. We acknowledge that alternative nominating schemes have their own virtues and discuss some of the options in the final section of this chapter. Instead, our focus has been South Carolina's place in the current system and empirical questions about the primary's basic dynamics. Simply put, any electoral scheme has tradeoffs, and we want to highlight the positive qualities with the existing system.

As a starting point, a common argument is that the current framework benefits from its predictability (Mayer 1996; Norrander 2010). Unlike what would occur with a switch to one of the many alternative schemes, there does not need to be a public relations campaign if Iowa, New Hampshire, and South Carolina remain in their current calendar slots. After all, voters in these states are accustomed to vetting the candidates by attending campaign events and asking questions (Fowler 2007; Moore and Smith 2015; Redlawsk, Tolbert, and Donovan 2011; Vavreck, Spiliotes, and Fowler 2002). Likewise, the critically important work of organizing an early contest will be easier if the the status quo is maintained. Party leaders and other officials in these states have proven themselves capable of handling the considerable logistics of holding one of the first contests, which tend to result in higher voter turnout as well as more frequent campaign events, debates, and media attention (Ridout, Rottinghaus, and Hosey 2009).[1] Holding a critically important early primary is no small endeavor, for voters and state officials alike, and as we note in chapter 2, some of the initial resistance to moving to a primary format in South Carolina had to do with the sheer logistics of the effort.

Another common argument in support of the current system is that underdog candidates who have less name recognition and financial support can compete and build momentum as they move through the campaign season (Norrander 2010). Like Iowa and New Hampshire, South Carolina has an easily accessible population. Each state's geographic size is small enough so that a candidate can drive from one side to the other for a day of campaigning. Iowa ranks twenty-third in the nation in its total land area, while South Carolina and New Hampshire come in fortieth and forty-fourth, respectively.[2] All three states have affordable media markets as well. The Columbia, South Carolina, television market is the largest in the three states, ranking seventy-fourth in the nation.[3] Obama's 2008 victory over Clinton in the Iowa caucuses—and subsequent victory in South Carolina—is often held up as a clear example of how a less popular candidate can benefit from the current system and defeat the establishment favorite (Redlask, Tolbert, and Donovan 2011). It is hard to imagine

Obama securing the nomination over Clinton, a candidate who had more endorsements and more money, in a national or even regional primary. It is worth noting that some who want to scrap the current system hope to *expand* this feature by front-loading other small states (see, for example, S. Smith and Springer 2009). If you value retail politics—meeting face to face, shaking hands, and answering questions—the current calendar featuring Iowa, New Hampshire, and South Carolina makes that possible.

Chapters 4–6 provide evidence that less well-known candidates can indeed compete on level playing field with presumed frontrunners in South Carolina. Although the evidence from our analysis in chapter 4 confirms the conventional wisdom about the importance of some factors—such as endorsements—it is also notable what is insignificant in our analysis. Namely, our model reveals that political newcomers and candidates with fewer campaign contributions have an equal chance of winning the South Carolina primary as rivals with greater experience and fund-raising advantages. Likewise, chapters 5–6 review a number of contests in which more experienced and better-funded candidates lost the South Carolina primary to a lesser-known candidate. In a national or even regional primary format, which would almost certainly be fought in the most populous states, candidates with fewer resources would have a harder time campaigning. No doubt some candidates would be discouraged from running in the first place, thus reducing the number of options available to voters.

The current system also forces candidates to make their case to a diverse array of voters with vastly different interests (Mayer and Busch 2004; Redlawsk, Tolbert, and Donovan 2011). In chapter 3, we document the characteristic features of Iowa, New Hampshire, and South Carolina and note that they are indeed unique in their demographic and attitudinal features. Not only does the diversity of the three early states allow voters to see the candidates perform in a variety of geographic settings, but it may help the candidates better appreciate the complexity of the American electorate. Alternative schemes, like a national primary, would allow candidates to ignore the diversity of the American public and cater to extreme factions within the party (Mayer and Busch 2004). On this point, it is important to remember that general elections are often fought exclusively in large battleground states—Florida, Ohio, North Carolina, Michigan, Virginia. Simply put, there are many benefits to voters and candidates alike when the primary election hinges on a diverse array of smaller states that otherwise have little electoral power.

A final worthwhile feature of a sequential nominating system is that it helps determine a candidate's viability and electability in the general election (Redlawsk, Tolbert, and Donovan 2011). Namely, the time-consuming and difficult act of campaigning state by state over a period of many months increases the likelihood that candidates are vetted and can withstand criticism from rivals, voters, and the press. Such a feature is important given that the nominees are seeking the highest office in the United States and will be involved in a deeply contested general election. Determining a candidate's viability and electability in early caucuses and primaries is also important insofar as it shapes voter perceptions in later contests. It is therefore critical that voters in early states are accustomed to vetting candidates and have the capacity to meet with the candidates face to face. Notably, determining a candidate's viability and electability is a major part of the campaign coverage as candidates vie for votes in Iowa, New Hampshire, and South Carolina. A number of proposed reforms—including a national primary—would likely curtail these benefits.

Positives of South Carolina

Although the current system has many positive features as a whole, South Carolina provides its own unique positive qualities. Perhaps most importantly, South Carolina's first-in-the-South primary offers a critical counterweight to the Iowa caucus and New Hampshire primary. As we document in chapter 3, Iowa and New Hampshire do not accurately resemble either party's nominating electorate in a demographic or attitudinal sense, but South Carolina does, making the characteristics of South Carolinians critically important. Notably, the lack of representativeness of citizens of early states is one of the most common critiques of the current system (see Altschuler 2008). Yet the ways in which South Carolina balances Iowa and New Hampshire is different for each party.

On the Republican side, South Carolina's primary electorate is far more representative of the national GOP nominating electorate than that of either Iowa or New Hampshire. In fact, South Carolina was third in our analysis of each state, while Iowa and New Hampshire ranked toward the very bottom. South Carolina's strength in Republican contests comes from its citizens' balanced mix of issue priorities (from the economy and social issues to world affairs) as well as its parity in the percentage of veterans and college graduates. Although the same is not true on the Democratic side, South Carolina adds critical balance to the three early states. Unlike Iowa and New Hampshire, which are disproportionately white, South Carolina has a large percentage of African American voters, a demographic that is vitally important to the Democratic Party. South Carolina also provides much needed balance in terms of the percentage of voters concerned with economic issues, which is higher than either of the other states, as well as with respect to voters' level of education and liberalism, both of which are lower than either of the other states.

The state's representativeness owes not only to the demographic and attitudinal characteristics of South Carolina's primary electorate but also to the fact it holds fully open primaries. In South Carolina, any voter can participate in either party's contest without registering, one of just eleven states in which this is possible.[4] Research shows that voters who participate in open primaries are often more moderate and more representative of their state's general election electorate (Kaufmann, Gimpel, and Hoffmann 2003). Iowa is only partially open, requiring voters to register but allowing them to switch the day of the election, and New Hampshire is semiclosed, requiring party registration but allowing undeclared voters to participate in either primary. Although the initial aim of holding an open primary in 1980 was to build a competitive Republican Party in a state dominated by Democrats, as noted in chapter 2, the decision has helped the Palmetto State balance its early state brethren.

Another positive quality of South Carolina's primary is that the state is an excellent barometer of outcomes in subsequent states. South Carolina is a harbinger of who wins in other southern states owing to the region's shared political culture and the bonds of southern identity (Black and Black 1987; Cooper and Knotts 2017; Key 1949; McKee 2018a; Woodard 2013). We have noted that this feature is especially important in the delegate race because nearly all southern primaries are early on the calendar, which helps candidates who do well in the region to quickly build an insurmountable delegate advantage (McKee 2018b). The state is also a powerful predictor, as we have indicated, of who ultimately secures a party's nomination.

We believe there are two main reasons why representativeness and predictive ability are beneficial in nomination contests. First, and perhaps most obvious, these qualities enhance the degree to which presidential elections are democratic in nature. Given that the two-party system is likely here to stay in the United States (Duverger 1963), these two qualities are especially important, since voters often have just two viable candidates to choose between in the general election. Representativeness and predictive ability help increase the extent to which voters' opinions are reflected in the candidates who ultimately compete in the general election. It is worth noting that these qualities take on extra importance when a state plays a critical tie-breaking role, as South Carolina so often does. Second, a state's representativeness and predictive ability are important for both parties and candidates. For parties, the ultimate goal in a nomination contest is to win the general election, and a skewed nominating scheme can result in candidates that deviate too far from the national median voter (Polsby 1983; Downs 1957). Likewise, candidates may adopt unpopular or extreme positions in a strategic effort to win the early states and secure their party's nomination (Key 1956). Representative states that prove to be good barometers of outcomes in other states can help compel candidates to adopt positions favored by a large portion of the population.

Lastly, South Carolina has a number of regional features that distinguish it from the current group of early caucus and primary states. First, South Carolina is located in a geographic region that is not represented among the early states. Just as the Northeast, Midwest, and West have distinct histories and political cultures, the South has a shared identity that has become increasingly open to both black and white southerners (Cooper and Knotts 2017). And while race continues to play an outsized role in its politics and society, the region's unique politics are also a result of economics and religion (McKee 2018a). Economic views structure the party system in the South, as a low tax/small government ethos dominates in many parts of the region. The South's exceptionalism is also derived from the ways religion shapes the region's politics. In the Bible Belt, conservative Christians continue to be a major influence in Republican politics, and black Protestants dominate Democratic politics.

The Future of the South Carolina Primary

In many ways, South Carolina's place on the electoral calendar is more secure than ever. When the South Carolina GOP adopted to a primary format back in 1979, there were, of course, many skeptics. However, the state's current party leaders and elected officials, both Republicans and Democrats, are uniformly committed to maintaining the state's privileged position. As we detail in chapter 2, getting the state's first-in-the-South status required South Carolina's party organizations to fight challenges from within the state, from other states, and from the national political parties, and keeping that status has likewise been a struggle. Additionally, there is a 2007 state law requiring that the state election commission conduct presidential primaries. Notably, this statute gives the state parties considerable power over the primaries, allowing them to set the election dates, polling place hours, and candidate filing requirements.

Perhaps equally important, South Carolina's first-in-the-South status has the endorsement of both national political parties. As we discuss in chapter 2, the Democratic National Committee named South Carolina and Nevada "carve-out" states prior to the 2008 primary season, along with the early state stalwarts of Iowa and New Hampshire (Kamarck 2016a). The Republican National Committee recently gave special status to the same four states as well. According to the "Rules of the Republican Party," approved at the 2016 convention, only Iowa, New Hampshire, South Carolina, and Nevada may conduct primaries prior to March 1 (Republican National Convention 2016).

Simply put, party leaders at both state and national levels agree that South Carolina's position on the primary calendar is secure. Nothing is guaranteed, of course, and there are certainly ways that South Carolina's privileged position could be challenged. Other southern states could, for example, simply leapfrog South Carolina in an effort to claim the title of first in the South. Florida, Georgia, and Louisiana have been the most aggressive in the past, and it is possible that another state could schedule a primary ahead of South Carolina. If this occurred, it is highly likely that South Carolina Republicans and Democrats would simply adjust their primary dates in an effort to remain the first southern contest. And under current national party rules, these challengers would receive sanctions from the national committees and risk losing delegates to national conventions. Moreover, when states break national party rules, candidates often bypass these states in an effort to stay in the good graces of party officials and voters in the rule-following states. Suffice it to say, although there are no legal barriers to doing so, other states would face significant obstacles if they sought to become the first southern state.

Various presidential nomination reform proposals, including those we have described, would also jeopardize South Carolina's first-in-the-South status. It is worth noting that the American public has expressed support for reforming the current system in the aggregate. For example, according to a forty-state survey during the 2008 primaries, 71.6 percent of respondents favored rotating the state primary order and 73.4 supported a national primary (Redlawsk, Tolbert, and Donovan 2011). Needless to say, these alternative nomination schemes would give South Carolina's voters much less influence than they have in the current system.

Although major nomination reforms are certainly possible, they are not very likely at the present time. One of the main reasons is that there are many competing interests (e.g., state parties, national parties, elected officials) that make change difficult. As Brookings senior fellow Elaine Kamarck (2016c, 8–9) puts it, "Some sort of more rational mega-system is unlikely to prevail mostly because the presidential nomination process is the result of the interplay of state and national political parties, legislatures, courts, reformers, and presidential hopefuls." Moreover, reform proposals seem less popular in recent years as other election-related issues have gained momentum. Reforming the Electoral College, campaign finance rules, voter identification laws, election system security, and redistricting have gotten more recent attention. In addition, such reforms would require an act of Congress and there are constitutional questions about whether the federal government can set election rules for state and local parties (Kamarck 2016a; Norrander 2010).

Efforts to restrict access to the ballot—which have proven to be easier to adopt—would also threaten the South Carolina primary. Voter suppression, including stricter voter identification requirements or excessive voter list purges, would negatively impact the primary. The South Carolina primary has always been an open contest, and both parties have worked to maximize political participation. Needless to say, restricting who can patriciate in the South Carolina primary would undermine this long-standing commitment. In addition, South Carolina has been a state where residents *do not* register to vote by political party and a place where any registered voter can participate in the primary. There are signs however, that this could change in future elections. In 2018, 82.4 percent the state's GOP voters supported registration by party on an "advisory" ballot question.[5] If party registration led to closed primaries, South Carolina would likely lose both its representativeness and predictive accuracy, especially on the Republican side

Barring a major overhaul to the presidential nomination system, however, South Carolina is likely to remain first in the South. Although there are certainly other ways to structure nomination contests, we believe that the current system, with South Carolina as the first southern state, has many positive qualities. And with the endorsement of both national political parties, in part a recognition of the state's beneficial features, the South Carolina primary will continue to play a pivotal role in selecting presidents.

APPENDIX A

South Carolina Primary Election Results since 1980

March 8, 1980

Republican Primary	Vote Total	Percent
Ronald Reagan	79,549	54.67
John Connally	43,113	29.63
George Bush	21,569	14.82
Other	1,270	0.87
TOTAL	**145,501**	

Source: Cook 2000

March 5, 1988

Republican Primary	Vote Total	Percent
George Bush	94,738	48.51
Bob Dole	40,265	20.62
Pat Robertson	37,261	19.08
Jack Kemp	22,431	11.49
Other	597	0.31
TOTAL	**195,292**	

Source: Cook 2000

March 7, 1992

Republican Primary	Vote Total	Percent
George Bush	99,558	66.89
Patrick Buchanan	38,247	25.70
Other	11,035	7.41
TOTAL	**148,840**	

Source: Cook 2000

March 7, 1992

Democratic Primary	Vote Total	Percent
William J. Clinton	73,221	62.90
Paul E. Tsongas	21,338	18.33
Tom Harkin	7,657	6.58
Edmund G. Brown	6,961	5.98
Uncommitted	3,640	3.13
Bob Cunningham	1,369	1.18
Charles Woods	854	0.73
Robert Kerrey	566	0.49
William Kreml	336	0.29
Angus W. McDonald	268	0.23
Lyndon H. La Rouche Jr.	204	0.18
TOTAL	**116,414**	

Source: uselectionatlas.org/RESULTS

March 2, 1996

Republican Primary	Vote Total	Percent
Robert Dole	124,904	45.13
Patrick Buchanan	80,824	29.21
Steve Forbes	35,039	12.66
Lamar Alexander	28,647	10.35
Alan Keyes	5,752	2.08

Republican Primary	Vote Total	Percent
Richard Lugar	1,017	0.37
Phil Gramm	467	0.17
Maurice Taylor	91	0.03
TOTAL	**276,741**	

Source: Cook 2000 and uselectionatlas.org/RESULTS

February 19, 2000

Republican Primary	Vote Total	Percent
George W. Bush	305,998	53.39
John McCain	239,964	41.87
Alan Keyes	25,996	4.54
Gary Bauer	618	0.11
Steve Forbes	449	0.08
Orrin Hatch	76	0.01
TOTAL	**573,101**	

Source: Cook 2007

February 3, 2004

Democratic Primary	Vote Total	Percent
John Edwards	132,660	45.15
John Kerry	87,620	29.82
Al Sharpton	28,495	9.70
Wesley Clark	21,218	7.22
Howard Dean	13,984	4.76
Joe Lieberman	7,101	2.42
Dennis Kucinich	1,344	0.46
Richard Gephardt	828	0.28
Carol Mosley-Braun	593	0.20
TOTAL	**292,843**	

Source: Cook 2007

January 19, 2008

Republican Primary	Vote Total	Percent
John McCain	147,733	33.15
Mike Huckabee	132,990	29.84
Fred Thompson	69,681	15.63
Mitt Romney	68,177	15.30
Ron Paul	16,155	3.62
Rudy Giuliani	9,575	2.15
Duncan Hunter	1,051	0.24
Tom Tancredo	121	0.03
Hugh Cort	88	0.02
John Cox	83	0.02
H. Neal Cap Fendig Jr.	23	0.01
TOTAL	445,677	

Source: uselectionatlas.org/RESULTS

January 26, 2008

Democratic Primary	Vote Total	Percent
Barack Obama	294,898	55.42
Hillary Clinton	140,990	26.49
John Edwards	93,801	17.63
Bill Richardson	726	0.14
Joe Biden	693	0.13
Dennis Kucinich	551	0.10
Chris Dodd	247	0.05
Mike Gravel	245	0.05
TOTAL	532,151	

Source: uselectionatlas.org/RESULTS

January 21, 2012

Republican Primary	Vote Total	Percent
Newt Gingrich	244,065	40.42
Mitt Romney	168,123	27.85
Rick Santorum	102,475	16.97
Ron Paul	78,360	12.98
Herman Cain	6,338	1.05
Rick Perry	2,534	0.42
Jon Huntsman	1,173	0.19
Michele Bachmann	491	0.08
Gary Johnson	211	0.03
TOTAL	**603,770**	

Source: uselectionatlas.org/RESULTS

February 20, 2016

Republican Primary	Vote Total	Percent
Donald Trump	240,882	32.39
Marco Rubio	166,565	22.40
Ted Cruz	165,417	22.24
Jeb Bush	58,056	7.81
John Kasich	56,410	7.59
Ben Carson	53,551	7.20
Rand Paul	929	0.12
Chris Christie	699	0.09
Mike Huckabee	497	0.07
Carly Fiorina	412	0.06
Rick Santorum	200	0.03
Jim Gilmore	49	0.01
TOTAL	**743,667**	

Source: uselectionatlas.org/RESULTS

February 27, 2016

Democratic Primary	Vote Total	Percent
Hillary Clinton	270,810	73.47
Bernie Sanders	95,737	25.97
Willie Wilson	1,317	0.36
Martin O'Malley	713	0.19
TOTAL	**368,577**	

Source: uselectionatlas.org/RESULTS

APPENDIX B

Methodological Approach

In chapters 3 and 4, we present a series of findings that stem from statistical analyses of various data sources. In the body of the chapters, we discuss the basic features of each analysis and make multiple references to additional information in this appendix. Here we present this additional information by chapter and section.

Chapter 3

Calculating a State's Predictive Accuracy

In the body of chapter 3, we note two models that examine a state's predictive ability in a nomination contest in light of its competitiveness and representativeness. Table B1 describes those models. Because the dependent variable is dichotomous—coded 1 for states that correctly selected the winner in a given year and 0 for states that chose incorrectly—the model was estimated via multilevel mixed-effects logistic regression that includes both year and party random intercepts (see also Kaufmann, Gimpel, and Hoffmann 2003). In plain English, this approach helps account for the considerable variation in the fifty states' ability to correctly select the winner due to a wide array of party- and year-specific factors.

Our competitiveness index combines into a single additive scale the two measures described in the body of the chapter (the number of days remaining on the calendar and the number of viable candidates still in the race). To create this scale, we first standardized the two variables so that they would have a common mean and standard deviation and then added them together into a single index. Higher values therefore indicate states with more days left on the calendar, more competitive candidates remaining in the race, or some combination of the two. Cronbach's alpha for these two variables is 0.75, which is generally considered acceptable for combining items into an index.

Our main finding in model 1 is the significant negative effect of the competitiveness variable, which reveals that competitive states have a lower likelihood of correctly selecting the winner, as we hypothesized. Our main finding in model 2 is the significant and positive effect of the representativeness variable, which reveals that representative states have a higher likelihood of correctly selecting the winner, also as we hypothesized. In the model we compute the inverse of a state's democratic and attitudinal deviation so that higher values indicate states that are more representative and lower values states that are less representative.

Table B1: State Predictive Accuracy in Nomination Contests (1980–2016)

Main Variables	Model 1 Coefficient	SE	Model 2 Coefficient	SE
Competitiveness	-0.83***	(0.17)	-0.78***	(0.18)
Representativeness	-	-	0.19**	(0.09)
Constant	1.15***	(0.29)	1.28***	(0.33)
Year/Party Variance	0.63***	(0.21)	0.80**	(0.34)
Observations	615		475	

Robust standard errors in parentheses
*** p<0.01, ** p<0.05, * p<0.1

Calculating a State's Demographic Representativeness

For the demographic items in our dataset, the National Election Pool (NEP) questions are usually the same across years and states, with only minor variation. On both sides of the aisle, items ask a respondent's sex, race, age, education, and income. We therefore have state-by-state data on the percentage of males to females, the ratio of whites to blacks, a six-category age range, the percentage of college graduates, and a four-category income range.[1] Because the NEP tailored its religion question to each party's base, for Republicans we use the percent of Christians who identify as born again and for Democrats we use the percentage of voters with who declare they have no religious affiliation. Lastly, given the importance of veterans in GOP contests, we include data on the percent of Republican voters who served in the military.

For the attitudinal items, our first predictor comes from a question that asks the direction and strength of a voter's ideology.[2] In Democratic contests, the scale ranges from very liberal to conservative, and in Republican contests, the scale ranges from very conservative to liberal. We also include three items that measure the importance of various policy issues. We have two items that apply to both parties: the economy and world affairs. On the Republican side, we include a third item that is the percentage of voters concerned about abortion, while on the Democratic side our third item is the percentage of voters who are concerned about health care.

In chapter 3, we note the creation of a measure that tells us how far a state deviates from the national average on a specific demographic indicator. Statistically, our measure is a z-score, which tells us how many standard deviations a state is from the national mean on that item. We compute the absolute value so that positive deviations (for example, too many white voters) do not cancel out negative deviations (for example, too few women) and make a state appear representative in the aggregate. Larger z-scores therefore indicate how far a state deviates from the national mean while a z-score of exactly 0 indicates a perfectly representative state. The z-score formula appears below.

$$\text{State Absolute Standard Deviation} = \left| \frac{(\text{State Mean-National Mean})}{\text{Standard Deviation of State Means}} \right|$$

Chapter 4

Election Outcomes Analysis

In chapter 4, we discuss a model used to predict which candidates perform well in South Carolina's contests. In the analysis we go back to 1988, rather than 1980, because a number of the factors we use to predict a candidate's performance are not available to us prior to this contest. We focus on contested elections, defined as those where the incumbent president was not on the ballot, giving us a total of six Democratic contests (1988, 1992, 2000, 2004, 2008, 2016) and six Republican contests (1988, 1996, 2000, 2008, 2012, 2016).

In the model in table B2, the dependent variable we use is a candidate's vote percentage. Because the response is bound between zero and one, we follow the recommendation to use a fractional logit model to estimate the results (Baum 2008; Papke and Woolridge 1996). In the model, a positive coefficient indicates that the factor increases a candidate's vote share while a negative coefficient indicates that the factor decreases a candidate's vote share.

We have sixteen variables in the model. Additional discussion can be found in the body of the chapter. *Competitive* is the number of a rival candidates who won 10 percent or more of the vote in Iowa and New Hampshire, and *New Hampshire Vote %* and *Iowa Vote %* is the candidate's vote share in these two states. Because the relationship between New Hampshire, Iowa, and South Carolina likely depends on party, we interact these two variables with a measure of which party's contest the candidate is running in labeled *GOP*. *Previous Vote* is a variable for a candidate's prior vote share in a South Carolina primary or caucus. *Media Attention* is the volume of a candidate's local and national media coverage in the week prior to the election. *Endorsements* catalogues the volume of endorsements a candidate has received from South Carolina officials. *Campaign Receipts* is our measure of fund-raising by a candidate's campaign. Lastly, we have five candidate characteristics that are described in detail in the chapter: *Southern, Neighboring State, Black Democrat, Evangelical,* and *Quality*.[3]

In the analysis, we tested whether any of the candidate characteristics interact with party affiliation, which would be an indication that the characteristic in question matters more in one party's contest, and found that none do. Given that there is not enough variation among the black Republican candidates, we are unable to interact it with party affiliation like as we can for the other variables.[4] For this reason, the race variable tests just the effect of being a black candidate in Democratic contests.

In the column labeled "Effect Size" we report the marginal effect (dy/dx) of the significant covariates in the model. We report these estimates in the body of chapter 4 as well. For variables on a continuous scale, we computed these effects by standardizing the variables. In other words, the effect size column reports the estimated increase or decrease in a candidate's vote share for a one standard deviation increase in the variable above its mean. For variables on a dichotomous scale, we computed a discrete change (0 → 1). For example, the effect of the neighboring state variable is the estimated increase in a candidate's vote share if they are from Georgia or North Carolina (coded one) as opposed to any other state (coded zero). As we explain in the body of chapter 4, placing the significant factors on a common scale allows us to estimate to what extent they matter relative to one another.

Table B2 contains the statistical results. According to the analysis, our model performs very well, explaining 82 percent of the variation in the candidates' vote share in South Carolina contests from 1988 to 2016.

Table B2: Candidate Vote Share in South Carolina Nomination Contests (1988–2016)

	Coefficient	SE	Effect Size
Competitive Contests	-0.28**	(0.14)	-3.4%
GOP	-0.16	(0.50)	
Iowa %	-0.55	(1.36)	-1.1% (D)
GOP * Iowa %	5.51***	(1.43)	16.0% (R)
New Hampshire %	3.44***	(1.29)	6.3% (D)
GOP * New Hampshire %	-1.26	(1.33)	6.4% (R)
Previous Vote	0.15	(1.20)	
Media Attention	8.13***	(1.98)	5.9%
Campaign Receipts	-1.47	(0.94)	
Endorsements	0.56***	(0.18)	4.7%
Southern Candidate	0.71***	(0.83)	7.5%
Neighboring State Candidate	1.36***	(0.74)	14.4%
Black Democrat Candidate	1.86***	(0.26)	19.7%
Evangelical Candidate	0.12	(0.59)	
Quality Candidate	-0.16	(0.28)	
Constant	-2.80***	(0.57)	
Observations	63		
R2	0.82		

Robust standard errors in parentheses

*** p<0.01, ** p<0.05, * p<0.1

NOTES

CHAPTER 1: Why South Carolina?

1. For further details on the history of nominating contests, see Kamarck 2009, Norrander 2010, and Steger 2015.

2. Though voters in Oklahoma, Kentucky, and West Virginia have been called "southern" in the past, we follow the lead of V. O. Key Jr. (1949) by defining the South as the eleven states of the old Confederacy (Alabama, Arkansas, Florida, Georgia, Louisiana, Mississippi North Carolina, South Carolina, Tennessee, Texas, and Virginia).

3. See uselectionatlas.org/RESULTS.

4. The original Super Tuesday took place in 1988, though talk of southern states holding primaries on the same day can be traced back to at least 1975 (Moreland and Steed 2012; Norrander 1992). Super Tuesday was created to counteract the trend of nominating liberal candidates who fared poorly in the general election (Norrander 1992).

5. We base this on GOP primaries held in 1980, 1988, 1996, 2000, 2008, 2012, and 2016. As we note in chapter 3, for analytical reasons we do not include Bush's 1992 victory in our analysis of the state's predictive ability.

6. We base this on Democratic caucuses and primaries held in 1984, 1988, 1992, 2004, 2008 and 2016. As we note in chapter 3, for analytical reasons we do not include Carter's 1980 victory or Gore's 2000 win in our analysis of the state's predictive accuracy.

7. See www.ncsl.org/documents/Elections/Primary_Types_Table_2017.pdf.

8. The lone exception is 1992, when both parties scheduled the primary on Saturday, March 7.

9. See uselectionatlas.org/RESULTS and https://www.cnn.com/election/2016/primaries/polls/sc/Dem

10. See abstract.sc.gov/index.html.

11. See uselectionatlas.org/RESULTS.

12. For this we used Google's trends tool, which allows users to search for newspaper articles by keyword. We searched for news articles that mentioned "primary" and either "New Hampshire" or "South Carolina" or the word "caucus" and "Iowa." A value of one hundred represents the maximum traffic, and every other value is the volume of news articles relative to that peak. For example, a value of fifty represents half the volume of news articles.

CHAPTER 2: Becoming First in the South

1. See www.scstatehouse.gov/member.php?chamber=H&session=103.

2. In this chapter the story of the birth of the South Carolina primary is told through the voices of the political leaders who fought to create and maintain the state's first-in-the-South status. We draw extensively on the South Carolina Political Collection's archives at the University of South Carolina, including the Republican Party of South Carolina Papers and the Democratic Party of South Carolina Records. The archives include a number of excellent primary sources such as personal papers, correspondence, and internal party memorandums. We also rely on press accounts from South Carolina's political reporters and insights from many of the state's leading political scientists.

3. See also uselectionatlas.org/RESULTS.

CHAPTER 3: South Carolina's Primary Electorate

1. As noted in chapter 1, we do not include 1992 in this calculation. While President George H. W. Bush received a primary challenge from Pat Buchanan and David Duke, Bush won all contests.

2. As noted in chapter 1, we do not include the results of the 1980 contest, since there was an incumbent president running for reelection. In addition, we do not include the results from the 2000 Democratic contest, since Gore won every state. Throughout this chapter, when we discuss a state's predictive ability on the Democratic side, we exclude the 2000 result.

3. See factfinder.census.gov/faces/nav/jsf/pages/index.xhtml.

4. factfinder.census.gov/faces/nav/jsf/pages/index.xhtml.

5. A National Public Radio piece by Asma Khalid (2016) attempts to quantify the "perfect state" in nomination contests using census data aggregated at the state level. Although the analysis is well done, an obvious limitation is that the data are not granular enough to pick out primary voters and variation by party within a state. On the second point, we have shown that some states—like South Carolina—can be highly representative of one party but not the other. Likewise, a piece by Nate Silver (2016) on the FiveThirtyEight.com website examines state-by-state racial disparities in Democratic contests. Although a solid analysis, the analysis is limited given that it only examines race and only examines Democrats.

6. All data used in this section came from a variety of sources: Rhodes Cook (2000, 2007), the Real Clear Politics website, the Federal Election Commission website, David Leip's Atlas of Presidential Elections, the FrontLoading HQ blog, and various newspapers including the *New York Times* and the *Washington Post*. In this thirty-six year period, we have seven Republican (1980, 1988, 1996, 2000, 2008, 2012, and 2016) and six Democratic (1984, 1988, 1992, 2004, 2008, and 2016) contests. All contests in South Carolina were primaries, except for Democratic caucuses in 1984 and 1988, which we include to create a common comparison with every other state.

7. Correct predictions were coded one and incorrect predictions were coded zero.

8. We considered candidates competitive if they received at least 1 percent of the vote in the first state on the calendar. We then identified the date these candidates suspended their campaign.

9. Iowa's performance is statistically normal given that its actual success rate is within the confidence interval of the estimated success rate.

10. Both New Hampshire and South Carolina's overperformance estimates are statistically significant given the confidence interval.

11. The model predicts all three states will correctly select the winner in Democratic contests more often than they will in Republican contests. According to the data, this is due to the fact that Democrats have had fewer candidates vying for their party's nomination since 1980. For example, the data we collected indicate that in Republican contests since 1980, an average of 4.9 candidates were still in the campaign by the date of the South Carolina primary. In Democratic contests since 1992, by comparison, an average of 3.0 candidates remained in the campaign by date of the South Carolina primary.

12. On the Republican side, this includes 2000, 2008, 2012, and 2016, and for Democrats, this includes 2000, 2004, 2008, and 2016.

13. We did this by simply averaging each item by state and then creating a population weighted average. Ideally, we would just average all responses, but unfortunately, we cannot do that in this case because some questions were asked of only half the NEP respondents. While larger states naturally have a greater effect on the profile of the typical Republican primary voter, the approach we used is consistent with the fact that big states have more delegates and thus greater influence on which candidate ultimately wins the nomination contest.

14. Because the NEP questions are on different scales (percentages, ranges, Likert scales) and have difference variances, we compute each state's absolute standard deviation from the national average.

15. For each state's mean deviation, we computed 95 percent confidence intervals as an estimate of variability. In other words, the estimate will fall within this interval ninety-five times out of a hundred.

16. The mean indicator for South Carolina is 0.5 standard deviations away from the national average. By comparison, both Iowa and New Hampshire have mean deviations around 1.0.

17. We do not have useable data on veteran primary voters in Iowa. While a veteran question was asked in 2000, that question asked whether a member of the voter's household ever served in the military. Veteran questions in all other states asked about the individual voter's military service. Needless to say, such a measure, if included with the others, would artificially inflate Iowa's deviation.

18. See factfinder.census.gov/faces/nav/jsf/pages/index.xhtml.

19. See demographics.coopercenter.org/national-population-projections.

20. See www.scvotes.org/election-results.

CHAPTER 4: Winners and Losers of the South Carolina Primary

1. See the October issue in election years of the American Political Science Association's journal *PS: Political Science and Politics*.

2. For this variable, we simply counted the number rival candidates who won 10 percent of the vote in both Iowa and New Hampshire. Higher values thus indicate that there were more competitive candidates and lower values indicate that there were fewer competitive candidates.

3. We compiled the endorsement data from the *Post and Courier* archives. An endorsement from South Carolina's governor counts as 1, that from a United States senator

as 0.5, that from a United States representative as 0.25, and that from a state legisla-tor's endorsement as 0.10. Additional endorsements identified in our search such as from the governor of another state or a former South Carolina politician count as 0.10.

4. Our state news source is the *Post and Courier,* and our national one is the *New York Times.* At the time these data were collected, the only South Carolina newspaper we could access for a sufficient time was the *Post and Courier.* For both newspapers we simply count the number of stories mentioning the candidate by name and then com-pute the percentage of the stories mentioning the candidate relative to the number mentioning any candidate. Our index simply multiplies percentage in both news-papers.

5. We are unable to measure a candidate's expenditures per se, though Federal Election Commission data records the amount of fund-raising by a candidate, which no doubt correlates with expenditures. Because of commission requirements for reporting fund-raising, we use a candidate's total campaign receipts on the December 31 filing deadline the year before the South Carolina primary. We admit that this is an imper-fect variable but believe it is the best option given the scope of our data.

6. In the analysis, we tested two ways of defining southern candidates: first, a Deep South variable, and second, a former Confederate states variable. We found that Deep South candidates—from Alabama, Georgia, Louisiana, Mississippi, and South Carolina—do not perform any better or worse in South Carolina. We note that this result is con-sistent with our earlier research (Craven, Ragusa, and Thevos 2017). However, in the revised analysis reported in this chapter, we do find that candidates from the eleven former Confederate states perform better in South Carolina. For this reason, here we report the results from the analysis using the former Confederate states variable.

7. As we explain in appendix B, we compute the effect sizes in table 4.1 using a standard deviation increase above the mean of that variable. For example, a candidate who does well in Iowa is one who earns 34 percent of the vote, while for New Hampshire it is 33 percent of the vote. Doing this allows us to place each of the continuous variables on a common scale and compare them to one another. For the dichotomous variables, the effect size is computed to measure discrete change in the variable.

8. As before, we use a standard deviation increase above the mean for all candidates as what constitutes large quantities for these two variables.

9. See factfinder.census.gov/faces/nav/jsf/pages/index.xhtml and https://www.cnn.com/election/2016/primaries/polls/sc/Dem.

10. Sharpton did have his best performance in the District of Columbia, however.

CHAPTER 5: Lessons from Key GOP Contests

1. In a low turnout affair with less than ten thousand votes cast, Al Gore won the March 9 Democratic caucuses, amassing 91.8 percent of the vote (uselectionatlas.org/RESULTS).

2. See uselectionatlas.org/RESULTS.

3. uselectionatlas.org/RESULTS.

4. uselectionatlas.org/RESULTS.

5. uselectionatlas.org/RESULTS.

6. See http://www.cnn.com/election/2012/primaries/epolls/sc/.

7. See http://www.cnn.com/election/2012/primaries/epolls/sc/.

8. uselectionatlas.org/RESULTS.

9. It is important to view the debate bounce claim with some caution, however. Evidence from the Clemson University's Palmetto Poll indicates that Gingrich had a lead in December 2011, the month before the CNN debate.

10. uselectionatlas.org/RESULTS.

11. In 1996, there were three candidates from the South vying for the GOP nomination in South Carolina as well. However, the field of candidates was larger as a whole. In 2016, exactly half of the candidates on the ballot were from the South, compared to 37.5 percent in 1996.

12. uselectionatlas.org/RESULTS.

13. uselectionatlas.org/RESULTS.

Chapter 6: Lessons from Key Democratic Contests

1. uselectionatlas.org/RESULTS.

2. uselectionatlas.org/RESULTS.

3. See http://www.cnn.com/ELECTION/2004/primaries/pages/epolls/SC/.

4. See http://www.cnn.com/ELECTION/2004/primaries/pages/epolls/SC/.

5. uselectionatlas.org/RESULTS.

6. uselectionatlas.org/RESULTS.

7. See http://www.cnn.com/ELECTION/2008/primaries/results/epolls/#SCDEM.

8. See http://www.cnn.com/ELECTION/2008/primaries/results/epolls/#SCDEM.

9. See http://www.cnn.com/ELECTION/2008/primaries/results/epolls/#SCDEM.

10. uselectionatlas.org/RESULTS.

11. uselectionatlas.org/RESULTS.

12. uselectionatlas.org/RESULTS.

13. See https://www.cnn.com/election/2016/primaries/polls/sc/Dem.

14. See https://www.cnn.com/election/2016/primaries/polls/sc/Dem.

15. uselectionatlas.org/RESULTS.

CHAPTER 7: The Case for the South Carolina Primary

1. See also www.electproject.org/2016P. Although voter turnout is low in Iowa, usually around 15 percent, it is far higher than in most states that hold caucuses. Likewise, turnout in New Hampshire is typically greater than 50 percent in its primaries, higher than general election turnout in some states.

2. See factfinder.census.gov/faces/nav/jsf/pages/index.xhtml.

3. See www.nielsen.com/content/dam/corporate/us/en/public%20factsheets/tv/2018–19-dma-ranker.pdf.

4. See www.ncsl.org/documents/Elections/Primary_Types_Table_2017.pdf.

5. See www.scvotes.org/election-results.

Appendix B: Methodological Appendix

1. A category of Hispanic/Latino was not used consistently enough with the race question for us to examine. Likewise, the inconsistent use of an "other" category prevents us from creating a "white/nonwhite" index.

2. On the attitudinal items as a whole, we face a series of challenges in that the NEP questions exhibit substantial variability across states and years. In some cases, the questions were asked consistently, but the response options varied. In other cases, different questions were asked entirely. In the former instance, we combined response options to establish a common scale. In the latter, we used questions that were closely related.

3. We identified evangelical candidates based on their stated denomination: Baptist (Southern Baptist, Independent Baptist, National Baptist Convention), Evangelical Methodist, Evangelical Lutheran, Assemblies of God, Church of God.

4. For example, every black Republican who ran in South Carolina is also classified as nonevangelical, which introduces collinearity into the model.

REFERENCES

Abramowitz, Alan I. 1988. "An Improved Model for Predicting Presidential Outcomes." *PS: Political Science and Politics* 21 (4): 843–47.

Abramowitz, Alan I. 1989. "Viability, Electability, and Candidate Choice in Presidential Primary Elections: A Test of Competing Models." *Journal of Politics* 52 (4): 977–92.

Abramowitz, Alan I. 2012. "Forecasting in a Polarized Era: The Time for a Change Model in the 2012 Presidential Election." *PS: Political Science and Politics* 45 (4): 618–19.

Adams, Jerry. 1979. "Ross Hits at Fowler, Pushes GOP Primary Plan." *News and Courier,* December 12, 6B.

Adkins, Randall E., and Andrew J. Dowdle. 2000. "Break Out the Mint Juleps? Is New Hampshire the 'Primary' Culprit Limiting Presidential Nomination Forecasts?" *American Politics Quarterly* 28 (2): 251–69.

Adkins, Randall E., and Andrew J. Dowdle. 2001. "How Important Are Iowa and New Hampshire to Winning Post-Reform Presidential Nominations?" *Political Research Quarterly* 54 (2): 431–44.

Aldrich, John H., and Michael Alvarez. 1994. "Issues and the Presidential Primary Voter." *Political Behavior* 16 (3): 289–317.

Allen, Jonathan. 2016. "Clinton Owes Her Commanding Lead to African American Women." *Roll Call,* March 16. www.rollcall.com/news/opinion/clinton-owes-her -commanding-lead-to-african-american-women.

Altschuler, Bruce E. 2008. "Selecting Presidential Nominees by National Primary: An Idea Whose Time Has Come?" *Forum* 5 (4): article 5.

Apple, R.W., Jr. 1988. "South Carolina Votes Today in Test of Bush's Momentum." *New York Times,* March 4, section 1, page 8.

Applebome, Peter. 1992. "The 'Bubba' Stereotype Is Vanishing as a Region Becomes More Moderate." *New York Times,* February 29, section 1, page 22.

Archibold, Randall C. 2004. "Playing to a Home Crow, Edwards Sticks to a Basic Pitch." *New York Times,* January 30, A19.

Associated Press. 1979a. "Democrat Questions GOP Primary Plans." *News and Courier,* October 24, 8B.

Associated Press. 1979b. "GOP Expected to OK Primary." *News and Courier,* October 13, 10B.

Associated Press. 1979c. "S.C. GOP Panel Adopts Primary Proposal." *News and Courier,* August 31, 13C.

Associated Press. 1979d. "S.C. Primary: Crane, Bush Interested." *News and Courier,* September 1, 1B and 12B.

Associated Press. 1979e. "S.C. Primary Favored at GOP Panel Hearing." *News and Courier,* August 10, 10C.

Associated Press. 1979f. "S.C. Republicans Set March Primary." *News and Courier,* October 14, 1A and 14A.

Associated Press. 1988. "Dole, Kemp Woo S.C. Voters Today." *State,* February 24, 1A.

Associated Press. 1991. "Georgia May Beat S.C. to '92 Primary." *State,* November 24, 10B.

Associated Press. 1992. "Georgia Votes to Move Primary up to March 3 Date, Preempts Southern States." *State,* January 16, 3A.

Associated Press. 2004. "Kerry, Edwards Ramp Up TV Ads." *State,* January 31, A10.

Associated Press. 2011. "S.C. High Court Upholds Presidential Primary." *State,* November 23, Business, 14.

Ayers, B. Drummond, Jr., 1992. "Wilder Ends Bid for Presidency, Citing Virginia's Fiscal Troubles." *New York Times,* January 9, section 1, page 1.

Ayers, B. Drummond, and Frank Bruni. 2000. "Candidates Say Crossover Voters Hold Key on Saturday." *New York Times,* February 14, A22.

"The Bad Outweighs the Good." 1980. *News and Courier,* September 11, 12A.

Balz, Dan. 2008. "Edwards Will Face a Moment of Truth after South Carolina Primary." *Washington Post,* January 12, A8.

Balz, Dan. 2012. "A Last-Minute Embrace of Santorum." *Washington Post,* January 15, A2.

Balz, Dan. 2013. *Collision 2012: Obama vs. Romney and the Future of Elections in America.* New York: Viking.

Bandy, Lee, 1987. "Jackson Prompts Primary Challenge." *State,* July 26, 4B.

Bandy, Lee. 1988a. "Robertson Looks for Win in S.C. to Keep Presidential Hopes Alive." *State,* March 4, 2C.

Bandy, Lee. 1988b. "Robertson Says Story Planted—Bush Blamed for Releasing Swaggart Report." *State,* February 24, 1A.

Bandy, Lee. 1992a. "The Candidates Have Georgia on Their Minds." *State,* March 1, 1A.

Bandy, Lee. 1992b. "Georgia Beats S.C. into Primary Season." *State,* February 16, 5B.

Bandy, Lee. 1992c. "Harkin Laying It All on Line in S.C." *State,* March 1, 4C.

Bandy, Lee. 1992d. "Tsongas Isn't Betting on Southern Wins." *State,* March 5, 15A.

Bandy, Lee. 1995. "S.C. Not Fretting Louisiana GOP's Leapfrog Caucus." *State,* December 17, D4.

Bandy, Lee. 1999a. "Date for Primary Debated—S.C. Democrats Rethink When to Make Presidential Selection." *State,* May 2, B1.

Bandy, Lee. 1999b. "Democrats Move Up Presidential Primary." *State,* June 16, B1.

Bandy, Lee. 1999c. "For Democrats, It's a Big Weekend—Annual Convention Set at Township Saturday." *State,* April 30, B2.

Bandy, Lee. 1999d. "S.C. Democrats Vote to Hold Primary in February 2000." *State,* April 15, A1.

Bandy, Lee. 1999e. "S.C. GOP Moving to Keep Its Primary First in South." *State,* February 26, B1.

Bandy, Lee. 2000a. "Campbell & Co. Won—Now They Must Heal." *State,* February 20, A1.

Bandy, Lee. 2000b. "Christians Could Be Bush's S.C. Salvation." *State,* February 13, D1.

Bandy, Lee. 2000c. "Complaint Threatens 2 Primaries." *State,* January 14, B1.

Bandy, Lee. 2000d. "Despite Suit, GOP Plans Primary." *State,* January 28, B1.

Bandy, Lee. 2000e. "Forbes Exits—Bush Scooping Up Rival's S.C. Troops." *State,* February 10, A1.

Bandy, Lee. 2000f. "It's South Carolina's Day—400,000 Voters Might Turn Out Today in a Frenzied Primary That's Already Made Political History in South Carolina." *State,* February 19, A1.

Bandy, Lee. 2000g. "McCain Faces Uphill Battle in S.C. Primary." *State,* February 2, A1.

Bandy, Lee. 2000h. "McCain's Poll Vault Erases Bush's South Carolina Edge." *State,* February 4, A1.

Bandy, Lee. 2002. "S.C. Democrats to Hold Primary Feb. 3, 2004." *State,* February 14, B3.

Bandy, Lee. 2003a. "Democrats Fired Up to Fight GOP." *State,* May 4, A10.

Bandy, Lee. 2003b. "S.C. Democrats Launch Run for the White House." *State,* May 2, A1.

Bandy, Lee. 2004. "S.C. No Longer Big Prize for Democrats." *State,* January 30, A13.

Bandy, Lee. 2006a. "Democrats Hope to Keep Early Primary." *State,* April 16, B1.

Bandy, Lee. 2006b. "2 S.C. Presidential Primaries Now Likely." *State,* December 17, B3.

Bandy, Lee, and Jeff Stensland. 2000a. "Poll Puts Bush, McCain in a Dead Heat for S.C.—Bauer Endorses Arizona Senator as GOP Rivals Enter Last Days of Frantic State Campaign." *State,* February 17, A14.

Bandy, Lee, and Jeff Stensland. 2000b. "Presidential Rivals Race into S.C.—New Hampshire Victory Lifts McCain, but Bush Still Leads in Palmetto Polls." *State,* February 3, A1.

Banks, Ann. 2008. "Dirty Tricks, South Carolina and John McCain." *Nation,* January 14. www.thenation.com/article/dirty-tricks-south-Carolina-and-john-mccain.

Barr, Andy. 2010. "Rove Denies Role in McCain Rumor." *Politico,* March 8. www.politico.com/story/2010/03/rove-denies-role-in-mccain-rumor-034075.

Bartels, Larry M. 1988. *Presidential Primaries and the Dynamics of Public Choice.* Princeton, NJ: Princeton University Press.

Bauerlein, Valerie. 2004. "How Edwards Made S.C. Believe." *State,* February 8, A1.

Baum, Christopher F. 2008. "Stata Tip 63: Modeling Proportions" *Stata Journal* 8 (2): 299–303.

Bawn, Kathleen, Marti Cohen, David Karol, Seth Masket, Hans Noel, and John Zaller. 2012. "A Theory of Political Parties: Groups, Policy Demands and Nominations in American Politics." *Perspectives on Politics* 10 (3): 571–97.

Beam, Adam. 2011. "Who Should Pay for State GOP Primary?" *State,* November 15, Front Page, 1.

Beam, Adam. 2012a. "Can Iowa Strategy Win S.C." *State,* January 5, Front Page, 1.

Beam, Adam. 2012b. "Gingrich Routs Romney." *State,* January 22, Front Page, 1.

Beam, Adam. 2012c. "$11.3 Million Spent on TV Ads – S.C. GOP Primary." *State,* January 14, Front Page, 1.

Beam, Adam. 2012d. "Romney Defends Record at Bain." *State,* June 15, Nation and World, 11.

Beam, Adam. 2012e. "Romney, Gingrich Spar, Take It on Chin." *State,* January 20, Front Page, 1.

Beam, Adam. 2012f. "Whose Army Will S.C. Vets Join?" *State,* January 19, Nation and World, 9.

Beam, Adam, Gina Smith, and Noelle Phillips. 2012. "Candidates Pitch Economy, Values." *State,* January 12, Nation and World, 5.

Behre, Robert. 2008. "McCain Wins—Senator Scores Crucial Victory in Bid for Nomination." *Post and Courier,* January 20, A1.

Berke, Richard L. 2000. "South Carolina: Bush Intensifies His Push Again." *New York Times,* February 12, section 1, page 1.

Black, Earl, and Merle Black. 1987. *Politics and Society in the South.* Cambridge, MA: Harvard University Press.

Black, Earl, and Merle Black. 1992. *The Vital South: How Presidents Are Elected.* Cambridge, MA: Harvard University Press.

Black, Earl, and Merle Black. 2002. *The Rise of Southern Republicans.* Cambridge, MA: Harvard University Press.

Booker, Brakkton, and Domenico Montanaro. 2016. "5 Things You Should Know before the New Hampshire Primary." NPR, February 5. www.npr.org/2016/02/05/465652879/5 -things-you-should-know-before-the-new-hampshire-primary.

Bosman, Julie. 2008. "After His Loss in Nevada, Edwards Keeps Marching." *New York Times,* January 21, A12.

Bowerman, Mary. 2017. "The Census Bureau Shows the Fastest-Growing Cities in the U.S. Are . . ." *USA Today,* May 25. www.usatoday.com/story/money/nation-now/2017 /05/25/census-bureau-shows-fastest-growing-cities-u-s/344945001.

Bowers, Paul. 2016. "Chelsea Clinton Stumps for Hillary at College of Charleston." *Post and Courier,* February 25. www.postandcourier.com/archives/chelsea-clinton-stumps -for-hillary-at-college-of-charleston/article_9a3a4907–0d79–5cf1-bdf4–70e4611a4 bf6.html.

Boyd, Robert S. 1988. "S.C. Voters to Pull 'Trigger'—Polls, Experts Say the Vice President Will Win Primary." *State,* March 5, 1A.

Broder, David S., and Mike Allen. 2000. "Bush Cites Regret on Bob Jones." *Washington Post,* February 28, A1.

Broder, David S., and Dan Balz. 2000. "Bush and McCain Clash." *Washington Post,* February 16, A1.

Brook, Nina, and Lisa Greene. 1992. "Clinton Predicting Big S.C. Win Saturday." *State,* March 5, 15A.

Bruni, Frank. 2000. "Bush and McCain, Sittin' in a Tree, D-I-S-S-I-N-G." *New York Times,* February 8, A20.

Bryant, Bobby. 1988. "Caucuses Lose Favor with Party." *State,* March 13, 1A.

Buell, Emmett H., Jr. 1987. "First-in-the-Nation: Disputes over the Timing of Early Democratic Presidential Primaries and Caucuses in 1984 and 1988." *Journal of Law and Politics,* 4 (2): 317–39.

Buell, Emmet H., Jr. 2004. "Back to the Future? Proposals for Change." In *Enduring Controversies in Presidential Nominating Politics,* edited by Emmett H. Buell and William G. Mayer, 253–64). Pittsburgh, PA: University of Pittsburgh Press.

Bullock, Charles S., III. 1994. "Nomination: The South's Role in 1992 Nomination Politics." In *The 1992 Presidential Election in the South: Current Patterns of Southern Party and Electoral Politics,* edited by Robert P. Steed, Laurence W. Moreland, and Tod A. Baker, 9–24. Westport, CT: Praeger.

Bumiller, Elisabeth. 2008. "McCain Parries a Reprise of '00 Smear Tactics." *New York Times,* January 17, A1.

Burns, Alexander, and Patrick Healy. 2016. "James Clyburn, Leading Black Politician in South Carolina, Will Endorse Hilary Clinton." *New York Times* blog, February 18. www .nytimes.com/politics/first-draft/2016/02/18/james-clyburn-leading-black-politician -in-south-Carolina-will-endorse-hillary-clinton.

Burns, Alexander, and Jonathan Martin. 2016. "Parallel Battles as the G.O.P. Travels South." *New York Times,* February 11, A1.

Burriss, Moffatt. 1980. "A Rare Opportunity for the South Carolina Republican Party in 1980." Unpublished manuscript. Republican Party of South Carolina Papers, South Carolina Political Collections, the University of South Carolina.

Byers, Dylan. 2012. "The John King–Newt Gingrich debate." *Politico,* January 20. www .politico.com/blogs/media/2012/01/the-john-king-newt-gingrich-debate-111596.

Cannon, Carl M. 1992. "Democrats Change Stance—On Crime and Punishment." *State,* March 1, 11C.

Carroll, Chuck. 2000. "Keyes Hoping to Seize S.C. Opportunities, GOP Presidential Can- didate Courting African Americans, Crossover Voters." *State,* February 5, A1.

Chozick, Amy. 2016. "Clinton and Sanders Turn Focus to South Carolina, Courting Black Voters." *New York Times,* January 17, A26.

Christian Broadcasting Network. 2018. "Pat Robertson." www1.cbn.com/700club/pat -robertson.

Clark. John A. 2009. "The 2008 Presidential Nomination Process." In *A Paler Shade of Red: The 2008 Presidential Election in the South,* edited by Branwell DuBose Kapeluck, Laurence W. Moreland, and Robert P. Steed, 17–31. Fayetteville: University of Arkan- sas Press.

Clark. John A. 2014. "The 2012 Presidential Nomination Process." In *Second Verse, Same as the First: The 2012 Presidential Election in the South,* edited by Scott E. Buchanan and Branwell DuBose Kapeluck, 21–36. Fayetteville: University of Arkansas Press.

Clark, John A., and Audrey A. Haynes. 2002. "The 2000 Nomination Process." In *The 2000 Presidential Election in the South Partisanship and Southern Party Systems in the 21st Century,* edited by Robert P. Steed and Laurence W. Moreland, 23–36. Westport, CT: Praeger.

Clark, Lesley, and Anita Kumar. 2016. "Clinton, Sanders Call Out Legacy of Racism in America." *State,* February 24, Nation and World, 1.

Clements, Mike. 1979. "S.C. GOP Approves Primary." *State,* October 14, 1A and 12A.

Clyburn, James E. 2014. *Blessed Experiences: Genuinely Southern, Proudly Black.* Colum- bia: The University of South Carolina Press.

Cobb, James C. 2005. *Away Down South: A History of Southern Identity.* New York: Oxford University Press.

Cohen, Marty, David Karol, Hans Noel, and John Zaller. 2008. *The Party Decides: Presi- dential Nominations before and after Reform.* Chicago: University of Chicago Press.

Cohn, Nate. 2016. "Iowa Caucuses: The Political Divides to Watch Out For." *New York Times,* February 1. www.nytimes.com/2016/02/02/upshot/iowa-caucuses-what-to -watch-for.html.

"Colbert's Advice: Eat Boiled Peanuts." 2016. *Post and Courier,* February 14, 8.

Cook, Lindsey. 2016. "Why New Hampshire Matters in Presidential Elections." *U.S. News and World Report,* February 2. www.usnews.com/news/blogs/data-mine/2016/02/02/ why-new-hampshire-matters-in-presidential-elections.

Cook, Rhodes. 2000. *United States Presidential Primary Elections, 1968–1996.* Washington, DC: CQ Press.

Cook, Rhodes. 2007. *United States Presidential Primary Elections, 2000–2004.* Washington, DC: CQ Press.

Cooper, Christopher A., and H. Gibbs Knotts. 2017. *The Resilience of Southern Identity: Why the South Still Matters in the Minds of Its People.* Chapel Hill: University of North Carolina Press.

Cothran, Thomas C. 1979. "Edwards, Thurmond Believe in Presidential Primary." *State,* September 17, B1.

Coyne, Amanda. 2016. "Trump Takes a Victory Lap, Reminds Supporters to Vote during Rally at Clemson." *State,* February 11, Local, 3.

Craven, Jamie S., Jordan M. Ragusa, and John-Anthony G. Thevos. 2017. "Palmetto State Primaries: An Examination of South Carolina's Nomination Contests." *Journal of Political Science* 45 (1): 33–53.

C-SPAN. 2008. "South Carolina Democratic Presidential Candidates' Debate," January 21. www.c-span.org/video/?203717–1/south-Carolina-democratic-presidential -candidates-debate.

Cutler, Fred. 2002. "The Simplest Shortcut of All: Sociodemographic Characteristics and Electoral Choice." *Journal of Politics* 64 (2): 466–90.

Davis, Michelle R. 1999. "Democrats Denied Early S.C. Primary." *State,* September 25, B1.

Davis, Michelle R. 2000a. "Bush-McCain Pits Old Guard vs. Young Turks in S.C. Republican Primary, Might Test the Power of Campbell's Political Machine." *State,* February 6, A1.

Davis, Michelle R. 2000b. "Bush, McCain Spar over Ads." *State,* February 9, A1.

Davis, Michelle R. 2000c. "Front-Runners Bush, McCain Clash at Columbia Forum." *State,* February 16, A1.

Davis, Michelle R. 2000d. "GOP Establishment Proves Its Power." *State,* February 20, A1.

Davis, Michelle R. 2000e. "Terms of Endorsement." *State,* January 30, D4.

"Democrats Wisely Opt to Open Up Process." 1991. *State,* April 11, 2D.

Dionne, E. J., Jr. 1988. "Bush's Move to the Front." *New York Times,* February 17, A1.

Dolan, Kathleen. 2004. "The Impact of Candidate Sex on Evaluations of Candidates for the US House of Representatives." *Social Science Quarterly* 85 (1): 206–17.

Dominguez, Casey B. K. 2011. "Does the Party Matter? Endorsements in Congressional Primaries." *Political Research Quarterly* 64 (3): 534–44.

"Don and Dan Show." 1979. *The State,* December 25, 16A.

Douglas, William. 2016. "Sanders, Clinton Scour Black Colleges for Votes." *State,* February 23, Front Page, 1.

Downs, Anthony. 1957. *An Economic Theory of Democracy.* New York: Harper and Row.

Drake, Johns C. 2004a. "Clark Suffers Setbacks in S.C." *State,* January 29, A7.

Drake, Johns C. 2004b. "Iowa Energy Boosts Edwards' S.C. Campaign." *State,* January 24, A1.

Dumain, Emma. 2016. "Sanders Backers Hope to Beat Odds, Test Clinton Strength on S.C. Black Vote." *Post and Courier,* January 24, 1.

Duverger, Maurice. 1963. *Political Parties: Their Organization and Activity in the Modern State.* New York: Wiley.

Eckholm, Erik. 2012. "Evangelicals Step Up Efforts to Unite on an Alternative to Romney." *New York Times,* January 7, A15.

Eckholm, Erik, and Jeff Zeleny. 2012. "Evangelicals, Seeking Unity, Back Santorum." *New York Times,* January 15, A15.

Edsall, Thomas B. 1988. "Dole Takes to Sidelines in South Carolina Primary." *Washington Post,* February 17, 1988.

Edsall, Thomas B. 1992. "S. Carolina Picks Bush, Clinton." *Washington Post,* March 7, 1992.

Edsall, Thomas B. 1996. "Dole Makes Inroads, but Rough Road Ahead." *Washington Post,* February 28, A1.

Efron, Sonni, and Paul Richter. 1992. "Two Clinton Rivals Level a Double-Barreled Attack." *Los Angeles Times,* March 7, 24.

"Elections 2012." 2012. *State,* Nation & World, January 12, 4.

Fair Vote. 2009. "The Delaware Plan." Presidential Elections Reform Program, December. archive.fairvote.org/?page=2064.

"Fake CNN Email Alert Sent in Attempt to Smear Gingrich." 2012. *Post and Courier,* January 19. www.postandcourier.com/politics/fake-cnn-email-alert-sent-in-attempt-to-smear-gingrich/article_f41bf1fa-cfae-51df-83e6-d5ef0c989ff9.html.

Fiorina, Morris P. 1981. *Retrospective Voting in American National Elections.* New Haven, CT: Yale University Press.

Firestone, David. 2000. "McCain Effort to Straddle Sensitive Southern Issue Leaves Position Unclear." *New York Times,* January 12, A20.

"First in the South." 2018. South Carolina Republican Party. www.sc.gop/about/first-in-the-south.

Flach, Tim. 2016. "Trump Vows to Protect Jobs in Trade Deals." *State,* 6.

Fowler, Linda L. 2007. "Did Voters Want a National Primary?" *Newsday,* May 13.

FrontloadingHQ. 2009a. "Presidential Primaries and Caucuses by Month (1980)," February 4. frontloading.blogspot.com/2009/02/1980-presidential-primary-calendar.html.

FrontloadingHQ. 2009b. "Presidential Primaries and Caucuses by Month (2004)," March 4. frontloading.blogspot/2009/03/2004-presidential-primary-calendar.html.

Funk, Tim. 2016. "GOP Candidates Carson, Cruz Woo Evangelicals in Rock Hill." *State,* Front Page, 3.

Gabriel, Trip. 2012. "Disdainful of Strategist, Gingrich Acts as His Own." *New York Times,* January 20. www.nytimes.com/2011/12/09/us/politics/gingrich-the-front-runner-is-still-selling-books.html.

Gabriel, Trip. 2016. "Race Goes to South Carolina, with No Clear Republican Threat to Trump." *New York Times,* February 10, A16.

Gaudiano, Nicole. 2016. "New Hampshire Braced to Take Center Stage in Presidential Race." *USA Today,* February 1. www.usatoday.com/story/news/politics/elections/2016/02/01/new-hampshire-take-center-stage-presidential-race/79640262.

Geer, John G. 1988. "Assessing the Representativeness of Electorates in Presidential Primaries." *American Journal of Political Science* 32 (4): 929–45.

"Gephardt to Drop Out of Race." 2004. *CNN,* January 20. www.cnn.com/2004/ALL POLITICS/01/19/elec04.prez.gephardt.

Germond, Jack W., and Jules Witcover. 1988. "South Carolina to Set Pace, Bush Has Edge in Saturday Primary," *The State,* March 2, 14A.

Gibson, Ginger. 2012. "Romney Clinches Nomination." *Politico,* May 29. www.politico .com/story/2012/05/mitt-clinches-gop-presidential-nod-076845.

Gooding, Richard. 2004. "The Trashing of John McCain." *Vanity Fair,* November. www .vanityfair.com/news/2004/11/mccain200411.

"GOP Creates Committee to Study S.C. Primary." 1979. *State,* April 21, 4B.

"A GOP Primary." 1979. *State,* August 19, 2B.

Gopoian, J. David. 1982. "Issue Preferences and Candidate Choice in Presidential Primaries." *American Journal of Political Science* 26 (3): 523–46.

Graham, Cole Blease, Jr. 1998. "Between a Rock and a Hard Place: South Carolina's Republican Presidential Primary." *Southern Cultures* 4 (1): 43–51.

Graham, Cole Blease, Jr. 2009. "South Carolina: A Paler Shade of Red?" In *A Paler Shade of Red: The 2008 Presidential Election in the South,* edited by Branwell DuBose Kapeluck, Laurence W. Moreland, and Robert P. Steed, 95–118,. Fayetteville: University of Arkansas Press.

Graham, Cole Blease, Jr., and Scott E. Buchanan. 2014. "It's Déjà Vu All Over Again." In *Second Verse, Same as the First: The 2012 Presidential Election in the South,* edited by Scott E. Buchanan and Branwell DuBose Kapeluck, 101–119. Fayetteville: University of Arkansas Press.

Graham, Cole Blease, Jr., and Scott E. Buchanan. 2018. "South Carolina: It's All about the Primary." In *The Future Ain't What It Used to Be: The 2016 Presidential Election in the South,* edited by Scott E. Buchanan and Branwell DuBose Kapeluck, 105–23, Fayetteville: University of Arkansas Press.

Graham, Cole Blease, Jr., Laurence W. Moreland, and Robert P. Steed. 2010. "South Carolina: The New Politics of the Palmetto State." In *The New Politics of the Old South: An Introduction to Southern Politics,* 4th ed., edited by Charles S. Bullock and Mark J. Rozell, 27–48. Lanham, MD: Rowman and Littlefield.

Grantham, Dewey W. 1992. *The Life and Death of the Solid South: A Political History.* Lexington: University Press of Kentucky.

Green, Donald Phillip, and Jonathan S. Krasno. 1988. "Salvation for the Spendthrift Incumbent: Reestimating the Effects of Campaign Spending in House Elections." *American Journal of Political Science* 32 (4): 884–907.

Grimaldi, James V. 2012. "Big Bucks for Gingrich from Las Vegas." *Washington Post,* January 8, A6.

Gurian, Paul-Henri. 1990. "The Influence of Nomination Rules on the Financial Allocations of Presidential Candidates." *Political Research Quarterly* 43 (3): 661–87.

Guth, James L. 1995. "South Carolina: The Christian Right Wins One." *God at the Grassroots: In The Christian Right in the 1994 Elections,* edited by Mark J. Rozell and Clyde Wilcox, 133–46, Lanham, MD: Rowman and Littlefield.

Guth, James L., and Oran P. Smith. 1997. "South Carolina Christian Right: Just Part of the Family Now?" In *God at the Grassroots 1996: The Christian Right in the 1996 Elections,* edited by Mark J. Rozell and Clyde Wilcox, 15–32. Lanham, MD: Rowman and Little-field.

Haberman, Maggie. 2016a. "Clashes and Surprises Emerge in Prelude to South Caro-lina Primary." *New York Times,* February 18. www.nytimes.com/politics/first-draft/2016/02/18/clashes-and-surprises-emerge-in-prelude-to-south-Carolina.

Haberman, Maggie, 2016b. "Donald Trump Escalates Rhetoric before South Carolina Pri-mary." *New York Times,* February 15. www.nytimes.com/politics/first-draft/2016/02/15/donald-trump-escalates-rhetoric-before-south-Carolina-primary.

Hadley, Arthur. 1976. *The Invisible Primary.* Englewood Cliffs, New Jersey: Prentice Hall.

Hamby, Peter. 2012. "Fake CNN Email Used as Dirty Trick in South Carolina." CNN, January 2012. politicalticker.blogs.cnn.com/2012/01/20/fake-cnn-email-used-as-dirty-trick-in-south-Carolina.

Hatuqa, Dalia. 2016. "How Important Are the South Carolina Primaries?" *Al Jazeera,* February 19. www.aljazeera.com/indepth/features/2016/02/south-Carolina-primary-important-election-republicans-democrats-160217105427419.html.

Haynes, Audrey A., and Paul-Henri Gurian, and Stephen M. Nichols. 1997. "The Role of Candidate Spending in Presidential Nomination Campaigns." *Journal of Politics* 59 (1): 213–25.

Healy, Patrick. 2008. "In S. Carolina, It's Obama vs. Clinton. That's Bill Clinton." *New York Times,* January 22, A17.

Healy, Patrick, and Amy Chozick. 2016. "Clinton Seizes on Policy Shifts in 4th Debate." *New York Times,* January 18, A1.

Healy, Patrick, and Jeff Zeleny. 2008. "Obama and Clinton Square Off." *New York Times,* January 22, A1.

Helderman, Rosalind S., and Dan Balz. 2012. "Gingrich Gains on Romney in S.C." *Wash-ington Post,* January 21, A1.

Helderman, Rosalind S., and Karen Tumulty. 2012. "Rivals Vie to Battle Romney from the Right—Alone." *Washington Post,* January 18, A6.

Heldman, Caroline, Susan J. Carroll, and Stephanie Olson. 2005. "'She Brought Only a Skirt': Print Media Coverage of Elizabeth Dole's Bid for the Republican Presidential Nomination." *Political Communication* 22 (3): 315–35.

Helfand, Candice Leigh. 2012. "RNC Hands Down Punishments to Florida for Early Primary Date, Starting 'Domino Effect.'" *CBS Tampa Bay,* January 13. tampa.cbslocal.com/2012/01/13/rnc-to-punish-convention-host-state-for-early-primary-date.

Hendin, Robert, Jennifer Pinto, Anthony Salvanto. 2011. "RNC to Punish Florida, but Says Goal of Primary Rules Have Been Met." *CBS News,* September 30. www.cbs news.com/news/rnc-to-punish-florida-but-says-goal-of-primary-rules-have-been-met.

Herrnson, Paul S., and Irwin L. Morris. 2007. "Presidential Campaigning in the 2002 Congressional Elections." *Legislative Studies Quarterly* 32 (4): 629–48.

Holbrook, Thomas M., and Scott D. McClurg. 2005. "The Mobilization of Core Support-ers: Campaigns, Turnout, and Electoral Composition in United States Presidential Elections." *American Journal of Political Science* 49 (4): 689–703.

Huffmon, Scott H., H. Gibbs Knotts, and Seth C. McKee. 2017. "First in the South: The

Importance of South Carolina in Presidential Politics." *Journal of Political Science* 45 (1): 7–31.

Hurtz, Howard. 2000. "GOP Right Sees McCain Coverage as a S.C. Weapon." *Washington Post,* February 6, A6.

Husted, Thomas, and David Nickerson. 2014. "Political Economy of Presidential Disaster Declarations and Federal Disaster Assistance. *Public Finance Review* 42 (1): 35–57.

Ifill, Gwen. 1988. "Dole Drops Out of Debate in Dallas." *Washington Post,* February 19, A9.

Iffil, Gwen. 1992a. "Can Clinton Soar outside the South?" *State,* January 5, 1D.

Ifill, Gweń. 1992b. "Clinton's Talk of Racial Unity Falls on Eager Ears." *New York Times,* March 7, section 1, page 10.

Isenstadt, Alex. 2016. "Lindsey Graham Endorses Jeb Bush for President." *Politico,* January 15. www.politico.com/story/2016/01/lindsey-graham-to-endorse-jeb-bush-for -president-217838.

Jackson, Gavin. 2016a. "Bill Clinton Rallies Pee Dee for Hillary." *Post and Courier,* February 14, 7.

Jackson, Gavin. 2016b. "Now for the Dems—Sanders Holds Rally in Greenville ahead of Saturday's Primary as Clinton Campaign Hosts Event in North Charleston." *Post and Courier,* February 22, 1.

Jackson, Gavin. 2016c. "Trump Fires up Rock Hill ahead of Debate." *Post and Courier,* January 7, 1.

Jackson, Gavin, and David Slade. 2016. "Sanders in Charleston Touts His 'Radical Ideas' for Change." *Post and Courier,* February 17, 1.

Jones, Jeffrey M. 1998. "Does Bringing out the Candidate Bring out the Votes? The Effects of Nominee Campaigning in Presidential Elections." *American Politics Quarterly* 26 (4): 395–419.

Kamarck, Elaine C. 2016a. *Primary Politics: Everything You Need to Know about How America Nominates Its Presidential Candidates,* 2nd ed. Washington, DC, Brookings Institution Press.

Kamarck, Elaine C. 2016b. "Iowa and New Hampshire: Where Winners Lose, and Losers Win." *Washington Post,* January 25. www.washingtonpost.com/news/the-fix/wp /2016/01/25/iowa-and-new-hampshire-where-winners-lose-and-losers-win.

Kamarck, Elaine C. 2016c. "Why Is the Presidential Nomination System Such a Mess?" Center for Effective Public Management, Brookings Institution, January. www .brookings.edu/wp-content/uploads/2016/07/primaries.pdf.

Kane, Paul. 2016. "How Tim Scott Chose to Endorse Marco Rubio for President." *Washington Post,* February 3. www.washingtonpost.com/news/powerpost/wp/2016/02/03/ how-tim-scott-chose-to-endorse-marco-rubio-for-president/?utm_term=.dbc862 0757fb.

Kaufmann, Karen M., James G. Gimpel, and Adam H. Hoffman. 2003. "A Promise Fulfilled? Open Primaries and Representation." *Journal of Politics* 65 (2): 457–76.

Key, V. O., Jr. 1949. *Southern Politics in State and Nation.* New York: Knopf.

Key, V. O., Jr. 1956. *American State Politics: An Introduction.* New York: Knopf.

"Keyes' Focus Too Narrow." 2000. *State,* February 14, A8.

Khalid, Asma. 2016. "The Perfect State Index: If Iowa, N.H. Are Too White to Go First, Then Who?" NPR, January 29www.npr.org/2016/01/29/464250335/the-perfect-state -index-if-iowa-n-h-are-too-white-to-go-first-then-who.

Kriner, Douglas L., and Andrew Reeves. 2015. "Presidential Particularism in Disaster Declarations and Military Base Closures. *Presidential Studies Quarterly* 45 (4): 679–702.

Kristol, Bill. 2008. "Desperate Husband." *New York Times,* January 28, A23.

Kropf, Schuyler. 2012. "S.C. Bigwigs Keep Quiet." *Post and Courier,* January 8, A1.

Kropf, Schuyler. 2016a. "Ambush Stunt Spotlights Clinton's Record on Race" *Post and Courier,* February 26, 1.

Kropf, Schuyler. 2016b. "Clinton to Confront Racial Disparities in S.C." *Post and Courier,* February 12, 1.

Kropf, Schuyler. 2016c. "Democrats Fry Fish, Roast Republicans." *Post and Courier,* January 17, 1.

Kropf, Schuyler. 2016d. "Graham's Bush Endorsement Geared toward Drawing Vets." *Post and Courier,* January 16, 10.

Kropf, Schuyler. 2016e. "Presidential Endorsements of Note in South Carolina Today." *Post and Courier,* February 3. www.postandcourier.com/politics/presidential-endorse ments-of-note-in-south-Carolina-today/article_8468bfb5–97d0–5abc-a90b-0dba953 aa278.html.

Kropf, Schuyler, 2016f. "Seven Candidates Make Main Stage for N. Charleston GOP Presidential Debate." *Post and Courier,* January 12, 4.

Kropf, Schuyler. 2016g. "Trump, Haley Bashed by Robocall Supporting Cruz." *Post and Courier,* February 20, 1.

Kuzenski, John C. 2003. "South Carolina: The Heart of the GOP realignment in the South." In *The New Politics of the Old South: An Introduction to Southern Politics,* 2nd ed., edited by Charles S. Bullock and Mark J. Rozell, 23–52, Lanham, MD: Rowman and Littlefield.

Lanier, Al, 1979. "Republicans Fear Democratic 'Raid.'" *News and Courier,* October 22, 10B.

"Late Night: Stephen Colbert Ends Presidential Campaign." 2012. *Los Angeles Time,* January 24. latimesblogs.latimes.com/showtracker/2012/01/late-night-stephen-colbert -ends-presidential-campaign.html.

LeBlanc, Cliff. 2000a. "Panel Hears Primary-Poll Complaint." *State,* February 14, A1.

LeBlanc, Cliff. 2000b. "Rulings Lift Cloud over Republican Primary." *State,* February 115, A1.

Lessem, Rebeccca and Carly Urban. 2015. "Local Economic Gains from Primary Election Spending." *Economic Journal* 126 (597): 2147–72.

Liming, Robert G. 1972. "Powell Re-Elected S.C. GOP Chairman." *State,* March 26, A1.

Lloyd, Joshua. 2016. "At Florence Rally, Trump Calls Politicians Stupid, Incompetent." *State,* February 6, Local, 3.

Lovler, Ronnie. 1980. "Their Styles Are Difference, but They All Play Politics." *State,* February 18, 1B and 7B.

Lundgren, Mark. 1979. "GOP Candidates Favor Proposes S.C. Primary." *State,* August 26, 1C.

Mackun, Paul, and Steven Wilson. 2011. *Population Distribution and Change: 2000 to 2010.* 2010 Census Briefs, C2010BR-01. Washington, DC: U.S. Census Bureau. www .census.gov/content/dam/Census/library/publications/2011/dec/c2010br-01.pdf.

Markoe, Lauren. 2004. "Kerry Playing Catch-Up in S.C." *State,* January 21, A1.

Martin, Jonathan, and Alexander Burns. 2016. "Poor Showings by Bush and Cruz Could Do Lasting Damage to Their Campaigns." *New York Times,* February 19, 2016.

Martin, Jonathan, and Astead W. Herndon. 2019. "For Democrats, South Carolina Already Looms Large for 2020 Race." *New York Times,* January 22.

Matthews, William. 1979. "S.C. Primary Study OK'd by Committee." *News and Courier,* April 4, 7B.

Mayer, William G. 1996. "Forecasting Presidential Nominations." In *In Pursuit of the White House: How We Choose Our Presidential Nominees,* edited by William Mayer, 44–71. Chatham, NJ: Chatham House.

Mayer, William G., and Andrew E. Busch. 2004. *The Front-Loading Problem in Presidential Nominations.* Washington, DC: Brookings Institution Press.

McCann, James A., Randall W. Partin, Ronald B. Rapoport, and Walter J. Stone. 1996. "Presidential Nomination Campaigns and Party Mobilization: An Assessment of Spillover Effects." *American Journal of Political Science* 40 (3): 756–67.

McCormick, John, and Mark Niquettte. 2016. "Republicans Take White House Fight to South Carolina after Trump Win." *Bloomberg Politics,* February 10. www.bloomberg .com/politics/articles/2016–02–10/presidential-primary-moves-to-politically-steamy -south-Carolina.

McKee, Seth C. 2018a. *The Dynamics of Southern Politics: Causes and Consequences.* Thousand Oaks, CA: CQ Press.

McKee, Seth C. 2018b. "The 2016 Presidential Nominating Contest." In *The Future Ain't What It Used to Be: The 2016 Presidential Election in the South,* edited by Branwell DuBose Kapeluck and Scott E. Buchanan, 23–40. Fayetteville: University of Arkansas Press.

Miller, Jeff. 1988a. "Bush Enlists Help of Goldwater in Push to Build S.C. Support." *State,* March 1, 2C.

Miller, Jeff. 1988b. "Campaign Proved Unbeatable in South Carolina." *State,* March 6, 1A.

Miller, Jeff. 1988c. 'Dole Says He Sees S.C. as 'Upset State' Kemp also Signs up for GOP's Big Bout." *The State,* February 19, 1C.

Miller, Jeff. 1992a. "Feeling's Mutual Blacks Not Focus for Democrats." *State,* March 5, 1A.

Miller, Jeff. 1992b. "Tsongas Tells S.C. He Can Win." *State,* March 4, 10A.

Mitchell, Alison, and Frank Bruni. 2000. "Spotlight Turns on Ugly Side of Politicking." *New York Times,* February 10, A 26.

Monkovic, Toni. 2016. "Clinton, Sanders, and the Underrated Power of the Black Vote." *New York Times,* February 17. www.nytimes.com/2016/02/18/upshot/clinton-sanders -and-the-underrated-power-of-the-black-voter.html.

Montopoli, Brian, and Sarah Huisenga. 2012. "Phony E-Mails Say Gingrich Forced Abortion on Ex-Wife." *CBS News,* January 20. www.cbsnews.com/news/phony-e-mails-say -gingrich-forced-abortion-on-ex-wife.

Moore, David W., and Andrew E. Smith. 2015. *The First Primary: New Hampshire's Outsize Role in Presidential Nominations.* Durham: University of New Hampshire Press.

Moran, Jack, and Mark Fenster. 1982. "Voter Turnout in Presidential Primaries: A Diachronic Analysis." *American Politics Research* 10 (4): 453–76.

Moreland, Laurence W., and Robert P. Steed. 2005a. "The 2004 Presidential Election and Southern Politics." *American Review of Politics* 26 (Spring): 1–23.

Moreland, Laurence W., and Robert P. Steed. 2005b. "South Carolina: Republican Success, Democratic Decline." *American Review of Politics* 26 (Spring): 109–30.

Moreland, Laurence W., and Robert P. Steed. 2012. "The South and Presidential Elections." In *The Oxford Handbook of Southern Politics,* edited by Charles S. Bullock III and Mark J. Rozell, 470–83. New York: Oxford University Press.

Moreland, Laurence W., Robert P. Steed, and Tod A. Baker. 1991. "South Carolina: Different Cast, Same Dram in the Palmetto State." In *The 1988 Presidential Election in the South: Continuity amidst Change in Southern Politics,* edited by Laurence W. Moreland, Robert P. Steed, and Tod A Baker, 119–40. New York: Praeger.

Nadeau, Richard, and Michael S. Lewis-Beck. 2001. "National Economic Voting in U.S. Presidential Elections." *Journal of Politics* 63 (1): 159–81.

Nagourney, Adam. 2003. "Democrats' First Presidential Debate Shows Party Fissures." *New York Times,* May 4, N30.

Nagourney, Adam, and Jim Rutenberg. 2004. "Candidates Turn away from S.C." *New York Times,* February 1, A21.

Neal, Terry M. 2000a. "Bush Dodges Confederate Flag Issue in South Carolina." *Washington Post,* January 7, A7.

Neal, Terry M. 2000b. "McCain Reverses Flag Stance." *Washington Post,* April 19, A10.

Neal, Terry M., and Thomas B. Edsall. 2000. "Polls Show McCain Is Surging in South Carolina." *Washington Post,* February 4, A1.

Newkirk, Vann R. 2016. "Sanders' Not-So-Southern Strategy." *Atlantic,* April 15. www .theatlantic.com/politics/archive/2016/04/sanders-race-south/478506.

Norrander, Barbara. 1989. "Ideological Representativeness of Presidential Primary Voters." *American Journal of Political Science* 33 (3): 570–87.

Norrander, Barbara. 1991. "Explaining Individual Participation in Presidential Primaries." *Western Political Quarterly* 44 (3): 40–65.

Norrander, Barbara. 1992. *Super Tuesday: Regional Politics and Presidential Primaries.* Lexington: University Press of Kentucky.

Norrander, Barbara. 2006. "The Attrition Game: Initial Resources, Initial Contests and the Exit of Candidates during the US Presidential Primary Season." *British Journal of Political Science* 36 (3): 487–507.

Norrander, Barbara. 2010. *The Imperfect Primary: Oddities, Biases, and Strengths in U.S. Presidential Nomination Politics.* New York: Routledge.

O'Connor, John. 2008a. "Choosing a President—Democratic Debate in Myrtle Beach—At Each Other's Throats Clinton, Obama in Bitter Debate as Primary Looms." *State,* January 22, A1.

O'Connor, John. 2008b. "Democrats' Eyes on Prize—Beyond Saturday Primary, Who Can Win in the Fall?" *State,* January 23, A4.

Olsen, Henry. 2015. "State of Play: South Carolina." *National Review,* November 20. www .nationalreview.com/corner/state-play-south-Carolina.

Papke, Leslie E., and Jeffrey M. Woolridge. 1996. "Econometric Methods for Fractional

Response Variables with an Application to 401(K) Plan Participation Rates." *Journal of Applied Econometrics* 11 (6): 619–32.

Parker, Ashely. 2012. "Romney Turns His Attention away from Gingrich and toward Obama." *New York Times,* January 20. thecaucus.blogs.nytimes.com/2012/01/20/romney-turns-his-attention-away-from-gingrich-and-toward-obama.

Parker, Ashley, and Michael D. Shear. 2011. "Nikki Haley Endorses Mitt Romney." *New York Times,* December 16. thecaucus.blogs.nytimes.com/2011/12/16/nikki-haley-endorses-mitt-romney.

Patterson, Thomas E. 1980. *The Mass Media Election.* New York: Praeger.

Peterson, Bill, and Jack Bass. 1980. "Reagan Crushes Connally, Bush in S.C." *Washington Post,* March 8, A1.

Polsby, Nelson W. 1983. *Consequence of Party Reform.* New York: Oxford University Press.

Pomper, Gerald. 1996. "Alive! The Political Parties after the 1980–1992 Presidential Elections." In *American Presidential Elections: Process, Policy, and Political Change,* edited by Harvey L. Schantz, 135–56. Albany: State University of New York Press.

Pope, Charles. 1988a. "Hopeful Shows Off Support, Ex-Governors Back Gephardt." *State,* March 2, 1C.

Pope, Charles. 1988b. "3 GOP Hopefuls Hit State—Bush and Kemp Stress Importance of Primary." *State,* March 4, 1A.

Prabhu, Maya T. 2016a. "Bill Clinton Touts Wife as a 'Change-Maker' for Workers, Women at S.C. Campaign Rally." *Post and Courier,* February 4, 7.

Prabhu, Maya T. 2016b. "S.C. Lawmaker Shifts Support to Sanders." *Post and Courier,* January 26, 1.

"Presidential or Advisory Primaries Act." 2007. South Carolina General Assembly, 117th Session, Act No. 81, June 27. www.scstatehouse.gov/sess117_2007–2008/bills/07actsp1.php.

Preston, Mark, Jeff Zeleny, Gregory Krieg, and Eric Bradner. 2016. "Martin O'Malley, Mike Huckabee End Presidential Campaigns" *CNN,* February 2. www.cnn.com/2016/02/01/politics/martin-omalley-to-suspend-campaign/index.html.

Prince, K. Michael. 2004. *Rally 'Round the Flag, Boys: South Carolina and the Confederate Flag.* Columbia: University of South Carolina Press.

Prokop, Andrew. 2016. "Why Do the Iowa Caucuses Matter? Because Everyone Thinks They Do." *Vox.com,* February 1. www.vox.com/2016/1/25/10817088/ iowa-caucus-2016-poll-trump-sanders.

Ragusa, Jordan, and Anthony Gaspar. 2016. "Where's the Tea Party? An Examination of the Tea Party's Voting Behavior in the House of Representatives." *Political Research Quarterly* 69 (2): 361–72.

Ranney, Austin. 1968. "The Representativeness of Primary Electorates." *Midwest Journal of Political Science* 12 (2): 224–38.

Real Clear Politics. 2018a. "Election 2016—Democratic Delegate Count." www.realclearpolitics.com/epolls/2016/president/democratic_delegate_count.html.

Real Clear Politics. 2018b. "Election 2016—Republican Delegate Count." www.realclearpolitics.com/epolls/2016/president/republican_delegate_count.html.

Recio, Maria. 2016. "South Carolina Tag Team Smackdown: Cruz, Trump, Rubio." *State,* February 15, Nation, 4.

Redlawsk, David P., Caroline J. Tolbert, and Todd Donovan. 2011. *Why Iowa: How Caucuses and Sequential Elections Improve the Presidential Nominating Process.* Chicago: University of Chicago Press.

Reed, John Shelton. 1983. *Southerners: The Social Psychology of Sectionalism.* Chapel Hill: University of North Carolina Press.

Reid, T.R. 1988. "Robertson Links Bush to Swaggart Scandal." *Washington Post,* February 23, A1.

Republican National Convention. 2016. *The Rules of the Republican Party.* Republican National Committee, January. prod-cdn-static.gop.com/media/documents/2016 -Republican-Rules-FINAL_1529681395.pdf.

"Republican Primary Blueprint Is Sound." 1979. *State,* October 17, 8A.

Ridout, Travis N., Brandon Rottinghaus, and Nathan Hosey. 2009. "Following the Rules? Candidate Strategy in Presidential Primaries." *Social Science Quarterly* 90 (4): 777–95.

"Riley and McNair to Endorse Gephardt Republican Candidates George Bush, Jack Kemp Campaign in South Carolina." 1988. *State,* March 1, 1A.

Roldan, Cynthia. 2016a. "Brother Goes to Bat for Bush." *Post and Courier,* February 15, 1.

Roldan, Cynthia. 2016b. "GOP Brawls in Greenville." *Post and Courier,* February 14, 1.

Roldan, Cynthia. 2016c. "Trump 'Fine' without Endorsement from Haley." *Post and Courier,* February 6, 1.

Roldan, Cynthia, and Schuyler Kropf. 2016. "Sanders Says He's Fighting Hard in Tough S.C. Race." *Post and Courier,* February 25, 1.

Root, Jay. 1999. "Bush's Quiz Performance Brings Criticism, Support." *State,* November 6, A4.

Rosen, James. 2015. "Predicting South Carolina GOP Vote Is a Challenge." *McClatchy DC Bureau,* June 17. www.mcclatchydc.com/news/politics-government/election/article 24722233.html.

Ross, Dan. 1979. "S.C. GOP Alive and Growing." *State,* August 28, 14A.

Ross, Daniel I., Jr. 2001. Oral history interview by Herbert J. Hartsook. South Carolina Political Collections, University Libraries, the University of South Carolina.

Ross, Janell. 2016. "The Fight for the Black Voter in South Carolina, Explained." *Washington Post,* February 27. www.washingtonpost.com/news/the-fix/wp/2016/02/27/the -south-Carolina-primary-is-all-about-the-black-vote-which-is-actually-pretty-rare/ ?noredirect=on&utm_term=.272850f709b3.

Rucker, Philip, and Dan Balz. 2012. "Romney Faces Mounting Pressure to Release Tax Returns Sooner." *Washington Post,* January 19, A5.

Rucker, Phillip, and David A. Fahrenthold. 2012. "Gingrich Comes from Behind to Win South Carolina Primary." *Washington Post,* January 21. www.washingtonpost.com/ politics/in-south-Carolina-a-sharply-tightened-race/2012/01/21/gIQAS6JIGQ_story .html?noredirect=on&utm_term=.c89f8358c678.

Rudin, Ken. 2008. "South Carolina's Role as GOP Kingmaker." NPR, January 16, www .npr.org/templates/story/story.php?storyId=18147641.

"Same Day Presidential Primaries." 2007. *Post and Courier,* June 19, A8.

"S.C. Politics Today." 2007. *State,* June 20, B3.

Scoppe, Cindi Ross, Lisa Greene, and Jeff Miller. 1992. "Clinton, Harkin, Duke Scour S.C. for Last-Minute Primary Support." *State,* March 7, 8A.

"S.C. Republicans to Study 1980 Presidential Primary." 1979. *State,* March 10, 15A.

Seelye, Katharine Q. 2004. "Kerry and Edwards Face a Critical Test in the South." *New York Times,* January 28, A1.

Seelye, Katharine Q., and David M. Halbfinger. 2004. "Democratic Contenders Attack Bush on Iraq, Terrorism, and Trade." *New York Times,* January 20, A19.

Self, Jamie. 2015. "SC Republican Lindsey Graham Drops Out of Presidential Race." *State,* December 21. www.thestate.com/news/politics-government/politics-columns-blogs/the-buzz/article50880210.html.

Self, Jamie. 2016a. "How Hillary Clinton Won South Carolina." *State,* February 28, Front Page, 1.

Self, Jamie. 2016b. "Mothers of Victims of Gun Violence, Police Violence Campaign with Clinton." *State,* Nation and World, 7.

Self, Jamie. 2016c. "Rubio Emerges as GOP's Anti-Trump, Anti-Cruz Option." *State,* February 18, Front Page, 1.

Self, Jamie. 2016d. "S.C. Democrats Not Feeling the 'Bern.'" *State,* February 17, Front Page, 1.

Shain, Andrew. 2016a. "Candidates: Wait on Justice." *State,* February 14, Front Page, 1.

Shain, Andrew. 2016b. "Carson Says He Plans to Focus Campaign More on SC Than on New Hampshire." *State,* February 2, Metro, 3.

Shain, Andrew. 2016c. "Cruz, Clinton Winning SC Money Fight." *State,* February 5, Front Page, 1.

Shain, Andrew. 2016d. "GOP Rivals Spar in SC Presidential Debate." *State,* January 15, 1.

Shain, Andrew. 2016e. "Is It Trump's Race to Lose?" *State,* February 20, Front Page, 1.

Shain, Andrew. 2016f. "Trump Cheers 'Beautiful' SC Win." *State,* February 21, Front Page, 1.

Shain, Andrew. 2016g. "Trump Targeted ahead of SC Republican Debate." *State,* February 13, Front Page, 1.

Shaw, Daron R. 1999a. "The Effect of TV Ads and Candidate Appearances on Statewide Presidential Votes, 1988–96." *American Political Science Review* 93 (2): 345–361.

Shaw, Daron R. 1999b. "A Study of Presidential Campaign Event Effects from 1952 to 1992." *Journal of Politics* 61 (2): 387–422.

Sheinin, Aaron Gould. 2003. "Candidates Target Bush, S.C. Issues in Columbia Debate." *State,* A1.

Sheinin, Aaron Gould. 2004a. "Democrats Lobby for Votes During Debate in Greenville." *State,* January 30, A1.

Sheinin, Aaron Gould. 2004b. "Edwards Takes S.C.—Kerry Grabs 5 States." *State,* February 4, A1.

Sheinin, Aaron Gould. 2004c. "Gephardt's Supporters Now Up for Grabs." *State,* January 20, A6.

Sheinin, Aaron Gould. 2004d. "Kerry Faces Uphill Battle in S.C." *State,* January 20, A1.

Sheinin, Aaron Gould. 2004e. "Lieberman, Clark Focus on S.C." *State,* January 15, A1.

Sheinin, Aaron Gould. 2007a. "Democrats in S.C. to Seek Jan. 26 Primary." *State,* October 17, A1.

Sheinin, Aaron Gould. 2007b. "S.C. Democrats Pursuing Earlier Primary Date." *State,* October 4, A1.

Sheinin, Aaron Gould. 2007c. "S.C. GOP Moves Primary to Jan. 19." *State,* August 10, B1.

Shurr, Maureen. 1988. "GOP Calls Record Turnout Indication of Party Growth." *State,* March 6, 12A.

Silver, Nate. 2016. "Clinton Is Winning the States That Look like the Democratic Primary." FiveThirtyEight, April 15. fivethirtyeight.com/features/clinton-is-winning-the -states-that-look-like-the-democratic-party.

Simon, Mark, and Zachary Coile. 2004. "Edwards, Still Upbeat, Admits His Run for the Presidency Is Over." *San Francisco Chronicle,* March 3. www.sfgate.com/politics/ article/THE-RACE-IS-ON-John-Kerry-clinches-Democratic-2786593.php.

Slackman, Michael. 2004. "Sharpton Fails to Achieve 2 Chief Goals in South Carolina." *New York Times,* February 4, A22.

Slade, David. 2018. "SC Accounts for Nearly Half the Nation's Growth in White Population." *Post and Courier,* July 9.

Smith, Andrew E., and David W. Moore 2016. "Five Myths about the New Hampshire Primary." *Washington Post,* February 5. www.washingtonpost.com/opinions/five-myths -about-the-new-hampshire-primary/2016/02/05/3f809d1e-caaf-11e5-ae11-57b6ae ab993f_story.html.

Smith, Bruce. 2012. "South Carolina Election: State Succeeds at Making Voice Heard on Primary Day." *Huffington Post,* March 22. huffingtonpost.com/2012/01/21/south -Carolina-election-_n_1221092.html.

Smith, Gina. 2011a. "S.C. GOP Sets January Primary." *State,* October 4, Front Page, A1.

Smith, Gina. 2011b. "State, GOP To Pay For Primary." *State,* October 6, Metro, 11.

Smith, Gina. 2012a. "Bain-Bashing Could Actually Help Romney." *State,* January 15, Front Page, 1.

Smith, Gina. 2012b. "Down and Dirty in S.C." *State,* January 12, Front Page, 1.

Smith, Gina. 2012c. "Front-Runner Romney Fends Off Rivals' Attacks." *State,* January 17, Front Page, 1.

Smith, Gina. 2012d. "Women's Firm a Key to Gingrich's S.C. Win." *State,* January 12, Front Page, 1.

Smith, Gina. 2012e. "Will S.C. Go Rogue? The S.C. Republican Primary." *State,* January 15, Metro, 19.

Smith, Oran P., and James L. Guth. 2018. "South Carolina: Integration and Challenge?" In *God at the Grassroots 2016: The Christian Right in American Politics,* edited by Mark J. Rozell and Clyde Wilcox, 161–80). Lanham, MD: Rowman and Littlefield.

Smith, Steven S., and Melanie J. Springer. 2009. "Choosing Presidential Candidates." In *Reforming the Presidential Nomination Process,* edited by Steven S. Smith and Melanie J. Springer, 1–22. Washington, D.C.: Brookings Institution Press.

Sobieraj, Sandra. 1999. "GOP Presidential Hopefuls Courts Christian Coalition." *State,* October 2, A4.

South Carolina Democratic Party. 1984. "The Report of the Committee to Study the Feasibility of a Presidential Primary for Democrats in South Carolina." Unpublished manuscript. Democratic Party of South Carolina Records, South Carolina Political Collections, the University of South Carolina.

South Carolina Democratic Party. 2004. "Key Facts about the SC Primary." Democratic

Party of South Carolina Records, South Carolina Political Collections, the University of South Carolina.

South Carolina Republican Party. 1979. "The Report and Recommendations of a Professional Preference Primary." Republican Party of South Carolina Papers, South Carolina Political Collections, the University of South Carolina.

South Carolina Republican Party. 1980a. "Official State Certification of Returns, South Carolina Republican Presidential Primary, March 8, 1980." Republican Party of South Carolina Papers, South Carolina Political Collections, the University of South Carolina.

South Carolina Republican Party. 1980b. "Poll Managers Handbook For the Conduct of the 1980 Republican Presidential Primary, March 8, 1980." Republican Party of South Carolina Papers, South Carolina Political Collections, the University of South Carolina.

Steed, Robert P., and Laurence W. Moreland. 2007. "South Carolina: Change and Continuity in the Palmetto State." In *The New Politics of the Old South: An Introduction to Southern Politics,* third edition, edited by Charles S. Bullock III and Mark J. Rozell, 29–48. Lanham, MD: Rowman and Littlefield.

Steger, Wayne P. 2000. "Do Primary Voters Draw from a Stacked Deck? Presidential Nominations in an Era of Candidate-Centered Campaigns." *Presidential Studies Quarterly* 30 (4): 727–753.

Steger, Wayne P. 2007. "Who Wins Nominations and Why? An Updated Forecast of the Presidential Primary Vote." *Political Research Quarterly* 60 (1): 91–99.

Steger, Wayne P. 2009. "Polls and Elections: How Did the Primary Forecasts Fare in 2008?" *Presidential Studies Quarterly* 39 (1): 141–54.

Steger, Wayne P. 2015. *A Citizen's Guide to Presidential Nominations.* New York: Routledge.

Steger, Wayne P., Andrew J. Dowdle, and Randall E. Adkins. 2004. "The New Hampshire Effect in Presidential Nominations." *Political Research Quarterly* 57 (3): 375–90.

Stensland, Jeff. 2000. "Oh, Democracy Is a Lonely Business." *State,* March 12, D4.

Stockley, Joshua. 2008. "Social Forces and the Primary Vote: Examining Race, Gender, Age, and Class in the 2008 Presidential Primaries." *Race, Gender, and Class* 15(3): 32–50.

Stone, Walter J., Alan I. Abramowitz, and Ronald B. Rapoport. 1989. "How Representative Are the Iowa Caucuses?" In *The Iowa Caucuses and the Presidential Nominating Process,* edited by Peverill Squire, 19–49. Boulder, CO: Westview Press.

Strope, Leigh. 1999. "S.C. Democrats Keep Distance from National." *State,* June 20, B7.

Stroud, Joseph S. 2000. "S.C. Saves Bush a Record 500,000 Vote." *State,* February 20, A1.

Stuckey, Tom. 2000. "Alan Keyes 'Always a Little More Driven.'" *State,* February 13, D4.

Sullivan, Andy. 2008. "Bill Clinton Takes on Obama, Media, on Race Comments." *Reuters,* April 22. blogs.reuters.com/talesfromthetrail/2008/04/22/bill-clinton-takes-on-obama-media-on-race-comments.

Surratt, Clark. 1982a. "Candidacy Overrides Primary." *State,* April 18, 1A.

Surratt, Clark. 1982b. "Democrats Considering '84 Primary." *State,* April 16, 2B.

Surratt, Clark. 1988a. "Democrats Favor S.C. Primary." *State,* March 11, 1A.

Surratt, Clark. 1988b. "Jackson Taps 'Power to Win.'" *State,* March 13, 1A.

Surratt, Clark. 1988c. "Primary a Hot Topic—For Now." *State,* March 17, 12A.

Surratt, Clark. 1991. "Democrats to Get '92 Primary Wish." *State,* March 28, 5B.

Taylor, Andrew J. 2010. "Does Presidential Primary and Caucus Order Affect Policy? Evidence from Federal Procurement Spending." *Political Research Quarterly* 63 (2): 398–409.

Tumulty, Karen, and Philip Rucker. 2012. "Romney Rivals Seize What May Be Last Chance." *Washington Post,* January 14, A1.

United Press International. 1979. "GOP Looking for Primary Volunteers." *State,* November 27, 16B.

United Press International. 2000. "Bauer Drops Out of Presidential Race," February 4. www.upi.com/Archives/2000/02/04/Bauer-drops-out-of-presidential-race/94619 49640400.

Van Natta, Jr., Don, and John M. Broder. 2000. "With a Still-Ample Treasury, Bush Builds a Green 'Fire Wall' against McCain." *New York Times,* February 21, A12.

Vavreck, Lynn, Constantine J. Spiliotes, and Linda L. Fowler. 2002. "The Effects of Retail Politics in the New Hampshire Primary." *American Journal of Political Science* 46 (3): 595–610.

Wallace-Wells, Benjamin. 2016. "Ted Cruz: The Empty Evangelical." *New Yorker,* January 25. www.newyorker.com/news/benjamin-wallace-wells/ted-cruz-the-empty-evangelical.

Walsh, Edward, and Thomas B. Edsall. 2000. "In S.C., Momentum v. Resources." *Washington Post,* February 2, A1.

Warren, Ellen. 1988. "QB Kemp Barks Out Abstract Game Plan." *State,* February 24, 1A.

Washington, Wayne. 2008a. "Choosing a President—S.C. Primaries Brought Plenty of Surprises." *State,* January 28, A1.

Washington, Wayne. 2008b. "Democrats Call a Truce—Clyburn Reaffirms Neutrality Candidates Pledge to End Racially Tinged Talk." *State,* January 16, A1.

Washington, Wayne. 2008c. "Hodges Backs Obama: 'He's the Real Deal.'" *State,* January 3, B3.

Washington, Wayne. 2008d. "'Truth Squad' Targets Clinton's Camp's 'Lies' about Obama." *State,* January 23, A1.

Washington, Wayne, and Gina Smith. 2008. "The Democratic Primary—For Women, a Choice and a Dilemma." *State,* January 25, A1.

Washington, Wayne, and Gina Smith. 2012. "Gingrich, Romney Race to the Wire." *State,* January 21, Front Page, 1.

Williams, Barbara S. 1987. "Demos Tempted by Super Tuesday, but . . ." *Evening Post,* July 19, 14A.

"Winners & Losers." 2016. *State,* February 28, Front Page, 9.

Wood, B. Dan. 2009. *The Myth of Presidential Representation.* Cambridge: Cambridge University Press.

Woodard, J. David. 2013. *The New Southern Politics.* 2nd ed. Boulder, CO: Lynne Reiner.

Yeip, Randy, Max Rust, and Jessia Ma. 2016. "The Many Faces of Iowa's Caucus Voters." *Wall Street Journal,* January 31. graphics.wsj.com/elections/2016/iowa-caucuses -demographics.

Zeleny, Jeff, and Marjorie Connelly. 2008. "Obama Carries South Carolina by Wide Margin." *New York Times,* January 27, A1.

Zeleny, Jeff, and Ashely Parker. 2012. "Romney Looks Past Weekend's Primary as Rivals Find New Hope." *New York Times,* January 18, A12.

Zurcher, Anthony. 2015. "Fees, Petitions, and 'Extortion' Make Getting on US Ballots a Challenge." *BBC News,* October 2. www.bbc.com/news/world-us-canada-34418041.

INDEX